Philip Nixon

Exploring Northumberland History

Published by Northern Heritage Services Ltd
and includes material from a Breedon Books Publishing edition 2006

Units 7&8 New Kennels, Blagdon Estate, Seaton Burn
Newcastle upon Tyne, NE13 6DB
Telephone 01670 789940

www.northern-heritage.co.uk

Text and photography copyright:
© 2019 Philip Nixon

Design and Layout:
© 2021 Ian Scott Design

Printed and bound in the China by Latitude Press Limited
British Library Cataloguing in Publication Data
A catalogue record for this book is available from the British Library.
ISBN: 978-1-9162376-0-5

All rights reserved.

No part of this book may be reproduced, stored or introduced into a retrieval system, or transmitted in any form or by any means (electronic, mechanical, photocopying, recording or otherwise) without the prior permission of the publisher, except in the case of brief quotations embodied in critical reviews and certain other noncommercial uses permitted by copyright law.

For my family:
*Val, Sophy, Mark, Nora, and Lizzy;
not forgetting Claude, the Boston Terrier.*

And in memory of my friend:
Denis Dunlop
1930 - 2019
"Never underestimate the power of prayer, Philip"

Acknowledgements

I would like to thank all the kind and friendly people I met when working on this book; without whose useful advice and encouragement it would not have been possible.

Particularly my wife Val, Sophy Nixon, Mark Nixon, Denis Dunlop, Tony Beaumont, John Stephenson, Dr Andrew Wilmott, and Chris Hartnell of Northern Heritage, who gave me the opportunity. And, of course, his excellent team whose tremendous support throughout the project was very much appreciated. and not forgetting Claude Monet Nixon 1st, my daughter's Boston Terrier.

Many thanks to Tony Beaumont and Mark Nixon for supplying additional photography and the Kemble Gallery in Durham for the use of their beautiful prints.

Thanks to English Heritage Trust, National Trust, Northumberland Estates, Ford and Etal Estates, Bamburgh Castle, Vindolanda Trust and the many owners and custodians of the fine buildings featured in this book.

Philip Nixon
Exploring Northumberland History

Contents

Acknowledgements	ii
Introduction	vii

Newcastle

All Saints Church	02
Bessie Surtees House	03
Blackfriars	04
The Black Gate	04
Bridges Over The Tyne	05-07
The Swing Bridge	
The Tyne Bridge	
The Millennium Bridge	
The High Level Bridge	
The King Edward VII Rail Bridge	
The Queen Elizabeth II Metro Bridge	
The Redheugh Road Bridge	
The Scotswood Road Bridge	
The Scotswood Rail Bridge	
The Blaydon Road Bridge	
The Castle	08-09
The Central Arcade	09
The Central Station	10
The City Walls	11
The Cooperage	12
Grainger Town	12-13
The Guildhall	14
Holy Jesus Hospital	14
The Keelmen's Hospital	15
The Literary and Philosophical Society ('The Lit and Phil')	16-17
The Moot Hall	17
St Andrew's Church	18
St Mary's Catholic Cathedral	19
St Nicholas' Cathedral	20-21
The Theatre Royal	22
The Town Moor	23
Trinity House	24
Victoria Tunnel Ouseburn	25-26

Northumberland Coast

Alnmouth	28-30
Amble	30
Bamburgh	31-33
Bamburgh	34, 35
St Aidan's Church	
Beadnell	36
Berwick-upon-Tweed	37-41
Blyth	42
Boulmer	43
Coquet Island	44
Craster	45
Cresswell	46
Cullercoats	47
Dunstanburgh Castle	48-49
The Farne Islands	50-52
Howick Hall	53
Howick	54
Church of St Michael & All Angels	
Longhoughton Church	54-55
Low Newton-by-the-Sea	56
Newbiggin-by-the-Sea	57
Seahouses	58
Seaton Deleval Hall	59
Seaton Sluice	60
St Mary's Lighthouse	61
Tynemouth Priory and Castle	62-63
Warkworth	64-68

Lindisfarne

Lindisfarne	69-77
Lindisfarne Castle	78-79
Lindisfarne Priory	80-81
St Mary's Church	82
St Cuthbert's Isle	82

The Tyne Valley

Acomb	84
Allendale and the Fire Festival	85
Allenheads	86-87
Aydon Castle	88
Bellingham	88-89
Beltingham	90-91
St Cuthbert's Church	
Black Middens Bastle	92
Blanchland	93
Bywell	94-95
Cherryburn - Mickley	96-97
Corbridge	98-99
Corstopitum	100
Falstone	101
The Goatstones	102
Haltwhistle	102-103
Bellister Castle	104
Haydon Old Church	104
Heavenfield	105
Hexham	106-108
Kielder Castle	109
Kielder Forest and Reservoir	110-111
Langley Castle	112
Linnel's Bridge	113
Low Cleughs Bastle	113
Ovingham	114
Prudhoe Castle	115
Stagshaw Bank	115
Stublick Chimney and Colliery	116
Tarset and Dally Castles	117
Thirlwall Castle	118
Warden	118-119
Wylam	120-122
Stephenson's Cottage	
West Wylam Bridge (Hagg Bank)	

Hadrian's Wall

Hadrian's Wall	123-124
Segedunum Roman Fort	125
Heddon-on-the-Wall	126
Brunton Turret	126
Chollerford Bridge Abutment	127
Chesters Fort	128-129
Temple of Mithras	129
Housesteads Fort	130-131
Housesteads Bastle House	131
Steel Rigg	132
The Sill	132
Vindolanda	133
Roman Army Museum and Magna Fort	134
Milecastle 42	134
Poltcross Burn	134

Mid Northumberland

Alwinton	136
Ashington	136-137
The Battle of Otterburn	138
Belsay Hall	139
Biddleston	140
Bothal	141
Brinkburn Priory	142
Cambo	143
Carter Bar	143
Cartington Castle	144
Elsdon	144-145
Harbottle Castle	146
Kirkharle	147
Kirkley Hall	148
Lordenshaws	148
Mitford Castle	149
Morpeth	150-152
Northumberlandia	153
Ottereburn Tower	154
Pegswood	155
Ponteland	155
Rothbury	156-157
Rothley Castle	157
Shittleheugh Bastle	158
Wallington	158-159
Winter's Gibbet	160

North Northumberland

Alnham	162
Alnwick	163-167
The Hotspur Tower	
The Percy Tenantry Column	
The Old Cross Inn	
St Michael's Church	
The Lion Bridge	
Alnwick Castle	
Alnwick Hulne Park	167-168
Brislee Tower	
The Alnwick Gardens	169
Battle of Flodden Field	170-171
Battle of Halidon Hill	172
Battle of Humbleton Hill	173
Chillingham Castle	174
Chillingham Wild Cattle	175
Cragside	176-177
Cuddy's Cave	178
Duddo Stone Circle	178
Edlingham	179
Etal Castle	180
Ford Castle	181
Ancient site of Ad Gedfin	182
Heatherslaw Mill	183
Ingram	184
St Michael's Church	
Kirknewton	184-185
Lady's Well, Holystone	185
Norham Castle	186-187
Norham	188
St Cuthbert's Church	
Preston Tower	189
Ros Castle	189
Roughtin' Linn	190
St Cuthbert's Cave	191
The Twizel Bridge	192
Union Suspension Bridge	193
Loan End	
Whittingham	194-195
Woodhouses Bastle	196
Yeavering	196-197
Endpiece	198

INTRODUCTION

Throughout our lives, we accept the constant changing of borders and boundaries brought about for political and administrative reasons. However, some borders are imprinted profoundly on the mind and it seems impossible that they should ever change. This impression has always been especially strong when crossing the River Tyne by that iconic symbol of the North, the Tyne Bridge. This was always, 'the Gateway to Northumberland' – indeed, a road sign proclaimed that very fact. You were entering a different county: a county of boldness and romance, of history and adventure; a place so different from Durham – the county you were leaving – and yet, in many ways, so closely linked in heritage.

The Romans were among the first to appreciate the importance of building a fort by the River Tyne; they had already built a bridge here, *Pons Ælii*, which carried the road north from Chester-le-Street to link with the Roman Wall. It was this bridge that gave its name to the fort, which was garrisoned by Roman auxiliaries from the Rhineland. The site attracted little interest until after the Norman Conquest, but in 1080 William the Conqueror's eldest son, Robert Curthose, built a wooden castle here on his way back from an incursion into Scotland. He called it the 'New Castle', the name the city has retained over many centuries.

This castle and its surrounding town seemed to change hands between the English and the Scots on a regular basis. Because of its defensive importance, the town continued to earn itself many royal favours and charters, and by 1216 it was given its own mayor. In 1400, the town was made a county in its own right, with a sheriff and law courts. It was during the English Civil War of 1642 to 1651 that, because of a heroic stand by the mayor Sir John Marley and his greatly outnumbered army, Newcastle earned the motto proudly displayed on its coat of arms: *"Fortiter defendit triumphans"* (Triumphing by brave defence).

Throughout its subsequent long history, the commercial prosperity of Newcastle steadily increased. The early days of wool, coal, salt, lime and glassmaking gradually developed into the heavier trades of the Industrial Revolution. The city has always been at the forefront of progress, and from 1850 it had gained a great reputation in shipbuilding and railways. It was this era of steam, iron ships and railways that provided the creative opportunity for the collective genius of such men as the Stephensons and Lord Armstrong. This fast pace of industrialisation in the city was matched by a change of architecture in the early 19th century until then, the character of Newcastle had been largely medieval. However, during the Victorian era, John Dobson, Richard Grainger and John Clayton created one of the best-planned city centres in England.

Newcastle upon Tyne is a place of great architectural variety, and there is much of interest; the imposing castle and impressive cathedrals blend with modern buildings and those of its early 19th-century centre, which in turn are further enhanced by the surviving ancient buildings close to the river.

The Quayside is a spectacularly modern development that still manages to share its character with the traditional aspects of the city. The tremendous drive and energy in Newcastle reflect in its ability to blend the old and the new – a delicate balance that has been so hugely successful.

Northumberland itself is England's most northerly county. However, it began its existence as a sort of no-man's land. Indeed, the Romans had built their vast wall in an attempt to cut it off from their empire altogether, designating it barbarian.

Roman Wall country near Steel Rigg

A post-Roman corn drying kiln incorporated into the granaries at Housesteads

Hobthrush, or St Cuthbert's Isle, Lindisfarne, at dawn

The Romans left in the fifth century and the north country once more became a lawless target for pillaging, plundering and invasion. In 547AD the Saxons swooped down on the defenceless coasts and firmly established themselves, under the leadership of a tough king significantly styled Ida the Flame-bearer. He made Bebbenburgh, or Bamburgh, as it became known, his seat of government.

Eventually, Edwin came to the throne of Northumbria and married Æthelburga, daughter of Æthelbert, King of Kent. The new queen was accompanied to her new kingdom by Bishop Paulinus who, through his teachings, converted the king and his subjects to Christianity. Some of the places where Paulinus baptised his converts are still regarded as secret places of great reverence. However, this 'golden time' was not to last, and Christianity was dealt a serious blow when King Edwin was defeated and slain by the combined armies of Cadwallon of Gwynedd and Penda of Mercia, causing Paulinus and Queen Æthelburga to flee to Kent.

It was a later Northumbrian king, Oswald, who defeated Cadwallon and Penda at the Battle of Heavenfield in AD 634. He immediately sent to Iona for Christian missionaries to convert his wild Northumbrian subjects. We are told, however, that the first monk who came was beaten by the "intractable nature of the people he had come to teach". The next man who arrived was a wise and gentle monk named Aidan, and it was he who, at the request of King Oswald, established a monastery on Lindisfarne in AD 635. His religious teachings reached out across all of Northumbria, and Lindisfarne became known as 'the Cradle of Christianity in the North'.

At the time of the Battle of Heavenfield a boy was born in the Border Hills. His name was Cuthbert. Inspired by Aidan, he too became a monk and played a major part in the spreading of Christianity, not only in the North, but also throughout Western Europe. He eventually became Bishop of Lindisfarne. Eleven years after his death, his body was found to be incorrupt; this incontestably established his worthiness to be a saint.

Cuthbert is perhaps the best-known and best-loved Northern saint; it was in his honour that the beautiful Durham Cathedral was built on the site of his last resting place. Dotted throughout the North – and well worth seeking out – are many holy locations associated with the saint's fascinating life, among them little-known places he visited in the high, wild Northumbrian hills during missions to convert the heathen tribes to Christianity.

During the turbulent centuries that followed, the warring factions of Saxons, Celts, Vikings and Danes crossed and recrossed the remote landscape, sometimes building, but more often destroying the early pockets of Christianity in such places as Lindisfarne, Tynemouth and Hexham. Northumbria was often described as a wasteland, and for much of its early history, it remained a useful buffer area between England and Scotland, sometimes taking sides, but owing allegiance to neither. It was not until AD 920 that the first submission to an English king took place, and in 954AD Northumbria moved permanently under the control of the English Crown.

In the border struggles between the 12th and 16th centuries that led to the eventual Union of the Crowns, Northumbria – now Northumberland – could so easily have been overlooked. The county was under successive control of Scotland and England, and its culture grew from the influence of these neighbours, adopting both the best and the worst traditions of each, from legends and songs to such bad habits as 'reiving' – the rustling of livestock and plundering of goods that grew into a local sport.

Bamburgh Castle from the north at dusk

To take the romantic view of Northumberland – as famous observers such as the novelist and poet Sir Walter Scott did – was to see only one side of the coin; in reality, Northumberland was a wild and dangerous place with a cold and bloody history with shocking stories played out on its isolated vastness that can still chill the soul. The many castles, bastles, pele towers and fortified churches that gave protection and shelter to families and their livestock remain as a poignant reminder of its grim past.

There have been a great many Northumbrian heroes who have played their part in the rivalry between England and Scotland. Probably the best-known of these are the Percy family and, in particular, the charismatic Harry 'Hotspur', who was immortalised by William Shakespeare in *Henry IV, Part 1*. 'Border clans' such as the Greys, the Fenwicks, the Milburns, the Charltons, the Armstrongs, the Nixons and the Swinburnes have also contributed to the county's unique history – so much so that even today many a Northumbrian considers their nationality as distinct from English or Scottish.

Some of the finest coastline in Britain is found in Northumberland, and complementing the vastness of its remote beaches is the intimate

Alnwick Castle

charm of its small islands, such as Lindisfarne where you can taste the wonderful mead brewed in the shadow of the great priory founded by St Aidan, or walk the causeway to the mainland, as the monks did, keeping a wary eye on the rising tide. The nearby Farne Islands, famous for their seals and seabirds, are an absolute paradise for lovers of natural history. Tales of the sea and ships abound, such as the heroic but sad story of Grace Darling who died of consumption four years after her famous lifeboat rescue. Further south lies Coquet Island, another isle rich in birdlife, which also supported an important religious community once visited by St Cuthbert.

The Cheviot Hills in the west rise to a height of around 3,000ft and have numerous beautiful little valleys that remain virtually unexplored, many of them hiding secret walks and waterfalls. These hills provided a great challenge to the Romans, and some of the modern roads follow their dead-straight switchbacks. Many of Britain's finest and most important Roman remains are to be found in Northumberland; Hadrian's Wall is a UNESCO World Heritage Site, and some of its less well-known sites are quite exceptional.

Northumberland has something for everyone, but, perhaps, more importantly, it offers a unique combination of space and secret corners where the pressures of today's overcrowded lifestyle can be put aside, at least for a while.

The famous beach huts, Blyth

The Author, Philip Nixon
Pic: Val Nixon

New Year Tar Barlin' Festival, Allendale

Kielder is one of the last strongholds for the Red Squirrel

EXPLORING NORTHUMBERLAND HISTORY:
NEWCASTLE-UPON-TYNE

ALL SAINTS CHURCH

A Gothic Church big enough to hold a congregation of up to two thousand people once stood on this site. The famous Roger Thornton was buried here in 1430 and it was the original home to the huge Thornton Memorial Brass which is now in St Nicholas' Cathedral. The building suffered badly during the severe winter of 1875 and parts of the structure began to develop dangerous cracks – it was decided that repairs would be much too expensive and the church was closed; the last service was held on 9th July 1786.

The current All Saints' Church was designed by local architect David Stephenson and was consecrated in November 1789, but it was another seven years before its tower was completed, bringing the final cost of construction to £27,000. The finance for the building of the church was raised by a combination of levies on tenants and landlords plus donations through public subscription – a good indication of the prosperity of the Quayside at that time.

The oval interior of the church is magnificent, with solid mahogany woodwork throughout. All Saints is the only elliptical church in England, and its box pews and curved gallery, which rests on Tuscan columns, lead the eye directly towards the eastern apse. The building stands in a prominent position at the very edge of the river valley, from where a series of narrow steps and *chares* (medieval alleys) lead steeply down to the Quayside. Before the Tyne Bridge was built in the 1920s, the church was generally regarded as the most dominant feature on the Newcastle skyline.

Unfortunately, the fortunes of All Saints' Church faded along with those of the Quayside, and, by the 1800s, money for the many urgently needed repairs was in short supply. A series of appeals were launched, but with little success, and the church continued to fall into disrepair; in 1961, it was deconsecrated. In 1984, the building was converted into offices and an auditorium for musical events; however, as a result of subsequent flood damage, it was placed on Historic England's 'At Risk' register in 2012.

However, the future of this Grade 1- listed building is assured; the Evangelical Presbyterian Church of England and Wales have signed a 150-year lease on the church and are planning to restore it to its former glory, an exciting addition to the backdrop of the re-generated Newcastle Quayside.

BESSIE SURTEES HOUSE

Opposite the Guildhall, on Sandhill, a group of fine old houses give some idea of how the Quayside looked in the 17th century. Surtees and Millbank Houses are possibly the best examples; they are now considered as one and known as Bessie Surtees House perhaps best known as the north-eastern headquarters of Historic England (English Heritage).

Robert Rhodes, the man who co-financed the building of the spire of St Nicholas' Cathedral, is believed to have owned Surtees House in 1465, although it is thought that he never actually lived there. He was a lawyer and man of great wealth; he died in 1474, leaving no heirs.

Just below the first-floor window on Bessie Surtees House a plaque tells the story of how Bessie, the eldest daughter of Aubone Surtees – a wealthy and powerful banker – descended by ladder from an upper window here on 18th November 1772 into the arms of her young lover, John, son of William Scott - a coal fitter – who lived in nearby Love Lane. Bessie was one of eight children and she was considered a great beauty. Even before she was eighteen, her hand in marriage was sought by many of the eligible sons of the local gentry. However, she fell in love with John Scott and they carried on their courtship in secret. On that cold November night, they eloped and ran off across the Border where they were married according to Scottish Law. John's prospects turned out to be good because he later became Lord Eldon and Chancellor of England. He became very wealthy and bought a large house in the fashionable part of London. With his success, he became one of Newcastle's favourite sons and a square in the city was named after him. Unfortunately, his fortune changed when the Corn Law was passed in 1815 and his family house in Bedford Square was attacked by an angry mob.

He and his wife were forced to make a hasty escape through a window into the grounds of the British Museum. Their previous experience with windows must have proved extremely valuable in this dire emergency.

Another tale of changing fortune is linked with Sandhill. In the middle of the open space, not far from Bessie Surtees House there once stood a magnificent burnished copper equestrian statue of James II. It was pulled down by an angry mob after the Revolution of 1688 and thrown into the nearby River Tyne. It was salvaged not long afterwards, melted down and cast into bells for the churches of St Andrews and All Saints.

First three floors of Bessie Surtees House, now Historic England Offices

The Dominican Monastery of Blackfriars carries on its principle of warm welcome

The ominous Newcastle Black Gate

BLACKFRIARS

Just behind the city walls, to the rear of Stowell Street, is the site of the 13th century Dominican Monastery of Blackfriars, founded in 1239 by Sir Peter Scot, a wealthy merchant who was to become Mayor of Newcastle in 1245. It flourished until 1539, although in 1250 the prior was heavily criticised by the General Chapter of the order for his architectural extravagance. The church was demolished during the Dissolution of the Monasteries in the mid 16th century, but a range of fine buildings can still be seen. Indeed, the priory must have been very comfortable and well-equipped, as it was the residence of choice for any royalty visiting Newcastle; it was in the church here, in 1334, that Edward Baliol paid homage to Edward III for the throne of Scotland.

Following the Dissolution, the property was sold to the mayor and burgesses of the city who, in 1552, leased it to *"the most ancient trades of the town":* bakers and brewers, fullers and dyers, smiths, tanners, butchers, cordwainers (shoemakers), saddlers, tailors, and skinners and glovers. The main building was the refectory, with the cloister behind, and in spite of many alterations over the years, the original outline can still be traced. Over the entrance to the Smiths' Hall, there is a coat of arms that dates from 1771 and bears the inscription: *"By hammer and hand, all artes do stand."*

Today, these historic buildings house a restaurant, craft workshops and several small businesses.

THE BLACK GATE

Across the Castle Garth, through the railway arches, stands the Black Gate, the original main entrance to the castle. Despite the dark connotations, its name is said to be derived from that of London merchant Patrick Black, a leaseholder of the building in the 17th century.

Built between 1247 and 1250 during Henry III's reign, the gatehouse was a very sophisticated defence at that time, protected by a drawbridge and a portcullis. If these did not deter attackers, there were also two large guardrooms in its towers. Just inside the Black Gate lies one of the castle's two prisons, the Heron Pit, a windowless underground dungeon named after Sir William Heron, High Sheriff of Northumberland and governor of the castle from 1247 to 1257; he was famous as the Hammer of the Poor and Persecutor of the Religious – he even spent £32.00 on rebuilding his 'Pit', probably to make it even less comfortable.

The sinister Heron Pit – Newcastle Black Gate

The prison reformer John Howard, who visited the castle's dungeons in 1787, told of men and women chained to rings in the walls and knee-deep in water and sludge for up to a week as they waited to stand trial at the assizes. He also reported that on the Sunday of the assizes they were exhibited to the public and *"the curious and the vulgar paid sixpence each for admission"*.

After falling into disrepair under various owners, the Black Gate was close to being demolished in the mid 19th century but was saved when the Society of Antiquaries of Newcastle upon Tyne took up the lease and converted the building into a museum.

BRIDGES OVER THE TYNE

Newcastle developed from what was an important Roman crossing point on the River Tyne, and, over the years, its geographical position, the development of transport and an increase in trade have encouraged bridge building on a grand scale. Originally there was a single river crossing in Newcastle; now, several centuries later, there are 10, a testament to the city's growth in status.

The first Roman bridge in Newcastle, most likely a wooden deck with side rails supported by stone piers probably stood on the site occupied by the present-day **Swing Bridge**. The city's first stone bridge was built sometime around the turn of the 13th century and would have had gatehouses, houses and shops incorporated into its construction. However, like most bridges in the North-east, this was badly damaged in the Great Flood of 1771, and by 1781 a new stone crossing was in place, designed by Robert Mylne, the architect behind London's Blackfriars Bridge.

By the late 1800s, it was decided that a different kind of crossing was needed: a swing bridge that would allow large, high-masted ships to sail up the Tyne, something that only the flat-bottomed keels had been able to do up until that point. The Swing Bridge was built between 1868 and 1876 by local engineering firm W G Armstrong and Company in association with the Tyne Improvement Commission. At the time of opening, it was the largest bridge of its type in the world. This iron superstructure is around 560ft long and weighs almost 1500 tons and is supported on metal rollers that can rotate to give two river openings of almost 100ft each on either side. It is still driven by Armstrong's hydraulic engines, but the original steam pumps have now been replaced by an electric version. Although the bridge does not open very often these days, it has been estimated that, over the years, almost half a million ships have passed through.

The Tyne Bridge was built between 1925 and 1928 and is the traditional iconic symbol of the City of Newcastle. Its construction was first proposed in 1921, not only as an addition to existing road crossings but also as a job creation scheme. Eager to benefit from a substantial government subsidy, the corporations of Newcastle and Gateshead granted permission in 1924, and work commenced the following year.

Engineering contractors Dorman, Long & Co of Middlesbrough had to devise special construction techniques for the project because the Tyne Improvement Commission insisted on full navigational clearance in both height and width throughout the work; this demand necessitated a single-span bridge with a level deck. Civil engineering firm Mott, Hay and Anderson, who were chosen to design it, came up with a scaled-down version of a bridge they had already conceived for Australia's Sydney Harbour. The Tyne Bridge has a two-hinged steel arch with a span of 531ft and a road deck suspended 84ft above the river. Most certainly a distinguished example of Northern engineering, it was Britain's largest single-span bridge at the time of its opening.

The Gateshead Millennium Bridge, which links Newcastle's Quayside with the Gateshead Quays, is the latest bridge to have been built across the Tyne; lifted into place by a huge floating crane at the end of 2000, it opened the following summer. This

The Swing Bridge

The iconic Tyne Bridge dominates the river view from the Millennium Bridge

The Millennium Bridge

The Millennium Bridge opens to allow a boat upriver

800-tonne construction comprises a pair of steel arches – one forms the deck, the other supports it with thin suspension rods. There are two lanes on the curved deck, one for foot traffic and the other for cyclists. Lights are built into these decks for night-time use and to illuminate the graceful, sweeping main arch, which echoes the shape of the nearby Tyne Bridge.

It has a clever design: when a ship requires passage, the bridge opens slowly and spectacularly like the lid of a huge closed eye, turning on pivots on either side of the river to form a gateway arch. A pleasant mile-long circular riverside walk can be enjoyed by using this and the Swing Bridge, further to the west.

The High Level Bridge is a perfect example of famed civil engineer Robert Stephenson's ability to use materials appropriate to their function. Many well-established designers and engineers, including John Dobson and Isambard Kingdom Brunel, had submitted proposals for both high- and low-level bridges to augment the existing crossing, but in 1845 the decision was taken to build a combined road and rail bridge at a high level to permit a link between the Newcastle to Berwick Railway and the Darlington to Gateshead line. Measuring just over 1,300ft in length and standing 120ft above the river, the High Level Bridge comprises six main spans, each 125ft long, plus several smaller arches on land. Masonry piers on massive timber piles support the whole structure; this was the first time that Scottish engineer James Nasmyth's patented steam hammer had been used for this sort of work. The bridge has changed little since its opening in 1849, except for some structural strengthening in 1922 to allow the passage of trams.

Eastwards along the Tyne is the **Queen Elizabeth II Metro Bridge**, built to carry the city's Metro system from Gateshead to Newcastle. This 1,160ft-long bridge cost just under £5 million to construct and was officially opened by the Queen in 1981. Next to this stands the King Edward VII Bridge, constructed between 1902 and 1906 to carry lines for the North Eastern Railway. Built at an estimated cost of £500,000, the bridge has four massive girder spans supported by stone piers and measures 1,150ft in length. Further east, the Redheugh Bridge is a graceful, modern concrete construction carrying four traffic lanes and one footpath high above the river on three spans. It was built between 1980 and 1983 at a cost of just under £16 million. Strong winds and the exposed location and can cause problems for high-sided vehicles and when it was first opened a double-decker bus was almost blown over the side.

Further upriver is **The Scotswood Rail Bridge** is now disused but was built in 1871 for the Newcastle and Carlisle Railway and is the fourth bridge on the site. The original timber-truss bridge was built in 1839 but unfortunately burned down in 1860 during a Board of Trade inspection. The Scotswood Road Bridge, constructed between 1964 and 1967 replaces an earlier suspension bridge – known as the Chain Bridge – dating from 1831. Furthest east on Newcastle's River Tyne is The Blaydon Road Bridge; a modern elegant concrete construction designed by Bullen and Partners. The Newcastle Western Bypass is carried over the Tyne by this 1088ft-long bridge built between 1987 and 1990.

The Metro and Railway Bridge from the Quayside

The disused pipeline, Scotswood Rail Bridge

The delicate span of the Scotswood Road Bridge

The Keep – Newcastle Castle

THE CASTLE

It was Emperor Hadrian who first realised the importance of establishing a fort beside the River Tyne. There was already a bridge here, *Pons Ælii*, which carried the road north from Chester-le-Street to link up with the Roman Wall. It was this bridge that gave its name to the fort which was garrisoned at first by German auxiliaries and later by other auxiliary troops from the Welsh border. Following the departure of the Romans in the early part of the fifth century, the fort fell into ruin. The Celts had no use for the settlement, although in Saxon times the area was referred to as 'Monkchester', a name taken from a community of monks that had settled in the vicinity.

The site seems to have attracted little further interest until after the Norman Conquest. After the Conquest William I allowed Waltheof, a Saxon lord, to remain as Earl of Northumberland, but changed his mind when he suspected Waltheof's loyalty and turned the lands over to one of his countrymen, Robert de Comines. He was not at all popular with the locals and was murdered – an event which was the signal for several punitive expeditions by the Normans that became known as "the Harrying of The North". Most of Northern England was laid waste and with mass retaliation on the population, it was reduced by nearly 75%. In 1076, William I combined the Earldom of Northumberland with the Bishopric of Durham under the control of William Walcher, who, even though he tried to pacify the angry Northumbrians by making no effort to catch the killers of de Comines, still managed to upset them with his religious control; in 1080, he too was murdered.

That same year Robert Curthose, William I's eldest son, made a further incursion into Scotland and, on his return, as the historian John Speed tells us, *"Laid the foundation of a castle whereby the town of Newcastle did afterwards bothe take her beginning and her name"*.

The chosen site of Robert Curthose's 'New Castle' could not have been better. On three sides, it was defended by very steep banks reaching down to the Lort Burn and the Tyne; the land to the west was comparatively flat, and a ditch was dug here to complete the defences. Nothing remains of this early Norman motte-and-bailey castle – constructed from earth and wood, it was not strong enough to withstand heavy attacks during the uprising of the Northern barons in 1095. The fort was strengthened by William Rufus after its recapture and a small community settled in the area. The King granted special privileges to encourage them to establish themselves permanently. However, Newcastle still fell into the hands of the Scots and it became the property of David I for 19 years.

It was Henry II who recaptured the castle for England in 1157, and again it was granted a special charter and re-established as a base to defend the country against the Scots. By this time, the town was walled, but it still suffered many attacks by the Scots, most notably in 1342 and again in 1388, when it was defended by Sir Henry Percy – popularly known as Harry Hotspur – just prior to the Battle of Otterburn.

Because of its defensive importance, Newcastle had earned itself many royal favours and charters over the years – in 1216, it was given its own mayor – and at the turn of the 15th century, the town was made a county in its own right, with a designated sheriff and law courts. In the Wars of the Roses, later that century, Newcastle remained neutral, but during the English Civil War of 1642 to 1651 it came down firmly on the side of the Royalists. The inhabitants refused to send their coal to London, and in 1644 the city came under siege for two months by more than 30,000 Scottish soldiers commanded by Lord General Alexander Leslie, the Earl of St Leven, fighting on the Parliamentary side. Sir John Marley, Newcastle's mayor and military governor, defended against these overwhelming odds with only 2,000 men but was forced to capitulate when the greater force broke through the city walls. However, Marley and his men fought heroically to the end of the siege, making a final stand in the Castle Keep. It was because of this celebrated resistance that the king conferred on the city the motto still seen on its coat of arms: *Fortiter defendit triumphans* (Triumphing by brave defence).

Still standing tall despite the upheaval of more than 800 years, the old sandstone Castle Keep occupies an imposing position above the world-famous River Tyne. Designed by Henry II's architect 'Maurice the Engineer' (who also devised the Grand Tower at Dover Castle), and built between 1172 and 1177, the construction measures 62ft by 56ft and stands 81ft tall, with a forebuilding on the Keep's east side.

Three corners of the building have square turrets, but the one on the north-west corner has been rounded; this would be to make the enemy believe it contained a stairway and was, therefore, a weak point to attack, when in fact it is the most solid corner. The interior of the Keep has three floors, each of which has a main apartment with smaller rooms and stairs set into the thick, strong walls. Entry to the Keep is via an external staircase, which was originally

The Southern Postern Gate

protected by three towers, although only the upper two remain. Ascending almost 40 steps to the second tower gives access to the main entrance.

The Great Hall measures 30ft by 24ft and has a high, arched ceiling; set into the south wall is the King's Chamber, lit by three windows and with the original fireplace still in place. In the north-east turret is a vaulted chamber known as the Well Room – the well is covered, but is almost 100ft deep, with more than 40ft of water.

At the bottom of the Mural Stair is the First Floor Apartment, which measures 27ft by 22ft and has four windows. In the north wall is the large room known as the Queen's Chamber, again with an original fireplace.

In the basement of the building is the Garrison Room – formerly the county jail – which is remarkable for its fine vaulting supported by a circular central pier. The whole of the basement below the forebuilding is taken up by the Chapel, a delicate architectural beauty that strikes a surprising contrast to the rugged severity of the rest of the Keep. It has a two-bay nave, and set at right angles at the northern end is a one-bay chancel that would have allowed the altar to be placed against the east wall.

Sadly, nothing remains of the stone curtain wall that once surrounded the courtyard of this magnificent building.

NEWCASTLE-UPON-TYNE

THE CENTRAL ARCADE

Newcastle's Central Arcade is a very elegant Grade II-listed Edwardian shopping arcade that dates from 1906 and was designed by respected architects Oswald and Son of Newcastle. The arcade is contained within the Central Exchange Building and connects Grainger Street and Grey Street. It was built by Richard Grainger between 1836 – 1838 to the designs of John Wardle and George Walker.

The triangular-shaped Central Exchange was originally intended to be a corn exchange but instead became a subscription newsroom. By 1870 the Institute for Promoting the Fine Arts had converted the newsrooms into a gallery, a concert hall and a theatre. This was replaced in 1897 by a vaudeville theatre but in 1901 a fire destroyed the original; after which the current Central Arcade was built within the original walls. Beneath the astounding glass barrel-vaulted roof of the Arcade, the shop fronts are adorned with exquisite examples of some remarkable faience tiling – moulded glazed terracotta blocks used as cladding.

The longest-standing occupant in the arcade is JG Windows, one of the oldest and most respected music businesses in the UK. The business was founded in 1908 and its friendly and knowledgeable staff have been selling an extensive range of musical instruments, accessories, sheet music, recorded music and film for over a century.

Newcastle's magnificent Central Arcade

Concourse of Newcastle Central Station

THE CENTRAL RAILWAY STATION

Newcastle is unusual among Britain's major cities in that it has only one mainline railway station, Newcastle Central Station, formally opened in 1850 by Queen Victoria. As early as 1836, a number of railway companies were planning to run their lines into the city, and Richard Grainger, one of the men responsible for the Victorian redevelopment of Newcastle, persuaded these operators to go for a *"concentration of termini"*. Thus, the new station was built for the recently amalgamated York, Newcastle and Berwick Railway Company.

Newcastle Central Station was designed by celebrated architect John Dobson; However, the grandeur of his design was not completed, possibly due to the financial difficulties of the Railway. But it would have been of grand scale, coupled columns were to mark the bays, and the columns of the portico were to have supported magnificent giant seated figures, but these ideas were all abandoned before construction started.

Behind the still impressive portico we see today, three arches lead to the amazing covered train shed with more than two miles of platforms. Spanning an area of around three acres, the construction is curved to a radius of 800ft and roofed in timber and glass on slender wrought-iron ribs, supported by cast-iron columns just under 25ft high.

This was the first train-shed roof to be constructed in this manner, although it has been copied many times in various forms elsewhere. Dobson explained that he had realised curved wrought-iron sections could be easily manufactured on a rolling mill with bevelled rollers. It was this innovation that made his design a commercial possibility and allowed him to create what is regarded as an outstanding example of 19th century ironwork. Despite the initial financial setback, Newcastle Central Station remains a magnificent tribute to the very special architectural talent of John Dobson and the railway engineering of the Industrial Revolution.

THE CITY WALLS

Newcastle's original Town Walls were very impressive, being 7-10ft thick and 20-30ft high, including the parapet and battlements. Access was permitted via six main fortified gates – West Gate, New Gate, Close Gate, Pilgrim Street Gate, Pandon Gate and Sand Gate – of which the first two were the most important. In addition to these, there were less significant water gates and posterns along the walls' length.

This formidable barrier was dotted with a total of 17 towers, all of the same style – rectangular on the inside of the wall, semi-circular on the outside, with three large loopholes. These rounded towers were much stronger than the early square design they replaced, with no blind spots that might benefit attackers. Additional shelter was provided between the towers by smaller turrets that were flush with the outer face of the wall, and a ditch around the outside provided an extra line of defence.

An excellently preserved section of the West Walls can be seen between Newgate Street and Westgate Road, complete with the remains of four towers and a turret. The most damaged of these – though nonetheless impressive – is the Ever Tower. The Morden Tower was once owned by the Company of Plumbers, Glaziers and Pewterers and used as the society's meeting place; it was they who added the picturesque upper storey in around 1700. Close by is arguably the best-preserved turret, of which the passageway and external staircase to the roof platform can still be clearly seen. The Heber Tower retains its original barrel-vaulted roof, although it's likely that its battlements were modified during the Civil War to allow the use of guns, and a large window was added to the building during restoration work by the Company of Curriers, Feltmakers, Armourers and Hatters in 1771.

Between Morden and Heber Towers, the stone-blocked remains of a postern can be seen; this was granted to the Black Friars in 1280 to allow them access to their garden outside the Town Walls. At this point, the West Walls turn south-east towards the Durham Tower – the best preserved on this section – which also retains its barrel-vaulted roof.

Newcastle West City Walls

The Corner Tower – Newcastle City Walls

Ever Tower – Newcastle City Walls

THE COOPERAGE

The Cooperage, a wonderful timber-framed building, is perhaps, one of the most unusual buildings on the Newcastle Quayside. Because of its close proximity to the town wall any extensions carried out to the original 16th century building were, by necessity, upwards rather than outwards. Each storey of the building was added at an interval of approximately a hundred years. Each succeeding higher floor, because the building is virtually built on a steep slope, is twice the area of the one below. Its construction is fascinating; the building's Dutch bricks are believed to have arrived in Newcastle as part of a ship's ballast. And it is generally thought that the timber framing used in the construction was reclaimed from a ship that had sunk in the mouth of the Tyne, interestingly, each beam is carved with a large Roman numeral, as a sort of "construction instruction".

The building, of course, takes its name from the fact that a cooper established a business here in the mid-1730s. By the 1800s it was George Dunlop who was the master craftsman and when he retired, he turned the business over to his apprentice, John Arthur.

The high-quality wooden casks his company produced were in great demand until the early 1970s. Progress dictated that metal casks became the standard and the business modernised and expanded, dictating a move to Throckley Industrial Estate on the outskirts of the City, but the name serves as a reminder of the use of this historic building.

The Cooperage, Newcastle Quayside

GRAINGER TOWN

The city of Newcastle has always been at the forefront of progress, and by 1850 it had gained a formidable reputation for its railways and shipbuilding. It was this era of iron ships, steam railways and heavy industry that provided a creative opportunity for the collective genius of civil engineers such as Robert Stephenson and Lord Armstrong.

The fast pace of industrialisation in Newcastle was matched by a change of architecture in the early 19th century – until then the character of the city had

Grainger Town architecture

been largely medieval. Three men were responsible for the ideas that gave Newcastle one of the best-planned city centres in England, with elegant stone-faced buildings gracing wide-open streets: architect John Dobson, builder/developer Richard Grainger, and town clerk John Clayton. The trio devised a redevelopment scheme for the city centre that included new markets and a new theatre, and models illustrating their plans were put on display for public approval. The verdict: 5,000 people in favour, only 300 against!

The whole scheme was completed in five years and gave rise to such fine streets as Grey Street, Grainger Street and Clayton Street, as well as the markets, the arcades, the Theatre Royal and, of course, the magnificent Central Station. Today, all these streets and buildings serve as a reminder of the vision of these great men. Grainger Town, which covers approximately 90 acres, boasts an architectural style that has been dubbed 'Tyneside Classical', and the great art historian Sir Nikolaus Pevsner once described Grey Street as "one of the finest streets in England". The area has many fine Georgian and Victorian buildings, in addition to a 13th century Dominican friary and a notable stretch of the historic town walls.

Grainger Town is almost wholly located within Newcastle's Central Conservation Area, one of the first to be designated in England. The area around Grey's Monument and Grey Street was built in 1749 and now consists mainly of high-quality shopping outlets selling designer clothes and jewellery. The magnificent Edwardian Central Arcade is also located in this vicinity, along with the architecturally impressive Theatre Royal, designed by John and Benjamin Green. After the junction with Mosley Street, Grey Street morphs into Dean Street and follows the route of the subterranean Lort Burn, which once flowed into the Tyne.

Perhaps the best observation on Grey Street came from late poet laureate Sir John Betjeman: *"As for the curve of Grey Street, I shall never forget seeing it to perfection, traffic-less on a misty Sunday morning. Not even Regent Street, even old Regent Street London, can compare with that descending subtle curve."*

Grey's Monument, a Newcastle landmark

The Guildhall

THE GUILDHALL

Newcastle's original Town Hall or Exchange was built on Sandhill in the early 1500s; beside it was the Town Court or Guildhall, which was almost in the style of a lean-to, supported by pillars and left open like a market. Most of the guild meetings of the city's incorporated companies were held here, in addition to numerous other civic occasions. This building also housed the Mayor's Court, the Sheriff's Court and Borough Courts, as well as the Quarter Sessions.

The old Town Hall was pulled down after being badly damaged by fire in 1639 and a new Guildhall built in its place. Designed by Yorkshire-born architect Robert Trollope, the new construction – built to house the Corporation, the Merchant Adventurers' Court and the Assize Court – was completed in 1655 at a cost of £10,000, five times the original estimate!

The Guildhall suffered the ravages of both rioting and fire in the second half of the 18th century, necessitating considerable repairs and restoration. It survived several subsequent decades of town development, but in 1823 the building was rebuilt – with the addition of a colonnaded fish market – by celebrated Newcastle architect John Dobson; this was one of his first major projects in the city.

Legend has it that the fishwives were less than pleased with this new market and demonstrated their dislike to Dobson by having nothing to do with him. With the onset of winter, however, they began to realise how much warmer and more comfortable the market was than their draughty open stalls scattered along the Quayside. By way of an apology, the women sent a delegation to Dobson's home to present him with a gift: a selection of the best quality fish.

The colonnades were enclosed in the late 1800s and the fish market turned into a newsroom. Today, the Guildhall is a meeting place for the Freemen of the City of Newcastle upon Tyne and is not open to the general public.

The Holy Jesus Hospital

HOLY JESUS HOSPITAL

Although it stands amid modern roads and concrete and glass buildings, the Holy Jesus Hospital is an absolute treasure. It stands on the site of what was once an Augustinian friary; the monks lived and worked here for almost 250 years, from 1291 to 1539. Following the Dissolution of the Monasteries, the building was retained by Henry VIII for use by his "Council of the North", as an alternative to York.

The Corporation of Newcastle bought the site in the early 17th century, and in 1681 it built the Holy Jesus Hospital to provide accommodation for 39 poor Freemen of the City, or, indeed, poor Freemen's widows and their unmarried children. Records show that in the early 1700s the residents were each given an income of £4.00 per year, which by the end of the century had been increased to £6.00; in addition, each received a ton of coal. By the late 1800s, each received £13.00 and four tons of coal.

The building was originally fronted by a large green, but most of this was lost when the City Road was built in 1882. To the north of the hospital in the 18th and 19th centuries were a poor house, a charity school and the House of Correction, all which have since disappeared. Towards the end of the 19th century, the police station adjoining the western side of the hospital was replaced by a soup kitchen, which proudly advertised, *"Finest Soup – A pound of beef to every gallon with vegetables and proper seasonings in proportion – on sale at one Penny a pint"*

The Holy Jesus Hospital was closed in 1937, and by the middle of the 1950s it was derelict, and plans were considered for its demolition. But, thanks to public opposition, the site was saved, and restoration began in 1968; in 1971, it reopened as the John George Joicey Museum of Local History. In 2000, the National Trust took over the lease from the council, refurbishing the building as offices and meeting rooms, some of which are available to hire.

THE KEELMEN'S HOSPITAL

The Keelmen were the group of men who were in charge of the "keels" or "lighters", the boats of a shallow draft that carried coal from the fairly shallow waters of the Quayside to the larger collier ships waiting in the mouth of the Tyne. First recorded as a fraternity as early as 1539, the group would go on to set up a charitable trust at the turn of the 18th century to support sick and aged keelman and their families. The construction of the Keelmen's Hospital on City Road, not far from the Quayside, was completed in 1701, and this two-storey brick building with its domed clock tower and dormer windows with scroll-shaped gables can still be seen. *"I have heard of and seen many hospitals, the works of rich men,"* the Bishop of Ely is said to have remarked at the time, *"but this is the first I have ever seen or heard of, which has been built by the poor."*

For many years, the keelmen and the hostmen – local businessmen who controlled the export of coal – were in dispute over the management of funds for the hospital's maintenance; although the institution had been built and paid for by the fraternity, in the 18th century it was difficult for such a working-class group to control its own affairs without interference from the hierarchy. However, by 1788, an Act of Parliament was passed to safeguard the funds and, as a consequence, better support the men and families who had fallen on hard times through accident, illness or old age.

At its peak, the keelmen would hold a 'head meeting day', when members would march through the city to a gala dinner in musical procession, clothed in their 'holiday dress' – a short blue jacket and slate-coloured trousers with a margin of white shirt sewn between them, plus a yellow waistcoat. By the 19th century, however, the keelmen's society was in decline. More modern methods were employed for loading the collier ships, and the keels, which were no longer needed, eventually disappeared. The Keelmen's Hospital overlooks the area in Sandgate where these men lived and worked – a monument to this once vitally important Newcastle trade, long since vanished.

The Keelmen's Hospital

THE LITERARY AND PHILOSOPHICAL SOCIETY ("THE LIT AND PHIL")

Not far from Newcastle Central Station is the impressive Greek Revival-style home of the city's Literary and Philosophical Society. The 'Lit & Phil', as it is affectionately known, has been a source of information, inspiration and enlightenment for inquiring *minds* for more than 200 years. The building houses one of the few remaining independent libraries in the country, with more than 170,000 books and the most comprehensive music collection in the north of England.

It has spacious rooms for work and research and hosts many varied events. The Lit and Phil enthusiastically continues its mission to interest and educate the people of Newcastle and the surrounding area.

On the wall beside the front door, a plaque proclaims that it was here on 5th December 1815 that George Stephenson gave the first demonstration of his Miners' Safety Lamp.

The late 18th early 19th centuries were a great time for scientific discoveries and inventions. This was being carefully observed by a keen and knowledgeable public and science became a public activity, nearly every major town and city had its own Literary and Philosophical Society. Newcastle's society was founded in 1793 and has played an important part in the education and history of the city.

Lit and Phil main entrance

In August of that year, a group of north-east coal owners had determined to find a solution to one of their biggest problems: gas explosions. Mining was a dangerous occupation at the best of times, but it was made especially so by the naked flame – either in an oil lamp or on a candle – that a miner took underground to light his surroundings. There was a constant threat that even the slightest wisp of gas, found in almost every coal seam, would ignite and create a fatal explosion. This danger had been present for many years, of course, but as coal production increased so did the number of horrific accidents.

The coal owners contacted Britain's most celebrated scientist at the time, Sir Humphry Davy, who travelled to Newcastle on 24th August 1815 to visit some collieries, then returned to London to consider the problem. On 9th November 1815, Davy presented a paper at the Royal Society in the capital, detailing the lamp that would guarantee his place in history.

By coincidence, at the same time that Davy was inventing his lamp, George Stephenson was busy devising his own in Killingworth, working by trial and error. The Northumbrian engineer came up with a safety lamp based on the same principles as that of his Cornish-born counterpart, and on 5th December 1815, his invention was publicly demonstrated at a meeting of more than 80 members of the Lit & Phil in Newcastle.

Being unaccustomed to public speaking, Stephenson had asked his friend Nicholas Wood – colliery manager at Killingworth – to present to the group on his behalf. However, after detecting errors in Wood's answers to the audience's questions, a frustrated Stephenson took over, explaining his lamp in minute detail, in strong Northumbrian tones. All those assembled were greatly impressed, and when Davy's lamp was exhibited in Newcastle it was judged to be a copy of Stephenson's. The 'Davy lamp' was adopted by coalfields across the country – except in the north-east, where miners stayed loyal to the device they considered to be the first and the best: the 'Geordie lamp'.

A heated argument over the true originator raged for many months, following the award of £2,000 to Davy *"in honour of his invention of the safety lamp"*, and newspapers were bombarded with letters from the rival camps – Stephenson was even accused of stealing Davy's ideas. Stephenson's supporters would have none of this, and they proved that although their man hadn't been first to announce his lamp, he had, in fact, reached his conclusions and produced several prototypes three months before Davy had made his first public speech on the subject.

Matters came to a head on 1st November 1817 at a meeting in Newcastle's Assembly Rooms,

Geordie Lamp at the Lit and Phil – *image by Tony Beaumont*

THE MOOT HALL

Designed by builder and architect John Stokoe, the Moot Hall was conceived as a replacement for the "inconvenient and unhealthy" courthouse facilities that existed at the nearby castle. The foundation stone of the building was laid by Earl Percy on 22nd July 1810 and construction took two years to complete.

The Moot Hall heard all of Northumberland's Crown Court cases prior to 1998, when the combined court complex on the Quayside was opened. Several famous inquiries and trials were held within its walls, including the inquiry into the loss of the *SS Ina Mactavish*, wrecked at Amble in 1907, and the trial of the then 11-year-old Mary Bell for the murder of two young boys in 1968. Other notorious cases heard at the Moot Hall include that of Robert Black, tried for killing four young girls between 1981 and 1986; and, in 1991, Albert Dryden for fatally shooting local government officer Harry Collinson because of a planning dispute.

With its pillared portico and stone steps leading up to the entrance, the Moot Hall is a most striking and interesting three-storey building. The

The Moot Hall

where a number of prominent industrialists lent their weight to Stephenson's argument. Their report concluded that he could not have stolen Davy's ideas, and, although they accorded the scientist great respect, the sum of £1,000 was presented to Stephenson, along with a silver tankard engraved to state that he was *"the first to apply the construction of the safety lamp principle"*. The dispute continued until 1833 when a House of Commons committee judged that it believed Stephenson's claim to be justified.

The Geordie lamp was trusted by miners in the north-east for many years, while the rest of the country kept faith with Davy's invention, despite a defect that made it's top prone to overheating; the lamp was also implicated in the deaths of 68 people – 13 of them children – in an explosion at Moorfield Colliery in Accrington, Lancashire, in 1883.

Stephenson's lamp can be seen on display at the Lit and Phil in Newcastle as a reminder of the skill and talent of this great Victorian engineer.

courtrooms on either side of the lobby have retained their original decorative wood panelling, and there's a balcony and offices on the first floor; more interesting is the suite of cells and offices in the basement.

The building is Grade I-listed and has been declared a scheduled ancient monument: it sits within the Castle Garth and on the former site of the Roman fort of Pons Aelius; two copper coins and two altars from the time of Emperor Antoninus Pius were unearthed during its construction. The Moot Hall has now been sold to North East-based property developers, although it is thought that HM Courts & Tribunal Service will need to lease it back until late 2022 at the earliest.

The Nave, St Andrew's Church

ST ANDREW'S CHURCH

St Andrew's Church is probably the oldest in the city and stands at the top of Newgate Street. Some historians believe there was originally a Saxon Church on this site but more certainly St Andrew's was built by King David when the city was under Scottish control; the style of the architecture and its dedication to Scotland's patron saint lend some credibility to this belief.

Part of the tower dates from the 12th century but incorporates some stones of Roman origin, and during the Siege of Newcastle in 1644 a gun was mounted here as part of the city's defences. The walls were breached by Scottish cannon in the battle, damaging the church so badly that it could not be used for a year afterwards.

There have, however, been many additions and alterations to the fabric of the building over the years, with many styles of ecclesiastical architecture in evidence. The oldest feature inside the church is the Norman chancel arch, which is richly embellished with the typical zigzag mouldings of the style. The nave arches date from the same period, and the interior of the building is wonderfully open in aspect.

Along the north side of the churchyard are remnants of the old City Walls and part of an old gate, surmounted by a ruined tower. Opposite the south entrance of the church is the grave of Charles Avison the well-known Newcastle composer, musician and teacher whose works included "An Essay on Musical Expression".

St Andrew's, the oldest church in the City

NEWCASTLE-UPON-TYNE

ST MARY'S CATHOLIC CATHEDRAL

On reflection, it seems quite remarkable that in the late 1830s Newcastle's Catholic population made plans to build a fine second church in the city, with seating for 1,200 worshippers; the community at that time was very poor and included many destitute refugees from Ireland (worse was to come when the dreadful Potato Famine struck in 1845).

The project was the brainchild of Father James Worswick (from whom Worswick Street, with its bus station, takes its name) – pastor of St Andrew's, the first public Catholic church established in Newcastle after the Reformation – with the support of his assistant, Father William Riddell. The main source of fundraising was halfpenny donations from the poorest people of the city and the diocese, which extended from Berwick-upon-Tweed to Stockton-on-Tees.

The services of the young but widely renowned architect Augustus WN Pugin were engaged, and by 1842 he had designed an impressive edifice in his favoured Gothic Revival style. The church, which stands in a prime position opposite the present-day Newcastle Central Station, was completed two years later, although a lack of funds precluded the inclusion of the steeple in Pugin's design. Sadly, Father James Worswick did not live to see his vision realised; he died in 1843 and was interred in the church as its construction progressed.

Father Riddell, having by this time been consecrated bishop, was appointed St Mary's parish priest, and when the diocese of Hexham was created in 1850 the church became its first cathedral. In 1861, when the title of the diocese was changed to Hexham and Newcastle, the cathedral was dedicated to 'Our Lady of the Assumption'. A tower with a 222ft-high, needle-like steeple – the missing feature from Pugin's original plans – was finally added in 1872, 20 years after the death of the great architect at the age of just 40.

Much of the fine stained glass in the south elevation was destroyed by bombing during World War II, but in 2004 a new window was unveiled, created by Leeds-born glass artist Cate Watkinson and dedicated to war hero Adam Wakenshaw, who was baptised and married in the cathedral. The window illustrates a sequence of scenes from Private Wakenshaw's birth in Newcastle in 1914 to his valiant death in Mersa Matruh, Egypt, in 1942, for which he was posthumously awarded the Victoria Cross.

This tribute to the tragically short life of a brave soldier will hopefully inspire more dedications within this great building – an important focus in the diocese for almost two centuries.

St Mary's Catholic Cathedral

Adam Wakenshaw memorial window – St Mary's Cathedral

Cardinal Basil Hume Statue – St Mary's Cathedral

ST NICHOLAS' CATHEDRAL

St Nicholas' Cathedral – also known as Newcastle Cathedral – stands on what is believed to be the site of a late 11th century Norman church founded by Osmund the Good, Bishop of Salisbury and nephew of William the Conqueror. The first record of this earlier church came in 1122 when Henry I included it in a list of Northumbrian churches assigned to the monks of Carlisle, and its first association with St Nicholas – the patron saint of sailors and merchants, among other professions – appears to have been in 1194. The building was destroyed by fire in 1216 and again in 1248.

Construction of the new church, built mostly in a Perpendicular Gothic style, was completed by 1350, except for the choir arcades and the tower with its famous spire, which were finished in 1400. The lower part of the tower was also completed by then, but the belfry, vaulting and crown took another 50 years.

The first important event connected with the church was the ratification of the truce between England and Scotland, which took place in the vestry in 1451. John Knox held the position of preacher at St Nicholas' for two years during the reign of Edward VI, and it was here that he made his defence to the Council of the North for teaching that mass was idolatrous. When James I was on his way from Scotland to assume the crown of England, he stayed for a time in Newcastle and attended services at St Nicholas'. Tobie Matthew, Bishop of Durham, preached before the monarch on one occasion, welcoming him to his new kingdom.

During the 1664 siege of Newcastle, Lord General Alexander Leslie, the Earl of Leven, threatened to destroy the lantern tower unless there was an immediate surrender from Sir John Marley, then-Mayor, who was defending the city with his small force. In response, Marley moved his Scottish prisoners into the tower; thus, if Leven wanted to raze the structure, he would also have the blood of his countrymen on his hands. The Earl did not carry out his threat, but eventually, Marley and his men were forced to capitulate in the face of overwhelming odds.

Construction in the middle of the 15th century of the tower and its magnificent steeple were co-funded by Robert Rhodes, the eminent lawyer who later owned Bessie Surtees House in the city. The tower has a base measuring just over 36ft by 35ft and is divided into three storeys. The first forms the entrance to the church; the second houses the clock, which has two dials, one facing north and the other south; and on the third are the bells. There are 12 bells in total; the largest is named the 'Major' – in memory of its donor, the philanthropist Major George Anderson – and is used for striking the hours. Another, named the 'Pancake Bell', is rung at noon on Shrove Tuesday, and the 'Thief and Reiver' bell chimes before annual fairs and gatherings to let all thieves and vagabonds know that they can enter the city without fear of being arrested or molested.

The spire is often referred to as the 'Scottish Crown' type, although it pre-dates and served as a model for those of St Giles' Cathedral in Edinburgh, King's College in Aberdeen and the Tolbooth Steeple in Glasgow. It comprises a remarkable

NEWCASTLE-UPON-TYNE

St Nicholas' Cathedral – Lantern Tower where a light burns every evening after dusk

St Nicholas' Cathedral – Quire screen

'lantern' supported by four flying buttresses and stands almost 200ft above street level. Every evening, after dusk, a light burns here. In the late 18th century, the parishioners decided to convert St Nicholas' to a more fashionable church, and a great number of drastic alterations were carried out at that time. Further restoration was carried out on the building by Sir George Gilbert Scott between 1867 and 1876.

In 1882, the church, which until that time had been the fourth largest parish church in England, was raised to cathedral status. As a result, the main fittings were refurbished, with a new reredos, choir and stalls, bishop's throne, sedilia and chancel screens to enhance the dignity of the setting.

The cathedral is entered by the north-west porch, where there is a memorial to Admiral Collingwood, Lord Nelson's friend and his successor at the Battle of Trafalgar. Along the north aisle, part of a Norman arch can be seen, and, in the crossing, the remnant of the 13th century pillar is visible on one of the piers.

There are many interesting and unusual attractions in the cathedral. The brass eagle lectern, an early 16th century work, is the only pre-Reformation lectern in the North of England. Below the north end of the transept, reached by steps, is the tiny crypt, a fine example of one of the very few remaining medieval charnel chapels.

In the south choir is the magnificent German brass of Roger Thornton and his wife; adorned with 92 figures, it is the only surviving 15th century specimen in England. Roger Thornton, who died in 1429, was the 'Dick Whittington' of Newcastle – he arrived in the city penniless and yet became Mayor nine times and a Member of Parliament on four occasions.

In the east window of St Margaret's Chapel is a roundel of 15th century glass depicting the Virgin Mary and Child – the only surviving fragment of medieval glass in the cathedral. The octagonal 15th century font at the west end of the tower is made from Frosterley marble, a much-prized polished black limestone from County Durham. A small memorial in the corner of the churchyard marks the site of the wood engraver Thomas Bewick's workshop.

THE THEATRE ROYAL

The Theatre Royal in Grey Street is one of Britain's most successful provincial theatres, staging more than 400 performances each year for an annual audience of around 400,000. The building, with its graceful portico boasting six Corinthian columns, is arguably the most striking on the smooth uphill curve of this much-loved street.

This is Newcastle's second Theatre Royal – the original opened on 21st January 1788 in nearby Mosley Street, just a five-minute walk away. However, the building stood in the path of the proposed new development of Grey Street, so Richard Grainger bought this and the surrounding properties for the sum of £45,000, on the understanding that he would build a new theatre for the city. The final curtain came down in Mosley Street on 25th June 1836.

Construction of the new Theatre Royal, designed by John and Benjamin Green, took place between 1836 and 1837, and it opened on 20th February 1838 with a performance of William Shakespeare's *The Merchant of Venice*. Minor alterations to the venue took place throughout the late 19th century, but then, in 1899, disaster struck when the interior was damaged by fire, following – spookily enough – a staging of 'the Scottish Play'. The highly respected theatre architect Frank Matcham was enlisted to redesign, rebuild and extend the theatre; it re-opened in 1901.

In the late 1960s, the Theatre Royal was bought by Newcastle City Council and leased to an independent trust that became responsible for its administration and upkeep. Many of the auditorium's original features were in poor condition, and the cramped backstage facilities were woefully inadequate. When restoration began, it was discovered that the structural condition of the theatre was much worse than had first been thought – in fact, most of the building was found to be unsafe. Extensive renovation and restoration work took 19 months and was completed in January 1988.

The total cost of the project was around £6.3 million, and the theatre reopened its doors in great style on 11th January 1988 with a very well-received performance of *A Man for All Seasons*, starring Hollywood legend Charlton Heston and noted British actor Roy Kinnear.

The Theatre Royal

THE TOWN MOOR

In medieval times, Newcastle's Town Moor was an area of common pasture outside the town. By 1400, Newcastle had a population of just 4,000, and many of the inhabitants made their living working the land. Each day, cattle would be driven out to pasture on the Town Moor, Castle Leazes and Nuns Moor, all of which provided public grazing.

By the 17th century, the Town Moor was still being used for this purpose, and the Corporation of Newcastle employed a variety of people with the necessary skills to ensure smooth running. 'Grassmen' were employed to police the moor, and a 'neateherd' supervised the four men who collected the cattle – they would walk through the streets at four o'clock in the morning, sounding trumpets as a signal to the people to drive their animals to the town gates. These men tended the cattle on the moor and returned them safely before dusk. This system was in use right up until the advent of the railways; however, it is interesting to note that as much as a third of Newcastle's milk supply was still being produced in the city as recently as 1895.

The Town Moor was not only used for grazing animals: in the 13th century, coal was mined there, and it provided a venue for cricket, horse racing and bull-baiting. It was also a favourite spot for public executions; one such event attracted a crowd of more than 20,000 to watch a female felon being hanged. The last public execution on the moor took place in 1844, when Mark Sherwood was executed for the murder of his wife, Ann.

Political groups such as miners and reformers held public meetings on the moor; in the late 19th century, the horse racing was moved to Gosforth and a large temperance meeting held in its place. This evolved into the famous Hoppings, a popular travelling funfair that returns to the moor in June each year.

The first publicly funded park was opened in Britain by Joseph Paxton (later to be Sir Joseph) in Birkenhead on 5th April 1847. This was brought about by a combination of pressure from the medical profession, who argued that clean air was important for good health and an increased demand from the general public for recreational facilities. In 1873, almost 36 acres of Castle Leazes became Leazes Park; soon after, Bull Park and Brandling Park were created, along with two more public parks at Elswick and Heaton.

In 1880, Lord Armstrong donated the park named after him, and this was followed three years later by the public opening of the adjoining Jesmond Dene, the wonderfully secluded dene of the Ouseburn where shady paths connect with the ruins of a banqueting hall, ruined flint mill, and an attractive gatehouse designed by architect Norman Shaw.

These parks not only provided space for pleasant walks, but they also made excellent venues for bowling, lawn tennis and quoits, and highly popular concerts on Sundays.

Cycling on the Town Moor

Cattle quietly grazing on the Town Moor, 1000 acres of public parkland in the centre of Newcastle

TRINITY HOUSE

Built in 1505 for the Guild of Masters and Mariners, Trinity House occupies an attractive courtyard just off Broad Chare. The site had been acquired by the seafarers' charitable guild in 1492 from local merchant Ralph Hebborn – the man from whom Hebburn takes its name. The south side of Trinity House was built in 1721, and behind that is a smaller courtyard and school. In the main courtyard are the almshouses *("for aged and infirm Brethren")*, the banqueting hall, the rigging loft and the chapel, which is still used once a year by the Brethren.

In 1536, Henry VIII granted the guild a Royal Charter of Incorporation, which allowed it to erect two lighthouses at North Shields – the High Light and the Low Light – lit by candles and constructed using stones from dissolved monasteries. The guild then levied a charge to enter the port: "fowerpence"(4 old pennies) for foreign ships and "tuppence" (Two old pennies) for English vessels. In subsequent years, Trinity House took even greater control of the river, appointing pilots, training mariners in its own school, and, of course, continuing to collect the levies and charges necessary to the profitable and efficient running of the port. In 1664, members of the guild were granted exemption from jury service and the obligation to bear arms, underlining the importance of their work.

Broad Chare was so named because it was wide enough to take a cart, unlike other chares in the city. A local legend tells of how sometimes, in the still of the night, the eerie rustle of a woman's long skirts can be heard in Broad Chare – the ghost of Martha Wilson, a mariner's widow who hanged herself in one of the almshouses in the early 1800s.

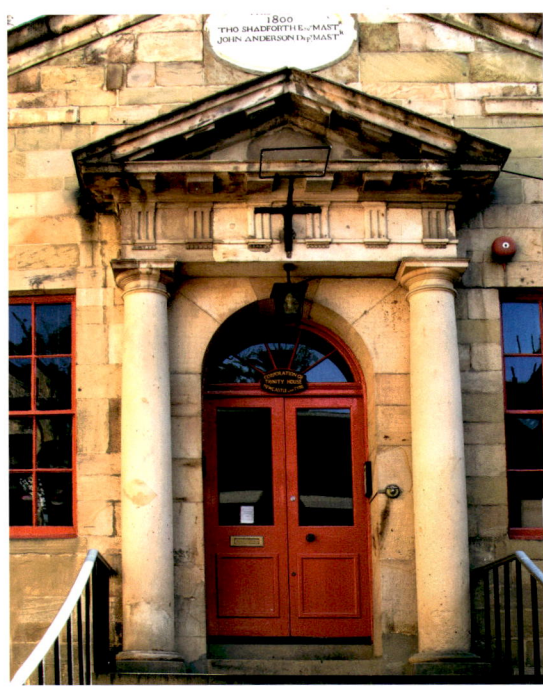
Trinity House – main entrance

Trinity House – street entrance

Trinity House courtyard – anchor from the Spanish Armada 1588

VICTORIA TUNNEL

The Victoria Tunnel carried a coal waggonway under the city; it was built between 1839 and 1842 and covered a distance of 2 and a quarter miles or 4 km from Leazes Main Colliery in Spital Tongues to the riverside coal staithes where its coal was loaded onto collier ships for export. The tunnel was 7' 5" (2.26 metres) wide, 6'3" (1.91 metres) high, had an overall drop of 222ft (68m) and at its deepest point was 85' (26m) below ground level. Today 766 yards or 700m is accessible.

The tunnel was driven through boulder clay with a base of coarse stone which supported a strong brick arch for the roof. Loaded wagons descended the incline by gravity and the empties were hauled back to the colliery by a powerful stationary steam engine. The colliery closed in January 1860 and the tunnel was largely abandoned until the start of the Second World War when it was pressed into use as an air raid shelter.

The Industrial Revolution was in full swing when Leazes Main or Spital Tongues Colliery was opened in 1835, the competition was fierce and the demand for coal was high. At first, the coal was carried on horse-drawn carts from the colliery to the river for shipping – but it was a slow process because the town still had its medieval layout of narrow, cobbled streets and, of course, high road taxes added to the problem. The Colliery owners, Mortimer and Latimer, employed a local engineer, William E Gillespie, to construct a wagonway. The first idea for an overground wagonway was rejected because the Freemen of Newcastle refused permission to lay tracks across the Town Moor. A more direct, overground route was also ruled out because the old Tyne Bridge prevented ships from sailing beyond Newcastle. This would mean building new staithes and having to pay the keelmen to take the coal downstream of the bridge before it could be loaded onto the colliers – again a huge chunk out of the profits.

An underground wagonway seemed to be the only answer – permission was granted in 1838 and work started the following year. John Cherry, a former lead miner, latterly employed at the Leazes Main Colliery, was appointed to manage the tunnelling. The building works were to be carried out by David Nixon, a builder from Prudhoe Street in Newcastle. The engineers would have excavated a shaft to the required level and then it would be tunnelled out to link up with the next section. The walls of the tunnel were lined in stone and a double brick arch supported the roof. It was made just large enough to accommodate the custom-built Chaldron Wagons.

The 200 workers employed in the construction of the tunnel at its completion were, as reported by Thomas Fordyce in his "Local Records" on 6th January 1842, *"Regaled with a substantial supper and strong ale, supplied by Mrs Dixon, the worthy hostess of the Unicorn Inn, the Bigg Market, Newcastle. The Albion Band attended and enlivened the joyous occasion with their music."*

The Tunnel was named after the popular young Queen Victoria. It was opened by the Mayor of Newcastle on 7th April 1842. A crowd of spectators including the Sheriff and important residents gathered on the quayside and at 1.00 pm cannons fired just as a train of eight wagons appeared from the tunnel – four of the wagons were loaded with coal and the others contained "a company of ladies and gentlemen and a band of musicians".

The Victoria Tunnel was a financial success and reduced the cost of transporting the coal from the colliery to the river by a staggering 88%. The colliery, unfortunately, was not a success and closed in 1860 – and although the tunnel took two and a half years to build it only operated for 18 years.

In 1939 Britain was preparing for war. People were advised to practice "Air Raid Precautions" to protect themselves from bombing raids by the German Luftwaffe. In Newcastle, the City Engineer made plans to convert the Victoria Tunnel into an air aid shelter for 9,000 people. It cost £57,000 to convert the tunnel – it was cleaned of coal dust, some of

Victoria Tunnel

the walls were whitewashed and a number of concrete blast walls were included to stop any flying bomb debris. A new concrete floor was laid and electric lighting installed. Wooden benches and about 500 bunk beds were fitted along the walls. Chemical toilets were enclosed in cubicles near the entrances, and the shelter was ready for anything Hitler could throw at them. Seven new entrances were made although originally 16 were planned. The tunnel was a dark, uncomfortable place to shelter and many people were afraid to use it, although those who did remember sitting with their families and neighbours, swapping stories and singing songs while apprehensively waiting for the "all – clear" to sound from above.

At the end of the war, most of the fittings were removed and all the entrances except Ouse street were closed. The Tunnel remains today as a monument and memorial to Victorian engineering and a tribute to the community who stuck together through their adaptability by using it as a protection from the ravages of war. Today the tunnel is in the care of the Ouseburn Trust which offers pre-booked tours and provides a most unforgettable experience.

Benwell Staith – print by permission of the Kemble Art Gallery - Durham

Ouseburn

EXPLORING NORTHUMBERLAND HISTORY:
NORTHUMBERLAND COAST

River Aln Estuary from Church Hill

ALNMOUTH

Alnmouth was, at one time, the port of the town of Alnwick, the principal seat of the Dukes of Northumberland. By the end of the 19th century, however, Alnmouth's fortunes as a seaport had dwindled; over subsequent years, it has developed into a coastal resort of the quieter kind – seemingly without any loss of character. The tall spire of the Church of St John the Baptist dominates the village, with the other buildings grouped pleasantly around it on a gentle slope leading down to the harbour.

In Saxon times, a chapel dedicated to St Waleric was built on Church Hill, just to the south of the river. The remains of an inscribed cross were discovered close to the site in 1789; one face is carved with scenes representing the Crucifixion, the other with the words *"Myredeh meh wo"*, meaning "Myredeh me wrought" – Myredeh is believed to have been an Irish sculptor. One of the edges is inscribed with the name of Eadulf, the Saxon chieftain who seized Northumbria in the early part of the 8th century. This hill is one of several locations that lay claim to having been the site of the synod of Twyford in AD 684, at which St Cuthbert was selected for the post of Bishop of Lindisfarne.

It was after the Norman Conquest that Alnmouth really began to develop in importance. The men of the port were required to keep their ships in a state of constant readiness for the protection of the realm and were also expected to light nearby beacons to give warning of any invasion. In 1336, Alnmouth was almost destroyed when it was attacked by the Scots during one of their frequent incursions following the Battle of Bannockburn. The village had barely recovered when, 12 years later, it was ravaged by the Black Death, losing a third of its population.

Measures put in place to protect the realm were relaxed at Alnmouth to a certain extent after the Union of the Crowns in 1603. It was then that the village developed an important trade in the export of corn, and by 1769 its granaries were thought to be the largest in the country.

Mortuary chapel, Alnmouth

There were 16 of these buildings, some of them three stories high; a number of these can still be seen, now converted into comfortable homes.

There was also a healthy trade in other goods, including timber from Norway. This prosperity, of course, led to the presence of privateers and freebooters in the waters off the Northumbrian coast, and there are records of several encounters in Alnmouth Bay. On 15th August 1779, a sea battle took place that lasted for two hours and was watched by a crowd from the shore. Two French privateers were chased off, but one of them came dangerously close to the shore. Fear of a landing brought a group of heavily armed volunteers and two mounted cannons at full speed from Alnwick Castle.

Another incident took place in the following month when the notorious freebooter John Paul Jones captured a small cargo ship within the sight of people watching from the shore. He then set off down the coast and fired a parting shot at the church; it missed its target, but the cannonball hit a nearby field with such force that it bounced three times and ripped through a farm, front to back.

An interesting barn-like building can be found about half a mile to the south of Alnmouth. Believed to have been built in the 18th century, the guano shed was a storage facility for the fertiliser, which was imported from Peru and, understandably, had to be kept as far from the village as possible because of its pungent smell. The structure was listed as a Grade II building in 1988.

In the middle of the 19th century, the trade in guano between South America and Europe became particularly important to British agriculture. The enthusiasm and demand for this natural product mushroomed due to its exceptionally high nitrogen, phosphate and potassium levels: all the nutrients essential for strong plant growth. These rich deposits were harvested

Alnmouth guano sheds

Lobster pots, Amble

for more than 30 years, and about 12 million tons of guano were exported to Europe. Around 16 ships a year delivered the fertiliser to the River Aln, most of them arriving via other ports such as London.

Teams of young girls worked the tides unloading the vessels by shovel and wheelbarrow, and when the easterly winds blew, the whole village knew what was going on. This gave rise to the lilting ballad *My Great Grandma Was a Guano Shoveller*, which is still heard in some of the more traditional folk and country clubs of Northumberland. These remarkable buildings at Alnmouth are the only known guano sheds in the county or, indeed, all of Great Britain.

On Christmas Eve 1806, a huge storm changed Alnmouth for ever, destroying the Church of St Waleric and altering the course of the River Aln. Until that day, Church Hill had been connected to the village by a spit of land and the river had entered the sea to its south. The storm caused the sandbank to be breached, creating a new channel that the Aln has followed ever since.

In 1870, a small mortuary chapel was built on the west side of Church Hill at a cost of £177.6s.3d., raised by public subscription, as part of a plan to reopen the cemetery on the site. In more recent times, the roof of the now Grade II-listed building has been deliberately removed by the National Trust to deter squatters. The ruined chapel can only be reached at very low tide from Alnmouth, or by a rough track on the other side of the Aln.

AMBLE

Situated at the mouth of the River Coquet, some 25 miles north of the River Tyne and standing at the northern tip of the vast Northumberland Coalfield, Amble developed as a port specialising in the export of coal. From here, the seams radiate southwards in a huge triangle reaching as far as Tyneside and Teesside. Coal has been worked in Northumberland since the 13th century, although the biggest and fastest development was during the 19th century when the coming of the railways provided the necessary transport. The harbour here – known as Warkworth Harbour – was constructed between 1838 and 1849, at a cost of £180,000, and was mainly used by Radcliffe and Broomhill collieries for the export of their coal.

The seams at Amble are so near to the surface and close to the sea that during stormy weather in the winter months they are uncovered, and the coal is spread along the shore – indeed, sea-coaling was once an important and rewarding local occupation. Now, by contrast, coal mining is almost non-existent in the county, and the port has further evolved to concentrate upon fishing, tourism and sailing.

The importance of this site has been recognised since the earliest times; indeed, several burial cists were discovered and opened here during the second half of the 19th century – one example, found close to the south pier, contained a perfectly intact human skeleton.

Fragments of an altar, uncovered during ploughing in 1856, would also suggest that there was some form of Roman camp here. The local names of Temple Hill, Chester House and Street Head indicate the possibility of a Roman road that ran from inland to the mouth of the Coquet.

A small Benedictine monastery, a satellite of Tynemouth Priory, was once established here, and the monks enjoyed the privilege of collecting the tithes of Amble, as granted by William the Conqueror. They also had the right to collect a toll from any ship or boat passing up the river. This lasted well into the 18th century – there is a record of a man in 1765 who failed to pay and, as a result, had to serve penance in the small chapel attached to the monastery.

The town of Amble has retained its interesting character, managing to combine an absorbing past with a promising, vibrant present. It most certainly deserves its billing as "the friendliest port".

Bamburgh Castle from the west

BAMBURGH

It was in AD 547 that Ida, King of Bernicia, built the first fortifications on the top of the huge outcrop of the Great Whin Sill, towering 150ft above the surrounding coastline. The king is said to have earned the colourful title of 'the Flamebearer' because of the utter destruction he brought upon the local Celtic tribes who dared to disagree with him.

The early fortifications were simply a wooden palisade surrounded by a thorn hedge and protected by a deep ditch. The settlement, known by the old British name of Din Guaydri, became the seat of the kingdom of Northumbria – which extended from the River Humber to the Firth of Forth – and this 'royal city' attained a position of importance second only to York itself.

Ida's grandson, King Ethelfrith the Destroyer – who, as his title suggests, further continued the family tradition of spreading devastation and destruction – gave the fortress to his wife, Queen Bebba. She renamed it Bebbanburg, from which it later became Bamburgh.

In his epic poem *Marmion*, Sir Walter Scott describes Bamburgh as:
"Thy tower, proud Bamborough [sic], mark'd they there,
King Ida's castle, huge and square."

However, the poet was guilty of a little over-enthusiasm, as the castle did not assume anything like the appearance we see today until more than 700 years after the reign of King Ida.

Bamburgh's status as a royal city lasted until the unification of the kingdom in the early seventh century. It was here that the Northumbrian kings were crowned, and both of the first two Christian monarchs, Edwin and Oswald, lived at Bamburgh. However, like all northern strongholds, Bamburgh has had a stormy history. In around AD 651, it was besieged by the Mercians, led by their pagan king, Penda, who killed both Christian leaders in battle and then tried to take their city by fire. Tradition has it that St Aidan, the first Bishop of Lindisfarne, was watching the attack from Inner Farne and prayed that the heathen ruler would be defeated. Immediately, the wind changed direction and threatened the attackers. The siege was stopped, and the city was saved.

From the late eighth to the mid-11th century, the Northumberland coast suffered repeated Viking raids, during which castles, churches and monastic establishments were over-run by these fierce invaders. But it would seem that Bamburgh escaped the full force of the raiding,

Trustees bell – Bamburgh Castle

Medieval suit armour in Bamburgh Castle

because it was still standing in 1069-70 when William the Conqueror carried out the Harrying of the North, leaving behind him a trail of devastation and destruction as bad as – if not worse than – that of the dreadful Viking incursions. In fact, only the cities of Bamburgh, Durham and York remained relatively unscathed, while the surrounding fields were scorched by the brutal Norman army.

King William granted Robert de Mowbray a large part of Northumberland, but before long Bamburgh was once again the centre of trouble. While William ruled the Northern Barons with an iron hand, they remained quiet in spite of the fact that they were ever eager for more land, more power and more money. That opportunity arose when William Rufus inherited his father's crown in 1087. Open revolt broke out, and the Earl of Mowbray was one of the first to defy the new king, with the result that in 1095 Rufus sent a large army to Northumberland. Mowbray managed to hold out at Bamburgh, even though he was greatly outnumbered, so a little cunning was applied. When the earl received a false message saying that he would be welcomed in Newcastle, he slipped quietly through the ranks of the siege army in an attempt to escape, but he was followed. Mowbray took sanctuary at a church in Tynemouth dedicated to St Oswin, but his rights were violated, and he was taken prisoner. His wife, Countess Matilda, held out at Bamburgh, but Mowbray was brought before her on a grassy knoll in front of the castle, and the lady was given the choice of surrender or seeing her husband's eyes gouged out on the spot. She capitulated, of course – the strength of the castle's fortifications was of little use in the face of such a threat.

Bamburgh then became a possession of the Crown, and much restoration work was carried out on the castle by Henry I. Both Henry III and Edward I visited the castle while on their excursions to wage war on the Scots.

During the Wars of the Roses, Bamburgh suffered more than one attack, although it remained in Yorkist hands for the majority of that time. It was taken by the Lancastrians in 1463, following a long siege by the forces of Margaret of Anjou, wife of the deposed King Henry VI. The king later found refuge at Bamburgh, but escaped after hearing of the fall of Dunstanburgh, where his chief henchman, Sir Ralph Grey, was captured, then taken to Doncaster and executed. The end of the Wars of the Roses also brought an end to the many sieges Bamburgh endured over those years.

Sir John Forster, Warden of the Middle March, was governor of the castle during the reign of Elizabeth I, and following the Union of the Crowns in 1603 the title passed to his grandson, Sir Claudius Forster, who James I also awarded the manor of Bamburgh. The family owned it for two hundred years but in 1715 they were implicated in the Jacobite Rebellion – Thomas Forster was the notorious Jacobite General. Not many Northumbrians supported this cause and the few that did fared badly. Indeed, the Forsters seem to have acted unwisely on several occasions, Sir William Forster and his sons got through their splendid inheritance with reckless extravagance. Eventually they reached such a state of insolvency that the buildings fell into neglect and disrepair and they were forced to sell.

In 1704, Bamburgh Castle was purchased by Nathaniel, Lord Crewe, Bishop of Durham, whose wife Dorothy was a Forster, and it fell to him to restore the castle to its former glory. He entrusted the work to Dr John Sharp – Archdeacon of Northumberland at the time – and following Lord Crewe's death in 1721 at the age of 88, a charity was set up to continue the restoration and the philanthropic work he had instigated.

In 1894, the castle came into the possession of the great Victorian industrialist Lord William Armstrong, whose family still owns the estate.

One of Bamburgh Castle's most interesting features is a well in a vaulted room on the ground floor of the keep. It descends to a depth of almost 150ft, cutting right through the Great Whin Sill and then through the sandstone of an even earlier age. This well is believed to be older than the keep itself – an account by

NORTHUMBERLAND COAST

Storm clouds over Bamburgh beach

the 12th century monk Symeon of Durham dates it to as early as AD 774. And, naturally, legend has found it a fitting setting for a grim tale – that of the Laidley Worm.

The story tells of how the radiantly beautiful Princess Margaret, daughter of King Ida, was turned into a 'laidley worm' (or loathsome serpent) by her wicked and jealous stepmother. A ballad written in the 18th century by the Reverend Robert Lambe, vicar of Norham, and supposedly transcribed from the manuscript by Duncan Frasier a 13th century Cheviot 'mountain bard', relates:

"For seven miles east and seven miles west
And seven miles north and south
No blade of grass or corn could grow
So venomous was her mouth.
The milk of seven stately cows
(It was costly her to keep)
Was brought her daily, which she drank
Before she went to sleep."

News of the dreadful devastation wreaked by this awesome creature spread far and wide. At length, it reached the ears of Margaret's brother, known as the Childe Wynde – 'Child of the Wind' – who was overseas, seeking fame and fortune. The prince immediately ordered the building of a sturdy ship to carry him and his men back to Bamburgh, and to protect them from evil he ordered the masts to be made from rowan. The evil queen, looking from her window, saw the Childe Wynde approaching and sent her witches to destroy the craft. When this failed, she ordered a boat loaded with armed men to stop the prince, but the magic of the rowan protected him.

The Childe Wynde eventually landed on the beach, only to be confronted by the monstrous creature breathing fire through its huge nostrils and whipping the sand into swirling dust with its enormous tail. The prince raised his sword to strike it a mighty blow, but stopped when he heard these words:

"O quit thy sword and bend thy bow,
And give me kisses three
For though I am a poisonous worm,
No hurt I'll do to thee."

The prince bravely did as he was bid, and the creature immediately vanished. In its place stood his beautiful sister, Princess Margaret. Overjoyed, the prince and princess set out to confront their wicked stepmother. She begged for mercy, but the Childe Wynde could not find it in his heart to forgive the dreadful curse she had inflicted on his sister. He cursed the evil queen, turning her into a huge and venomous toad. The creature was banished forever to the very bottom of the deep castle well, only emerging to scare the unwary traveller:

"And now on the sand near Ida's tower
She crawls a loathsome toad
And venom spits on every maid
She meets upon her road."

St Aidan's Church, Bamburgh

BAMBURGH, ST AIDAN'S CHURCH

St Aidan's, Bamburgh is one of the largest parish churches in Northumberland. It is certainly one of the most beautiful, and generates the most wonderful sense of warmth and peace upon entering. The church dates mainly from the late 12th century and was built on the site of the Saxon chapel constructed for St Aidan, of which there are now scant remains.

However, throughout the interior of the church are reminders of Northumbrian saints and heroes depicted in stained glass and on memorials. In the north aisle is a monument to Grace Darling that once stood in the churchyard, but had to be repaired in 1885 after being damaged in a gale. The original was brought into the church and a replacement placed in the monument outside.

Unusually long in proportion to the nave, the chancel of St Aidan's is possibly one of the church's finest features. Displayed high on its north wall are the sword, helmet, breastplate and gauntlets of Ferdinando Forster, who was killed by John Fenwick on the streets of Newcastle in 1701. In 1837, a crypt containing the bodies of several members of the Forster family was discovered, revealing that the chamber must have been used as a mausoleum. In earlier days, it would have served as a place for the safe-keeping of relics, and for the anointing of the sick and the dying. Consequently, this would have been a place of pilgrimage; the pilgrims would have entered through the chancel, passed down through the crypt and out into the churchyard. Today, the crypt is entered by a doorway in the outside wall, at the end of a short passage reached by a flight of stone steps.

The site of St Aidan's death, Bamburgh Church

The Grace Darling memorial in the churchyard was placed a short distance to the north of her grave so that it might be seen from vessels at sea. Grace's heroic actions really captured the imagination of the public, and numerous newspaper articles carried reports of her deeds. The publicity was overwhelming: books and poems were written about her, portraits were painted, and she received several offers of marriage. Grace died of tuberculosis on 20th October 1842, only four years after the rescue. By 1844, enough money had been raised by public subscription to erect the monument in the churchyard overlooking the sea; Queen Victoria was among the first to contribute to its cost.

The RNLI Grace Darling Museum, situated just across the road from the church, houses many of the relics connected with the rescue and its subsequent publicity. Pride of place goes to the boat that was used – a traditional Northumberland coble, 21ft long and 6ft wide.

Detail of St Aidan, west window, Bamburgh Church

Grace Darling's grave St Aidan's churchyard, Bamburgh

BEADNELL

Believed to date back to Saxon times, the village of Beadnell has always been an important fishing village. Indeed, records from the 16th century indicate that the population was larger then than it is today. In the 18th century, Beadnell – in common with many villages along the Northumberland coast – was a popular haunt for smugglers.

Its harbour, which was constructed in the late 18th century, has the distinction of being the only west-facing harbour on the east coast of England. Standing almost on the edge of the harbour is an extremely impressive group of disused limekilns. The earliest, built by Richard Pringle in 1798, measures 24ft high and 16ft in diameter at the top, tapering to a width of 9ft. The limestone and coal were extracted from landowner John Wood's nearby estate at Beadnell Hall, and it was he who carried out the maintenance to keep the kiln in good working order. A thousand cartloads of lime were produced per year, and these were exported by sea to other ports along the English and Scottish coasts. Sales of the lime exceeded all expectations; so much so that Wood had another two kilns built to keep pace with demand.

Coal and limestone were transported to the top of the kilns by wagons running on a tramway; it took one load of coal to burn two loads of limestone. Each kiln had a large pot that was filled from the top with alternating layers of limestone and coal. The coal was lit, and the stone burned slowly over several weeks to produce the quicklime. Each kiln had three or four "draw arches" at the base, and each of these had an "eye" from which the lime was extracted when the process was finished. The kilns, which are in the care of the National Trust, are now used by local fishermen for storage.

Just to the north-east of the harbour, on Ebb's Nook, there once stood a small medieval chapel dedicated to St Ebba (or Æbbe), Abbess of Coldingham, Saxon princess and sister of the Northumbrian kings Oswald and Oswy. Several grassy mounds and scant sections of masonry are all that now remain of the chapel, which is thought to date from the 12th or 13th century in its current form, although its isolated position on the headland suggests the site was established much earlier – some historians believe it could have been one of the earliest Christian chapels in Northumberland. Each year, on the closest Sunday to Ebba's Feast Day (25th August), the people of Beadnell still come here to worship.

The village church, also dedicated to St Ebba, was built in around 1740 and then enlarged in 1792. The spire, most notable for the unusual octagonal panelled stone screen around its base, looks 18th century, but was in fact added in 1860.

Close by is The Craster Arms, Beadnell's village pub. Incorporated into the fabric of this 18th century building is a pele tower that was built two centuries earlier, with walls almost 8ft thick – indicating that, prior to that date, fortification was a greater priority than socialising.

Beadnell Harbour and Lime Kilns

Ebb's Nook, Beadnell

Castle remains, Berwick-upon-Tweed

BERWICK-UPON-TWEED

Berwick's history dates back to the kingdom of Bernicia, founded by Ida in AD 547, although the first documented evidence of its existence comes from the ninth century. The town was claimed, along with the River Tweed, by the Scots under King Malcolm II following the Battle of Carham in 1018, and was quickly developed as a port. By the time of King David I, it was the most important of the four royal burghs: Berwick, Roxburgh, Edinburgh and Stirling. It remained so until 1174 when King William I of Scotland – known as William the Lion – was captured while retreating from a raid into Northumberland and forced to yield the town to his English captors as part of his ransom; for the next 15 years, Berwick was forced to accept England as her master.

The town remained a subject of dispute between England and Scotland for the next three centuries. In 1189, King Richard I of England – Richard the Lionheart – sold the Scots their independence to raise money for his crusades, but in 1216 trouble flared when King John entered Berwick on his way back from crushing military unrest in the border country. He enjoyed the hospitality offered by the locals, but committed barbarous atrocities and burned the town before he left.

In spite of this, by the middle of the 13th century the Port of Berwick enjoyed great commercial success, and the town became an important centre of commerce and administration – one of the wealthiest in Scotland. It was at Berwick Castle, in 1292, that King Edward I of England declared his decision on the matter of the disputed Scottish crown, ruling in favour of John Balliol, who swore an oath of allegiance to the English monarch.

The loyalty of the new king of Scotland was short-lived, however: in 1296, as a result of grievances and humiliations, Balliol broke into open rebellion and invaded Northumberland. Furious, Edward advanced north to inflict a terrible vengeance, and the first blow fell on Berwick. A combined attack by land and sea proved unstoppable; Edward himself, mounted on horseback, was the first to leap the dyke protecting the town, inspiring his men. All the horrors of war were unleashed on Berwick, the rich, well-populated, commercial town ravaged by a savage army led by a commander thirsty for vengeance. It is said that as many as 15,000 men, women and children were put to the sword – reputedly Berwick's streets ran red with blood for two days – and the churches, in which many inhabitants had sought sanctuary, were defiled, robbed of their sacred artefacts and used as stables by the English cavalry. This ruthless massacre caused a sensation all over the country, especially on the borders where it fomented much of the bitter hostility with which the English were regarded ever after. Edward had lit the fuse.

The English monarch ordered the building of new walls to defend the town, and much of this construction was still going on during the reign of his successor, Edward II. When finished, they stood 22ft in height and had 19 defensive towers and five gates in their 2½-mile length. However, in spite of the new walls, revolts and uprisings still occurred. To harass and despoil the English was looked upon as an almost sacred duty; first, William Wallace took up

Berwick-upon-Tweed Town Walls

the challenge, then Scottish king Robert I, better known as Robert the Bruce. In 1312, a stealthy move by Bruce to take the town was thwarted when a barking dog alerted guards, and he had to wait another six years for victory. Further fortification of Berwick's defences was made following the Scots' successful siege in 1318.

It was in Berwick that, prior to the town's taking by the Scots, a barbaric punishment was inflicted on Isabella MacDuff, Countess of Buchan. The countess, who had crowned Bruce at Scone, was imprisoned for four years in the castle, suspended from one of the towers in an iron cage that exposed her to the scorn, mockery and abuse of all passers-by.

The people of Berwick have witnessed many desperate and shocking events over the centuries; numerous kings and queens have passed through the town en route to glorious victory or miserable defeat, or in search of sheer bloody retribution. Edward II fled to Berwick after his humiliating defeat at Bannockburn in 1314; almost 20 years later, the longbowmen of his successor, Edward III, inflicted a devastating and satisfying revenge on the Scots at Halidon Hill.

In 1377, a band of desperate reivers, apparently only eight in number, crept into the castle at night, murdered the governor, Sir Robert de Boynton, and overcame the garrison. They were joined by about 40 of their associates and succeeded in holding the castle for eight days against 7,000 English archers and 3,000 cavalrymen.

Eventually, artillery was beginning to dominate warfare, so, in 1558, Queen Mary I engaged the famous military engineer Sir Richard Lee to improve Berwick's defences further, although most of this work on the new walls was completed during the reign of her successor, Queen Elizabeth I. The reivers in this part of the border country had taken to skirmishing

King James Bridge - Berwick-upon-Tweed

with the English soldiers on a regular basis, and the extra fortifications would no doubt reduce any chance of success with their incursions. The Elizabethan walls were constructed within those built during the Edwardian period and took more than 20 years to complete. These ramparts were the most expensive project undertaken during the reign of Elizabeth I, costing almost £130,000 pounds - nearly £38 million pounds in today's money - not surprisingly the Queen was quite taken aback by this large sum.

Holy Trinity Church Berwick-upon-Tweed

Holy Trinity Church pulpit, Berwick-upon-Tweed

On his way to being crowned King of England, James VI of Scotland experienced a perilous crossing of the Tweed across the rickety wooden bridge that had been built for Henry VII. Although a shrewd and cunning man, James was reputed to be a bit of a physical coward, and he was seized with abject fear and panic when crossing the bridge. The king flung himself off his horse, onto the planking, and called upon God to save him. He was half carried, crying and screaming, to the other side where he sank to his knees and kissed the ground. Here, James is reputed to have declared, *"What a shoogly [dangerously unsteady] brig! Is there ne'er a man in Berwick whae can werk stane to mak a brig o'er the Tweed?"*

Construction on a new bridge started in 1611, was finished, but not usable by 1626 and finally opened in 1634 at a total cost of £16,750. It is of red sandstone construction with fifteen segmental arches, its highest one being off centre to the north, in line with the deep-water channel.

The stone King James bridge is not shoogly.

Following his unhappy crossing of the original rickety wood bridge on 27th March 1603, James VI united England and Scotland in the Union of the Crowns and became James I of England; the dying wish of his mother, Mary, Queen of Scots, had been fulfilled. He immediately went to church to return thanks for his safe and peaceful entry into his new dominion, after which Toby Matthew, Bishop of Durham, preached an excellent sermon.

With the Union of the Crowns, James sought to put an end to the violent unrest and feuding that had kept the region in utter turmoil since the reign of Edward I. He prohibited the use of the term 'Borders', declaring that this should be replaced with "Middle Shires". The king also abolished the post of Warden and ordered that all places of stronghold – except, of course, the dwellings of nobles – were to be demolished. He limited any garrison to 100 men and declared that *"all rebels and disorderly persons, including their wives and bairns, will be prosecuted with fyre and sword"*. At a stroke, James had introduced the diligent persecution and speedy retribution that was to put an end to the dominance of the border reivers.

Oliver Cromwell was in Berwick during the Civil War, although he was never welcomed as a visitor because of the upscuttle and destruction his troops left behind. The Lord Protector's lasting legacy to the town is the Church of the Holy Trinity with St Mary, which opened in 1652 and said to be the only parish church built during his Commonwealth; it was greatly restored and enlarged around 200 years later. Holy Trinity's panelled pulpit is Elizabethan and came from the old parish church at St Mary's Gate; it is traditionally believed that the famous Scottish reformer John Knox preached from here when he was in Berwick in 1548. A small black marble monument marks the burial place of one of Cromwell's friends and officers, Colonel George Fenwick, Governor of Berwick, who, it says, *"was the principal instrument of causing this church to be built and died March 16, 1656. A good man is a public good"*.

When it was first built, Holy Trinity had no altar, no organ, no font, no stained glass and no bells; until 1951, when finally the church had its own installed, the congregation

The Royal Border Bridge

were summoned to worship by the bells at the Town Hall.

The Town Hall was built in the 1750s to a design by London architects Samuel and John Worrall. Confusingly, however, above the entrance the architect is named as one Joseph Dodds. It would seem that despite paying the Worralls for their work, the Guild of Freemen rejected their designs, handing the job instead to Dodds, a local carpenter and member of their committee; Dodds then satisfied the guild's demands by following the Worralls' plans, albeit with slight alterations. Originally the building was not only used for council meetings, it also housed the police station, law courts and jail. The Town Hall dominates the centre of Berwick – almost church-like in appearance, its giant portico and clock tower surmounted by a 150ft-high spire can be seen from almost everywhere on the town walls. Its eight bells date from 1754 – in fact, the curfew bell is still rung at 8pm every evening to signal that all good citizens should be retiring for the night.

Despite the historic uncertainty over which country it belonged to, Berwick today enjoys and accepts the best of both worlds: it stands at the mouth of the most romantic of all Scottish rivers, the Tweed, and yet the town itself is English. Having once belonged to neither side, it now belongs to both.

Berwick has always been centred around the river and its salmon; as far back as the 14th century, the "King's Fisheries" stood on the north bank and the "Bishop's Fisheries" on the south. By the 16th century, there were 12 fisheries on the river, and one barrel of salmon out of every 12 caught was paid to Queen Elizabeth I as a royalty. The fishing business thrived, controlled by the town's merchant guild, and fisheries changed hands for huge amounts of money. In 1636, the Moore Brothers bought the King's and the Bishop's Fisheries for almost £7,000.

In the first half of the 1800s, business boomed with record catches and enormous demand, fuelled by the use of ice and the coming of the railways, which allowed fish to be sent anywhere in the country quickly. Overfishing eventually prompted the introduction of the Tweed Acts in the late 1850s; these led to the close season being extended and severe restrictions being placed on the type of nets used, dramatically reducing the catch. Salmon fishing is still carried on in Berwick, though on a much-reduced scale.

All of Berwick's bridges are of note: in addition to the King James Bridge crossing the mighty Tweed, there's also the Royal Tweed Bridge, a concrete construction built to ease traffic congestion in the town. The bridge, which has four arches spanning 1,405ft and cost £180,000, was opened in 1928 by the then Prince of Wales. The Royal Border Bridge, designed by Robert Stephenson, is regarded to be one of the world's finest railway viaducts. More than 126ft high, with a total length of 2,160ft and 28 arches – each with a span of just over 60ft – it cost around a quarter of a million pounds to build. A workforce of more than 2,000 men was employed in the bridge's construction, which began in 1847. It was opened officially by Queen Victoria and Prince Albert on 29th August 1850; on its completion, Stephenson described the bridge as *"the final act of union"* – there is an inscription of this at the railway station nearby.

Berwick has always held an attraction as a popular holiday destination. The noted artist LS Lowry was especially fond of the town and visited many times from the mid-1930s until shortly before his death in 1976. From his base at the Castle Hotel in Castlegate, Lowry would spend his days exploring the Elizabethan walls and the back lanes; he found the architecture fascinating, especially the imposing Georgian Town Hall, which features in a number of his sketches and paintings. The artist produced a series of more than 30 drawings and paintings of the area, and it is thought that at one time he considered buying the early 19th century building known as The Lions House, but found it to be damp so unfortunately didn't pursue the purchase.

Dewar's Lane today and as drawn by Lowry in 1936

Harbour Walls, Berwick-upon-Tweed

Blyth beach huts and pier

Blyth – wind turbine & dock gate

BLYTH

The town of Blyth dates from the 12th century and stands at the mouth of the river of the same name. Around 150 years ago, the Blyth Harbour Commission was formed to improve the town's harbour facilities, which resulted in it attaining a position second only to Newcastle. Shipbuilding and large-scale coal exporting were the main activities, although herring fishing continued to thrive alongside the heavier industries. The port still imports large quantities of paper and pulp from Scandinavia for the newspaper industries of England and Scotland. With the decline of mining, and its consequences, it was necessary for the town to attract smaller, lighter industries while taking excellent steps to turn itself into a highly popular seaside resort; the glorious beach, golf course, caravan and camping sites, outstanding sailing facilities, traditional fish-and-chip shops and excellent restaurants, plus delicious home-made ice cream, all help to attract many visitors. The famous Blyth beach huts are instantly recognisable as one of Northumberland's most photographed attractions.

The Quayside has also seen a lot of redevelopment and has been transformed into a peaceful open space, the centrepiece of which is a sculpture commemorating the industry that once thrived there. The town has also become prominent in the production of power. On the opposite side of the river, along the harbour wall, stood the 300KW wind turbines of the famous Blyth Harbour Wind Farm. The nine original turbines have now been demolished, but there is still one larger turbine on the North Blyth side.

Wind-generated power continues to attract more and more interest, and in 2018 the EDF Group officially opened the 41.5MW Blyth Offshore Demonstrator Wind Farm, which comprises five MHI Vestas 8.3MW turbines installed on hybrid Gravity Based Foundations (GBFs) some 5km off the coast of Blyth. These are believed to be the world's largest foundations and are pushing the civil engineering boundaries in offshore structures. The construction firm BAM has used several different innovative techniques and methods to produce five ground-breaking GBFs. This pioneering design is the first time the specialist "float and submerge" method has been successfully used on an offshore wind farm. It's a great idea, and its simplicity belies its genius. The GBF is a hollow base constructed on land, then floated out to sea and submerged at its final location. The base is then ballasted with sand so that wind turbine loads can be placed upon it. This method does away with piling out at sea, and the simplified construction of these innovative structures will pave the way for more cost-effective renewable energy solutions worldwide. Each Gravity Based Foundation weighs 7,500 tonnes when floated. Once ballasted with sand, they provide stable foundations on the seabed and weigh a massive 22,300 tonnes each. There is no need for piling, heavy lift or jack-up vessels during the whole operation. After the 25-year lifespan of the foundations, the sand can be removed and the GBFs can be re-floated and towed back to land for demolition. EDF calculates the turbines are producing enough electricity to power around 34,000 average British households. Offshore wind-generated energy is expected to become an increasingly major contributor towards power supply in Britain. Research has shown that Britain has the ideal conditions to produce more than 33% of the potential output for Europe – enough to power the country three times over.

Boulmer fisherman's cottage

BOULMER

The tiny fishing village of Boulmer lies about halfway between Alnmouth and Craster. Although nowadays it is perhaps best known for its Ministry of Defence air surveillance centre, Boulmer once suffered a shocking reputation. This was where, in the 18th and 19th centuries, smugglers from inland Northumberland and the Scottish Borders would come to collect supplies of illicit liquor brought from the continent by dishonest sea captains and their crews – an activity known as "rum-running". Some of the older houses in the village have secret hiding places where contraband was stored, and, in the late 19th century, casks of spirits that had been buried on the beach in bygone times and forgotten by their owners were sometimes dug up by accident!

As many as 20 or 30 smugglers, mounted on horseback, would come to Boulmer for gin, whiskey, rum, or bolts of silk and other valuable textiles to carry back to the wilds of Northumberland or the Borders, running the gauntlet of narrow escapes and lively action with the excise officers. The dare-devil exploits of Wull Balmer, Jock Melvin, Ruthor Grahamshaw, Laird Cranstoun of Smailholm and Will Faa, King of the Gypsies, from Kirk Yetholm are recorded in several old Northumbrian ballads:

"Blind Wull Bawmer o' Jethart
His grips are no guid to come in;
He felled a' the gaugers i' Jethart
When comin' frae Boomer wi' gin"

Coquet Island

COQUET ISLAND

Coquet Island lies about a mile offshore from the fishing port of Amble and is an RSPB sanctuary for about 40,000 birds, including the rare Roseate Tern. It was known as Cocwaedae in Saxon times when a monastic foundation was established there. It is a low and level strip of land which tapers to fine point at its northern and southern ends and covers about sixteen acres in area. Geologically it is part of the Northumberland coalfield being composed mainly of red sandstone lying on a thin layer of coal and shale. John Leland, the Northumbrian historian, reports that: *"the isle of Coquet standith on a very good vayne of secoles and in the ebbe men dig in the shore by the clives."*

There was a small Benedictine monastery here in AD 684, occupied by monks from Tynemouth Priory. Evidence also points to a hermitage on the island in the distant past because, buried at Tynemouth, lies "Henry the hermit of Coquet Island"

This was the place where Ælflæd, Abbess of Whitby and sister of King Ecgfrith, had an important meeting with St Cuthbert; she was to try and persuade him to accept the bishopric offered to him by the king. She is reputed to have extracted a reluctant promise; however, it was Eata of Melrose who finally tipped the balance by offering to exchange his new appointment as Bishop of Lindisfarne for the Bishopric of Hexham offered to Cuthbert.

Another important event took place during the Civil War in 1643 when the Scots took the island from Colonel Curset and his men and established a garrison of 70 officers, 200 men and 7 pieces of artillery.

The old defences were converted in to a lighthouse on 1st October 1841 because the underlying rocks were treacherous to ships – on 4th November 1821 *The Catherine* of Sunderland was wrecked on the rocks on the northern end of the island and the crew of nine men clung to the rigging for hours desperately calling to a large group of people who listened helplessly to their cries, unable to rescue them because there was no lifeboat available. The ship broke up during the night and sadly all the poor crew were lost. Grace Darling visited her brother who was lighthouse keeper on the island but tragically during her stay she contracted the illness which would eventually cause her death.

Rabbits over- populated the island after being introduced by the Duke of Northumberland, however they were eradicated after the lighthouse was built.

CRASTER

Craster is a typical Northumbrian fishing village, with red-roofed houses clustered around a tiny harbour. It has been the home of the Craster family since the 11th century, and records show that a William de Craucestr held the estate in 1272. The village has been a fishing haven since at least the 17th century, although the present harbour was built by the Craster family as late as 1906, in memory of their son killed while on active service in India. A bronze plaque reads:

> CRASTER MEMORIAL HARBOUR
> CONSTRUCTED IN MEMORY OF
> CAPTAIN JOHN CHARLES PULLEINE CRASTER
> 16TH PUNJABIS
> WHO FELL IN ACTION DURING THE THIBETAN EXPEDITION
> JUNE 1904
> HE TOOK A DEEP INTEREST IN THE PROVISION OF A HARBOUR
> AT CRASTER, AND HIS BROTHERS AND SISTER CHOSE THIS WAY
> OF PERPETUATING HIS MEMORY
> A.D.1906.

In 1914, three 90ft silos supported by a concrete arch were added to the harbour to facilitate the shipment of whinstone chippings; these were demolished in 1936 and only the arch is left to serve as a reminder of a once-thriving business. The worked-out quarry is now used as a car park for visitors to the village. Little fishing is done from the harbour these days, but the world-famous Craster kippers – a great favourite of the late Queen Mother – are still cured here in a mid-19th century smokehouse, using a closely guarded traditional process.

About half a mile to the west of the village, a mysterious four-centred Gothic arch spans the road. This is the gateway leading to Craster Tower, the family seat of the Craster family. The nucleus of the house is an ancient, three-storied pele tower; built solidly from basalt, this has a characteristic basement vault with an entrance lobby. Sadly, the house is not open to the public, but in the grounds is a small garden centre with a tearoom situated in the old stables.

Leading north from Craster to Dunstanburgh Castle is a pleasant route along a grass-covered path on the edge of the rocky coast, which is considered by some to be the finest walk in all of Northumberland.

Unloading the catch, Craster

Lobster pots and harbour, Craster

CRESSWELL

Cresswell lies about nine miles to the north-east of Morpeth, on the southern tip of Druridge Bay. The little fishing village takes its name from the Cresswell family, who have lived here since the reign of King John. In the 1800s, the family name became Baker-Cresswell after Addison John Cresswell inherited the property of his wife's cousin, John Baker; one of their descendants, Joe Baker-Cresswell, was commanding officer of the Royal Navy ship *HMS Bulldog* that seized the famous Enigma machine from German submarine *U-110* during WWII.

Cresswell Tower was constructed in the late 14th or early 15th century and, although partly ruined, is a fine example of its kind, three storeys high and in a good vantage point overlooking the sea. In the 1820s, Cresswell Hall, a manor house designed by noted architect John Shaw, was built to incorporate the tower; however, this building was partly demolished in 1937, leaving only part of the doorway and a column arcade. Cresswell Tower is now undergoing restoration so that it can be used for various village events.

Cresswell Tower

According to folklore, the tower has its own ghost: the White Lady of Cresswell. The story goes that one beautiful young member of the family was at the top of the tower when she witnessed her lover, a Danish prince, being murdered by her three brothers on the nearby shore. So distressed was she that the poor girl refused to eat again and starved herself to death in the building. It is said that she can be seen weeping and gazing out from the tower in the forlorn hope of seeing her prince again.

Records show that in August 1822 a 60ft sperm whale was washed ashore near Cresswell and became the subject of considerable argument between Addison John Baker-Cresswell and one Ralph Atkinson, landowner of nearby Lynemouth. Both laid claim to the carcass, believing that the beast had first landed on their respective beach. The argument was settled when the Admiralty seized the whale meat and its oil; the skeleton was removed to the grounds at Cresswell.

Early in January 1876, a Swedish steamer, *The Gustav*, ran aground at Cresswell, necessitating the rescue of its crew and passengers by local fishermen. Three young fisherwomen – Margaret and Mary Brown, and Isabella Armstrong – distinguished themselves as heroines that cold, storm-lashed winter's night by running five miles along the beach, often wading through the incoming waves, to reach the next lifeboat station and get assistance for the mission.

NORTHUMBERLAND COAST

CULLERCOATS

Cullercoats retains the atmosphere of a small fishing village. Standing on the sandy beach here, it's easy to imagine those exciting and romantic days of smugglers and wreckers; no wonder the picturesque harbour has provided great inspiration for artists such as the local-born Myles Birket Foster and renowned American landscape painter Winslow Homer, whose residence in Cullercoats is commemorated by a blue plaque at the site of his first lodgings.

At one time, however, Cullercoats – a name thought to have derived from the Old English *"culver-cotes"*, meaning "dovecotes" – was more than simply a fishing village: salt, coal and gravel were among the many goods exported here. A wagonway ran from the nearby Whitley Colliery to the harbour, where coal was loaded onto ships from a wooden jetty. At one time, because of a difficult docking dispute, cartloads of coal were transported from a colliery at North Shields for loading at Cullercoats. The last shipment from the port was 21 tonnes of salt, which left aboard *The Fortune of Whitby* on 18th July 1726.

In the late 1800s, there were around 40 cobles (inshore fishing boats) working out of the harbour. They must have been a wonderful sight gliding into the bay with their red-brown sails billowing in the sea breeze. Each boat had a crew of three men and a boy, but the success of the operation also depended on the womenfolk, who would prepare the bait, help with the nets, and sell the catch in Tyneside towns. The Cullercoats fishwife was a familiar sight, dressed in her blue serge jacket, short petticoats with ample skirts, a large apron and a black straw bonnet. She would trudge from place to place with a heavy creel (basket) of fish on her shoulder, musically calling for people to buy her wares.

Cullercoats Bay

Old postcard image of Cullercoats Bay

DUNSTANBURGH (English Heritage)

Dunstanburgh Castle occupies an extensive and isolated hilltop site on a ridge of basaltic cliff rising straight up from the sea, with roaring waves pounding the deep recesses. Although now reduced to a dramatic ruin, Northumberland's largest castle is still very impressive – its situation has inspired great artists such as JMW Turner and Thomas Miles Richardson. Dunstanburgh was given to the National Trust in 1961 by Sir Ivan Sutherland, but is cared for by English Heritage under a deed of guardianship.

When it was built in the 14th century, Dunstanburgh must have been a formidable fortress, indeed almost impregnable; at that time, the sea came right up to the foot of the cliffs, and the tiny harbour was widened to a ditch more than 80ft wide and about 13ft deep and excavated all the way around the hill to Embleton Bay, affording even greater protection. A drawbridge guarded by a small gatehouse dominated this access at the point where the footpath from Craster crosses on its way to the castle.

There is a reason to believe there was an ancient British stronghold and later a Roman fortification on this site, but it was Thomas, Second Earl of Lancaster, who started the building of the present castle in 1313 as a private home. He obtained a licence to crenellate the building in 1316, having been appointed Commander-in-Chief against the Scots. However, the earl did little to control their incursions, and King Edward II, who was Lancaster's cousin, suspected him of "having secret dealings with the Scots". In 1322, the king marched north and, after defeating Lancaster at Boroughbridge, imprisoned him in Pontefract Castle – which, ironically, the earl also owned – until his execution. Lancaster was eventually canonised, and his place of execution became known as St Thomas' Hill.

Dunstanburgh became a stronghold against the Scots, and in 1362 it came into the possession of John of Gaunt, Duke of Lancaster. He enlarged the castle and blocked up the gatehouse, converting it to a great keep while placing the new main entrance to the north-west side. Unsurprisingly, Dunstanburgh took on a new role the following century – as a fortress for the Lancastrians during the War of the Roses. In these troubled times, the castle was taken and retaken five times.

In 1462 Dunstanburgh was garrisoned for Queen Margaret of Anjou by Sir Richard Tunstall and 200 men, but the castle came under siege from the large forces of Lords Wenlock and Hastings and the occupants are reported to have eventually "made an honourable capitulation". In 1464, After the Battle of Hexham, Dunstanburgh was attacked again, this time by the army of Warwick the Kingmaker, Earl Richard Neville, and after three days of fierce artillery bombardment it was finally overrun. After that, the castle seems to have been abandoned and by the 16th century it was in a state of decay. It is said that the Captain of Dunstanburgh, John Gosse, was taken to York where he was beheaded with a hatchet

On the eastern side of Dunstanburgh is a fearful abyss with a vertiginous view down the steep cliffs to the sea, which seethes and boils with a deafening roar into a cavern in the black rocks. In stormy weather, the tide crashes in, pounding the waves onto the rocks, the tremendous force lifting the foaming spray high into the wind. These huge, stormy fountains can be seen and heard from a great distance, giving this boiling chasm a fearsome reputation with the locals – here is a place that resounds with the wail of malignant spirits. No wonder, then, that it has spawned a tale of the supernatural. This is the story of Guy the Seeker…

Legend has it that Sir Guy was lost in a dreadful storm one night and rode towards the castle in search of shelter. On arrival, he discovered the building was a ruin, but nonetheless took refuge in its gateway. Sir Guy was immediately confronted by a powerful wizard with flaming hair, who told him a beautiful lady was imprisoned in the building and asked the knight if he had the courage to rescue her. When Sir Guy consented, he was led up a long, winding staircase, through a strong wooden door guarded by a huge serpent, and into an immense hall where a hundred black marble war-horses stood waiting with a hundred marble knights asleep beside them. At the far end of the great hall, in a crystal tomb guarded by two gigantic skeletons, was the captive lady, begging for help, tears streaming from her eyes.

The wizard offered Sir Guy the choice of a huge falchion or a large curved horn, declaring that the lady's fate depended upon his decision. After a moment's hesitation, the knight blew the horn with all his might. The lady screamed, the marble horses reared up, and the marble knights sprang to arms. Sir Guy reached for the sword, but it was too late, and the wizard addressed him with scorn, declaring, "Shame on the coward who sounded a horn when he might have unsheathed a sword!" At this, the knight fell unconscious. He awoke to find himself back in the ruined gateway, the beautiful lady lost to him for ever.

At night, when the wind howls among the eerie ruins, it is said that Guy the Seeker can be heard groaning and crying for the wizard's sword. Local children won't go near the castle when darkness is approaching for fear of an encounter with this ghostly, remorseful knight.

Dunstanburgh Castle Gatehouse (English Heritage)

Dunstanburgh Castle and Embleton Burr

Inner Farne

FARNE ISLANDS (National Trust)

The Farne Islands are situated just off the coast near Bamburgh, although they are most easily reached by boat from Seahouses. The islands vary in number from around fifteen to about twenty-eight, depending on the state of the tide. The two main groups, the Inner and Outer Farnes, are separated by the mile-wide stretch of water known as Staple Sound.

The Farnes are the most easterly point where the Great Whin Sill outcrops. This intrusive sheet of hard dolerite runs westwards for about 70 or 80 miles across Northumberland and the north of England, notably outcropping at Lindisfarne, Bamburgh and Hadrian's Wall. The geomorphology of the area dictates that the islands have high sea cliffs or rocky faces to the south and west, but slope gradually to the north and east. This means the islands are an ideal habitat for breeding seabirds – more than 23 species have been recorded. The islands also support a colony of Atlantic grey seals regarded to be one of the world's most important and which has lived here for more than 800 years.

According to the earliest records, monks and hermits have lived on the island of Inner Farne since the seventh century. The best known of these is St Cuthbert, who moved here as a hermit in AD 678 after serving 12 years as Prior of Lindisfarne. He lived on Inner Farne for 10 years until he was persuaded to take the position of Bishop of Lindisfarne. Unfortunately, his health deteriorated, and Cuthbert returned to his beloved little island just before Christmas AD 686; he died three months later on 20th March. He was eventually buried in Durham, but his influence remained, and the huge cult following that developed after his death meant that for many, many years Inner Farne was a place of pilgrimage.

Some of the later hermits here came from the religious community at Durham, and by 1255 a small "daughter" community, the House of Farne, had been established. Usually, there were two monks in residence – the master and the associate – together with perhaps a couple of servants.

Apart from the lighthouse, all the buildings on Inner Farne are from the monastic period.

Farne Islands, the Stacks

St Cuthbert's Chapel, Inner Farne

The Longstone lighthouse, The Farne Islands

Inside of St Cuthbert's Chapel, Inner Farne

St Cuthbert built a guest house for his visitors, and its remains – a small stone *"Fishehouse"* – can still be seen. Originally there were two chapels on the island, but the one dedicated to St Margaret has all but disappeared. St Cuthbert's Chapel was built in around 1370, but by the 1840s the roof had gone, and it was falling into disrepair.

It is thanks to restoration work commissioned by the Venerable Charles Thorp, Archdeacon of Durham, who went on to purchase the Farnes in 1861, that it has survived. The fine 17th century wooden stalls were brought here from Durham Cathedral in 1848, and the stained-glass window in the chapel includes some fine examples of Flemish glass. The altar, which was added early the following century, carries the tiny wooden-mouse trademark of its maker, Robert "Mousey" Thompson of Kilburn, North Yorkshire.

More imposing than St Cuthbert's Chapel is Prior Castell's Tower, named after the Durham churchman who commissioned its construction in around 1500, and said to stand on the site of St Cuthbert's original cell. Following the Dissolution of the Monasteries in 1536, the Farnes became the property of the Dean and Chapter of Durham Cathedral.

The islands have always been a dangerous area for shipping, and many vessels have been wrecked on the rocks. In 1673, King Charles II granted a licence for four lighthouses to be built along the east coast of England, including one in the Farnes. It is recorded that a beacon was constructed at the top of Prior Castell's Tower for this purpose, though there is no evidence that it was ever lit. The islands' first purpose-built lighthouse was a square tower constructed on Staple Island, and again a beacon fire was used; however, this tower was destroyed in 1783 and a replacement (later wrecked by storms) was built on nearby Brownsman.

Inner Farne got its first modern lighthouse in 1810, alongside the construction of another on Brownsman. However, the latter proved to be more of a danger to shipping; by 1826 it had been demolished and replaced by the Longstone Lighthouse. Longstone will forever be linked with the name Grace Darling, the lighthouse keeper's daughter who, on 7th September 1838, helped rescue the crew and passengers of the stricken *SS Forfarshire*. The steamer had run aground on the rocks of one of the islands, Big

Harcar, so Grace and her father William rowed half a mile from the Longstone in driving rain, raging seas and howling wind to save the nine survivors. Five were recovered safely on their first journey, then William returned with two crew members for the remainder. Conditions were so bad that the whole party had to stay at the Longstone for four days before they could get back to the mainland.

Grace's actions captured the public imagination and she was hailed a national heroine. As a result of her repeated exposure to the dreadful conditions, however, she contracted tuberculosis and sadly died in 1842 at the age of 26, only four years after the dramatic rescue.

In 1925, following a public appeal, the Farne Islands were bought from William Watson-Armstrong – the great-nephew of the previous purchaser, renowned industrialist William Armstrong – and placed in the care of the National Trust. Under the trust's expert management, this important wildlife sanctuary will be preserved for the pleasure and enjoyment of future generations.

Top Row; Guillemots and Kittiwakes - Fulmar Petrel
Middle row: **Kittiwake** *(pic: Mark Nixon)* Puffin with sand eels
Bottom Row; Razorbill, Arctic Tern, Grey Seal

HOWICK HALL

Built in 1782, Howick Hall is situated in a beautifully wooded park at the head of a lovely dene that comes out on the coast in the seclusion of Howick Haven. The modern house succeeded an ancient tower, the Turris de Howyke, which is mentioned in the county records of 1416. Howick has long been the historical home of the Grey family, several members of which have been famous and public-spirited individuals.

The two most famous, perhaps, are Charles Grey and his descendant Sir Edward Grey.

Charles, the Second Earl Grey, was Prime Minister at the time of the Great Reform Act of 1832 and is commemorated by a monument in the centre of Newcastle, at the head of the street that bears his name. Grey College at Durham University is also named after the earl; indeed, all of the Grey family's historical documents are in the care of the university. Howick is also the home of Earl Grey tea, which, it is said, was specially blended for Charles by a Chinese mandarin, who added bergamot to offset the taste of lime in the spring water at the estate. The tea proved very popular and eventually the blenders Twinings came to market it worldwide; unfortunately, the Greys failed to register the trademark and have never received any royalties….This splendid blend can still be enjoyed, however, with a tasty scone, in the excellent Earl Grey Tea House at Howick.

Sir Edward Grey was born at nearby Falloden, from which he took his title when he was made a peer. Viscount Grey of Falloden was Foreign Secretary in 1914 when WWI broke out, and his famous pronouncement, "The lamps are going out all over Europe", will be remembered for ever in the annals of the Great War. The viscount was a great lover of the countryside, especially birds – in 1927, he wrote a delightful book titled *The Charm of Birds*, and he also created an excellent sanctuary at the family seat in Falloden. Sadly, toward the end of his life, Sir Edward became blind; he died in 1933 at the estate in his beloved Northumberland.

The gardens and arboretum at Howick are an absolute delight; the gardens cover roughly 25 acres, while the 65-acre arboretum offers long and short walks and is planted with more than 12,000 trees and shrubs from all over the world.

It was while staying as a guest at Howick that the author Matthew "Monk" Lewis wrote his famous 1808 ballad *Sir Guy the Seeker*.

Howick Hall Gardens

Howick Hall

St Michael and all Angels Church, Howick

HOWICK, Church of St Michael and All Angels

Not far from Howick Hall, on the edge of the wooded ravine, is the Church of St Michael and All Angels. It was in 1748 that the Norman place of worship standing on this site was replaced by a new church, and this was remodelled and extended in the Romanesque style for Henry Grey, the Third Earl Grey, just over a century later. In the chancel is a beautiful marble tomb, which originally had an ornate canopy of Caen stone, although only one panel now remains. A former rector of Howick was Dr Isaac Basire, an unusual, and slightly eccentric character who lost his job just prior to the Protectorate in the 1650s and consequently led an adventurous, itinerant life as a missionary among the Greeks, the Arabians and the Egyptians.

LONGHOUGHTON
The Church of St Peter and St Paul

About a mile to the west of Boulmer is the quiet agricultural village of Longhoughton. Its church, dedicated to St Peter and St Paul, dates from the time of Henry I and was often used as a storehouse for contraband brought ashore by the smugglers known as the "Rum Runners". The building also served as a pele tower, its castellated tower and 4ft-thick walls affording great protection to the villagers during border raids. The head of the ancient village market cross is mounted on the east wall; after being lost for many years, it was discovered in a smuggler's grave. In the churchyard is a mysterious small stone cross that is believed to be pre-conquest in age and almost certainly marks the site of a grave.

Another feature is the large "squint" in the wall between the nave and the chancel to allow members of the congregation seated in the south aisle a view of the altar.

There is an unusual and interesting headstone on the left-hand side of the path, about halfway down. It is the grave of 29-year-old Peter Ford Miller, who *"accidentally met his death on the railway between Longhoughton and Little Mill on the night of Tuesday, May 23rd 1882"*. Miller was buried in the churchyard by order of the coroner, and his stone is carved with the advice, *"Take ye heed watch and pray for ye know not when the time is."*

The Reverend George Duncan, who was incumbent from 1696 to 1719, was most

Peter Ford Millers gravestone and the Saxon Cross, Longhoughton

certainly not a believer in keeping his personal thoughts about his parishioners to himself, and his entries in the parish registers make fascinating and unusual reading. Almost every entry is accompanied by some caustic observation on the character of the persons concerned. Most of the comments are in Latin, although a few are in English: Robert Pringle, a day labourer who died in 1712, is described as *"a bad son of a bad father"*; William Gray as *"a very ignorant and bad sinner"*; Henry Elder, a smith, is said to have been *"very unhappily married"*; while Anne Wilson, a mendicant widow, is condemned out of hand as being *"a vile, drunken, female sinner"*. Thomas Story, a shepherd of Sharpley, who was married in 1706, is described as *"a very brutish and wicked fellow"*; another shepherd from the same district is said to be *"obstinate, ignorant and wicked"*. However, some parishioners received glowing reports: Nicholas Davison, also a shepherd, is described as *"a very serious and religious herd"*, and one Thomas Gustard as *"a knowing good man"*. These accounts make very interesting reading, but it seems a great pity that no one wrote an observation on the vicar's character, just to complete the appreciation!

St Peter and St Paul's Church, the nave squint

St Peter and St Paul's Church, Longhoughton

Low Newton-by-the-Sea

LOW NEWTON-BY-THE-SEA

The fishermen's cottages at Low Newton-by-the-Sea form three sides of a square clustered around a green that looks out to sea and are generally regarded as the finest example of this type of small settlement on the Northumberland coast. They stand right on the edge of the wide sands of Embleton Bay, the shallow water ideal for bringing the little fishing cobles almost to the front doors of their owners. The cottages were originally built in the 1700s, but were modified in the middle of the next century with the addition of small gabled dormer windows.

The only two-storey building in the square is The Ship Inn, which stands in the northwest corner. The whole of this tiny fishing settlement is now in the care of the National Trust; it was purchased between 1980-82 as part of the trust's Enterprise Neptune project, an appeal originally launched on behalf of the Trust by HRH the Duke of Edinburgh in 1965. The project was so successful in its efforts to purchase large stretches of the country's coastline that it was re-launched as the Neptune Coastline Campaign with even greater endeavour in 1999.

St Mary's Church was built as a mission room in the late 19th century and is still used as a church and a meeting room. This unusual building is fabricated from corrugated galvanised iron. Many buildings like this were developed during the 19th century and referred to as "tin tabernacles". Urgency for religious devotion was uppermost and a lot of churches, chapels and mission halls were hastily built in new industrial areas, in pit villages and near railway works. Isolated rural and coastal locations were also considered paramount, and landowners or employers often donated plots of land; very often, they met the cost of the building if it wasn't covered by public subscription. The tin tabernacles proved very popular: one supplier, Francis Morton & Co, had a specialist church-building department, and its 1879 catalogue listed almost 70 churches, chapels and schoolhouses built in the United Kingdom.

St Mary's Church, Low Newton-by-the-Sea

NEWBIGGIN-BY-THE-SEA

Newbiggin-by-the-Sea is situated on a beautiful broad bay that sweeps between two rocky promontories, forming a natural harbour – indeed, Newbiggin was once a town of great maritime significance. As far back as 1352, there was a pier on the north side of the harbour, which was regarded as so important that an "indulgence of forty days" was granted to all who helped keep it in good repair. While England was at war with Scotland during the reign of Edward II, the town of Newbiggin was required to supply "a warship with eighty oars" to contribute to the strength of his navy. The king stayed here for three days, from the 13th to the 17th July 1319, when he was on his way to besiege Berwick; he made a brief return visit on 8th September 1322.

Although fishing has always been an important industry in the town, at one time large quantities of corn were shipped from here and it was a common sight to see large ships riding in the harbour waiting to be loaded.

In August 2007 Newbiggin's new sea defence system was completed - a £10,000,000 renovation scheme to replace the fast disappearing beach.

The project was expertly described in the news: *"500,000 tonnes of sand were brought from Skegness, delivered by the trailing suction hopper dredger (TSHD) Oranje and deposited on the beach through a pipe approximately 1 metre (39 in) in diameter. A new offshore breakwater was installed to accompany the matching breakwater on the opposite side of the bay".*

It was also the installation of the UK's first permanent offshore sculpture by artist Sean Henry. It is of two figures almost, 5 metres tall, standing on a breakwater looking out to sea. The piece was commissioned by the South East Northumberland Public Art & Design Initiative (INSPIRE) and, during high tides, it gives the impression of the couple standing on the surface of the water. The bronze and brass statue is anchored 300 meters off the shore and stands just over 12 metres high.

His inspiration for Couple came from the scale of the breakwater. The artist decided the project should have three distinct elements: the tapered steel pier platform and the two figures.

"I always wanted to have more than one figure to reflect a shared experience and intends to create an air of mystery by keeping the figures anonymous - looking out to sea with their backs to the shore," he said.

St Bartholomew's Church stands prominently on Newbiggin Point, visible for miles along the coast it serves as a useful landmark for sailors. Traditionally the church is built on a site that is said to have been founded by the Monks of Lindisfarne, its location would certainly support this, being in a position that was much favoured by religious communities in Celtic times. The church dates mainly from the 13th century although there are some features that would suggest an earlier origin, such as the long and narrow proportions of the nave and the unusual small western tower.

The churchyard was once in a wild and neglected state. Several tombs were ravaged by high seas and even in the mid-1800s, it was not unusual to find fragments of human bones lying about in the loose sand outside the churchyard wall.

St Bartholomew's Church, Newbiggin-by-the-Sea

Puffins on posts - Newbiggin-by-the-Sea

"Couple" sculpture, Newbiggin-by-the-Sea

Farne Island Tour Boats, Seahouses Harbour

Seahouses Lifeboat Station

SEAHOUSES

Seahouses is a busy fishing port with hotels, guesthouses, restaurants and shops. Originally a part of the adjacent village, North Sunderland, Seahouses has expanded in its own right over the past two centuries; no longer is it the small herring fishing port described, somewhat unkindly, by the noted historian William Weaver Tomlinson in 1888 as a *"malodorous place where fish-curing is extensively carried on"* he went on, it seems, to grudgingly admit that the work to the harbour would see it "much improved"!

Lime burning was also carried out in Seahouses – the bank of large lime kilns on the quayside testify to this. The lime trade ceased in the mid-19th century, but the kilns are still used by fishermen as storage sheds.

Seahouses is also the point of embarkation for the Farne Islands. In his 1873 Handbook for Travellers in Durham and Northumberland, writer John Murray gave some useful advice about visiting the islands: *"A boat to go thither costs about ten shillings and the boatmen expect to be fed during the day. To visit all the islands a pass must be procured at Bamborough (sic) Castle. Strangers are not allowed to shoot the birds or to take the eggs. It will be well not to undertake this excursion unless the weather be settled and the sea calm, as visitors have often been detained for days together upon the islands by stress of weather."*

In 1844, a violent display of public feeling emphasised the spirit of the community. A Doctor Belaney, who had practised in the area for several years, was arrested and brought to trial on suspicion of poisoning his lovely young wife and her mother. He was acquitted much to the surprise of the local people, who firmly believed he was guilty. On his return home, they assembled in front of his house carrying an effigy, loudly proclaiming his guilt in spite of the court's decision – he was so angered by this that he fired a pistol into the crowd before making his escape by the back door. The crowd, further angered by his action, ransacked the house and burned it to the ground.

Also in 1844, at Snook Point, just south of Seahouses, a small cave was discovered in a working limestone quarry. The floor was neatly paved, and it looked as if every effort had been made to make it pleasantly habitable. A pipe, possibly for communication – or more probably, for ventilation – connected the cave with a cottage above.

It was thought that since the cave was in the area of Dunstanburgh and Bamburgh Castles – the last Lancastrian strongholds in the north during the War of the Roses – it could have been a hiding place for Queen Margaret when she fled to the coast with her son, Prince Edward, after the Battle of Hexham in 1464.

Seaton Deleval Hall from the gardens

SEATON DELAVAL HALL (National Trust)

Seaton Delaval Hall was designed by Sir John Vanbrugh, the celebrated architect of Blenheim Palace and Castle Howard, for the wealthy Admiral George Delaval in the 1720s. This Grade I listed country house, seemingly built without any restriction on cost, serves as a monument and memorial to Sir John's great talents – and also indeed the life of its patron – as, sadly, both died before it was completed in 1728.

The Delaval family existed before the Norman Conquest – Guy Delaval married the daughter of Robert, the Earl of Montaigne, and niece of William the Conqueror. Gilbert Delaval was one of 25 barons sworn to see the Magna Carta – granted by John at Runnymede in 1215 – confirmed by the Pope. From then until the reign of William III in the mid-to late 17th century, the Delavals served their country either on the field of battle or in politics.

However, the family became better known for the fun and frolics they indulged in during the 1700s – a jolly notoriety that earned them the tag 'the Gay Delavals'. During the time of Sir Francis Blake Delaval and his brother John, the First Baron of Delaval, the house was the scene of wild and extravagant revelry, with a stream of guests suffering an uninterrupted barrage of practical jokes. Beds were suspended on pulleys over trapdoors so that sleeping guests were plunged into darkness and cold water. Bedrooms were arranged so that as the ladies and gentlemen were undressing for bed, partitions could quickly be drawn back, revealing them to each other in a highly embarrassing state of disarray. It was said that "With a host so handsome, gay and frolicsome it is not surprising that Seaton Delaval was a centre of attraction to the fashionable world, for there a series of amusements was provided of endless variety, from a grinning match and sack race to a masquerade and carousal."

Such was their appetite for unusual fun and entertainment that, on one occasion, the Delavals hired the Drury Lane Theatre in London to stage their own family production of Shakespeare's *Othello*. But perhaps the most outrageous scheme undertaken by Sir Francis was when he set himself up as a fortune teller and magician with a close friend, the actor Samuel Foote, as his assistant. The pair soon established an excellent reputation thanks to their 'talent' – revealing secrets they had discovered about fellow members of society and passing them off as psychic revelations.

Probably the most successful hoax Sir Francis pulled off was persuading the wealthy widow of the late politician Lord Nassau Paulet that it was mystically ordained she should marry him. Lady Isabella accepted his proposal, and her new husband came into a fortune of more than £90,000, although they were divorced soon after, by mutual consent.

Many amusing stories are also told about his brother, Lord Delaval, but he is better known for the remarkable beauty of his daughters – particularly Sarah Hussey Delaval, Countess of Lady Tyrconnel, whose hair is said to have been so thick and luxuriant it floated on her saddle as she rode.

When the male Delaval line became extinct in the mid-18th century, the estate passed to Sir Jacob Astley, the 16th Baron Hastings – the grandson of Rhoda, daughter of Sir Francis Blake Delaval. On Sir Jacob's death in 1859, he was succeeded by his eldest son, Jacob Henry Delaval Astley, who himself passed away on 9th March 1871. Seaton Delaval Hall is now in the excellent care of the National Trust and its future is assured; it remains a worthy monument to its architect and his patron.

The site of Seaton Sluice

SEATON SLUICE

In the mid-1600s, to help his ships with the export of coal and salt, Sir Ralph Delaval built a pier to protect the small, natural harbour at Hartley. In time, the pier caused the river to silt up, so the baronet arranged for the installation of sluice gates that would trap water during high tide and then release it during low tide, scouring the harbour. The sluice system was installed on a site just below the new road bridge; because of this, the harbour came to be known as Seaton Sluice. It was such a success that a similar system was installed at Margate in Kent.

As trade increased, the little harbour, which had always been difficult to enter, required further modification. So, in the 1760s, Sir John Hussey Delaval devised a plan to cut through the solid rock on the southern part of the headland, from the harbour to the sea, creating a channel 900ft long, 30ft wide and more than 50ft deep. At either end were lock gates, making the new cut a small, sheltered wet dock.

By the late 18th century, in addition to the coal and salt shipped from this unusual harbour, the Delavals had begun to export bottles from their Royal Hartley Bottle Works, which eventually became the largest of its kind in the country. However, in 1862, disaster struck when a pit accident at the Hartley Colliery brought coal shipments to an end, and when the bottle factory closed nine years later, all exports stopped.

All that remains today are the quiet little harbour and the dramatic, disused cut – reminders of a unique engineering achievement.

The "Cut" through to the sea, Seaton Sluice

Curry's Point and St Mary's Lighthouse

ST MARY'S LIGHTHOUSE

St Mary's Island is only an island at high tide when the 200-yard causeway that provides access is under water for four or five hours, so it is important to note the state of the tide to avoid being stranded. The island is dominated by the 150ft-high St Mary's Lighthouse, although there is also a gift shop and visitor centre, together with some small cottages.

The monks of Tynemouth Priory once maintained a chantry here and displayed a lamp to warn mariners of dangerous offshore rocks and reefs. There was also a tower with a bell that was rung to summon help in the event of a shipwreck, and a small cemetery (maintained up until the mid-1700s) where unfortunate storm victims were buried. The only clue to the location of the sacred spot where the chantry stood is a small inlet named St Mary's Bay, where fishermen still take refuge from storms

St Mary's Island seems an odd place to connect with the discovery of a large and valuable diamond, however there are records of one being found here - in the stomach of a woodcock, shot in the winter of 1765.

The island has also been known as Bait Island, which is thought to be a misspelling of the name of former owner Thomas Bates, a surveyor for Northumberland under Elizabeth I. The small headland directly opposite the island is known as Curry's Point, and a blue plaque at the site reveals the origin of the name: it was where the body of one Michael Curry was suspended in chains from a gibbet after his execution on 4th September 1739 for the savage murder of a pub landlord in Hartley. Standing on the point at twilight, it is easy to imagine this gruesome sight, displayed as a chilling reminder of his dreadful crime.

St Mary's Lighthouse

Tynemouth Priory

TYNEMOUTH PRIORY (English Heritage)

The ruins of Tynemouth Priory are strategically sited on a steep cliff that overlooks the North Sea and guards the entrance to the River Tyne. The Saxon name for this headland was *"Pen Bal Crag"*, and it is thought that originally an Iron Age fort occupied this site. Indeed, the Romans also found need for seaward protection and established a small camp here which was probably serviced from the garrison at Wallsend.

There was a monastery here at the time of the Venerable Bede, founded in the early-to mid-seventh century by either King Edwin or his eventual successor, Oswald. Viking incursions were causing destruction along the Northumbrian coast, and the Priory at Tynemouth was a tempting target. By the time of the reign of King Ecgfrith, these raids were becoming more determined, and he saw his monastery destroyed by fire; however, the king was not one to give up easily, and he soon had it rebuilt.

In AD 865, while occupied by the nuns of St Hilda, who had fled from Hartlepool in search of refuge, the Priory was again subjected to a horrendous Viking attack. The invaders burned and plundered, murdering the holy sisters during their rampage. By AD 870, a complete ransacking had left the Priory derelict and unoccupied. It remained so for almost 200 years.

Following the Norman Conquest, the ruins of the monastery were given by Waltheof, Earl of Northumbria, to the brothers of Jarrow. Several years later, a party of monks from Durham came to Tynemouth and began rebuilding the ancient building. Unfortunately, their bishop quarrelled with Robert de Mowbray, a successor of Waltheof, and the monks were removed. They were replaced by Black Canons from St Albans in Hertfordshire, making Tynemouth merely a cell to this southern monastery; it remained so until the Dissolution in 1539, a situation that gave rise to much ill-feeling between St Albans and Durham.

In 1138, when King David I of Scotland made incursions into Northumberland, the monks of Tynemouth had to pay a large ransom to save their possessions from being ravaged by the invading army; because of this payment, the king granted them a charter of peace and protection. Two centuries later, in October 1346, King David II of Scotland – who had been

Tynemouth Castle

captured after the Battle of Neville's Cross, near Durham – was brought to Tynemouth as a prisoner en route to Bamburgh, prior to his removal to the Tower of London.

In 1523, one Robert Lambert, accused of the murder of a man named Christopher Radcliff in the diocese of Durham, claimed the right of sanctuary here. Cardinal Wolsey, outraged by the evasion of justice for such a terrible and serious crime, urged Thomas Dacre, Lord Warden of the Marches, to do everything in his power to bring the criminal to justice.

On 12th January 1539, the Priory was surrendered to the Crown by Robert Blakeney, its last prior. The ruins of this monastery stand today as a reminder of the despoliation of the agents of King Henry VIII. Interestingly, three monarchs were buried within these walls: Oswin, King of Deira, in AD 651; Osred II, King of Northumbria, in AD 792; and Malcolm III, King of Scotland, in 1093. This is commemorated by the three crowns that today adorn the North Tyneside coat of arms.

Tynemouth Priory through the main door

Warkworth Castle (English Heritage)　　　St Lawrence Church, Warkworth

WARKWORTH

About a mile inland from the port of Amble, the River Coquet forms a great loop to encompass the town of Warkworth on three sides. Here, red-roofed houses and cottages huddle together on a narrow river peninsula rising to a lofty hill on which the magnificent castle stands.

The Saxons saw the advantage of such a site. Their small, stockaded village, hidden in a little hollow, was naturally protected from the coast, and, consequently, raiders from across the seas appear to have left it alone. The first historical record of Warkworth dates from AD 737 when King Ceolwulf, who was about to give up his crown and become one of the brethren of Lindisfarne, granted the monks ownership of *"Wercewode"* and five other villages.

The abdicating monarch was a devout Christian, and it is said that it was he who established the first church at Warkworth.

The present building on the site, the Church of St Lawrence, was mostly built in the early 12th century and is perhaps one of the most complete Norman churches in Northumberland, with a whole range of architectural styles – some of these were directly influenced by those in Durham Cathedral.

The north wall of the nave and the chancel are late Norman, while the tower belongs to the Transitional period (Romanesque to Gothic) and the spire is Decorated Gothic. The vestry is most probably Early English, and the Perpendicular south aisle and porch were added during the 15th century. Warkworth has one of the few vaulted 12th century chancels in England; the vaulting is reinforced with a zig-zag pattern, a style seen in Durham Cathedral. In the south aisle, there is the cross-legged effigy of a knight, thought to be Sir Hugh de Morwick, who gave the common of Warkworth to the burgesses.

A strange window in the vestry has three narrow slits through which, it is thought, an anchorite, walled up for life in the inner chamber, would be able to communicate with the outside world. The south porch has rib-vaulting and an upper chamber that is reached by a stair turret. In his 1888 *Comprehensive Guide to Northumberland,* historian William Weaver Tomlinson draws attention to the fact that the porch is *"well-peppered on the outside with bullet marks";* however, it would seem that this damage is not only confined to the porch, for the whole of the outside of the church carries the scars

St Lawrence Church, Warkworth, musket ball holes

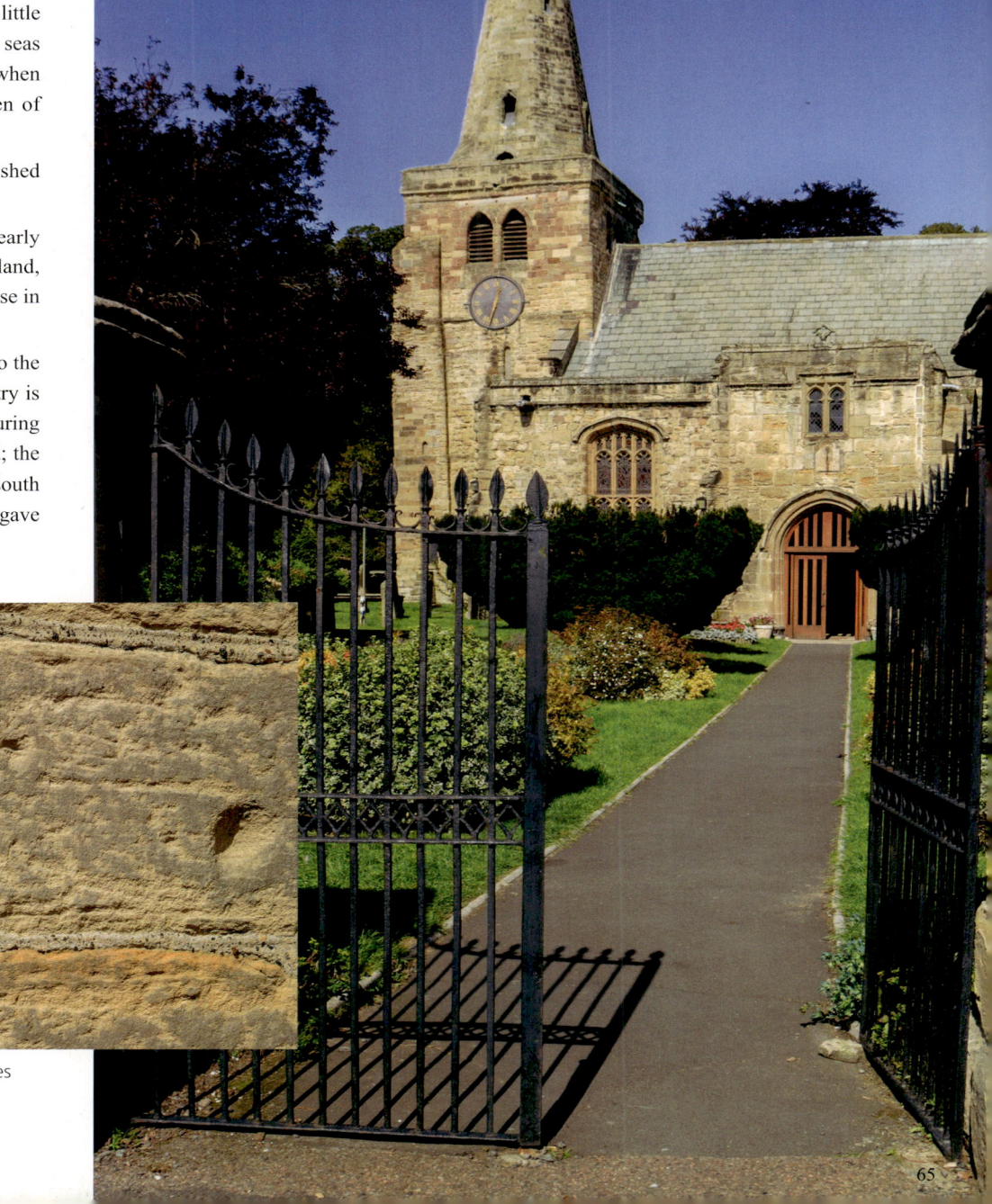

of musket ball holes.

Further back in its history, in 1174, the Church of St Lawrence was the scene of a dreadful massacre when a division of Scottish King William I's army under the command of Duncan II, Earl of Fife, attacked and burned the town of Warkworth, putting to death more than a hundred – some historians say it could have been as many as 300 – men, women and children who had taken refuge in the sanctuary and the vicarage.

Crossing the River Coquet a short distance from St Lawrence's is the 14th century Warkworth Old Bridge. Believed to be the only surviving fortified bridge in England, and now restricted to foot traffic, the structure has an imposing gatehouse at its southern end and bears the arms of the Percy family. It was in the vicinity of the gatehouse, near to what is now called Monks Walk, that a chantry was erected by Nicholas de Farnham, Bishop of Durham, during the reign of King Henry III, although this building has now disappeared.

Warkworth Castle occupies a carefully chosen position that both overlooks the town and offers a magnificent commanding view of the mouth of the Coquet. Although it is generally believed that a wooden fortress of sorts was erected here by the Saxon Ceolwulf, it was during the reign of King Henry II that Roger fitz Richard, son of the constable of Chester, replaced it

Lion Tower, Warkworth Castle (English Heritage)

with a more substantial building soon after he had been granted the lands in 1157. Ownership of the castle reverted to the crown during the reign of Edward II, but in 1345 it was given to the powerful Percy family. It would appear that the decision, made by then-monarch Edward III, was influenced by the idea that placing an excellent stronghold such as Warkworth in the hands of such a powerful family would create a tremendously strong centre of resistance to the Scots in such turbulent times – indeed, Henry, the Second Baron Percy, held the important position of Warden of the March.

In the late 14th century, Warkworth was the home of the gallant and charismatic Harry Hotspur, who, two centuries later, would be romanticised – along with the castle – by William Shakespeare in his play *Henry IV*. Things had gone well between the Percies and the Crown until Henry's reign when, following Hotspur's victory at the Battle of Homildon Hill, there was a heated dispute about who should have the ransom for prisoners. Hotspur rebelled against the king and marched his forces to Shrewsbury, but he was killed and his army defeated and; this ended any favour the family held with the Crown, and their estates were forfeited for high treason.

In 1405, Henry IV himself came north to lay siege to the castle. He expected a long struggle, but Warkworth had never been invincible from a military point of view, and the garrison surrendered after only seven rounds had been fired. The castle passed into the hands of Sir Roger de Umfraville, but the Percys were restored to ownership in 1414, only to forfeit their estates again by supporting the House of Lancaster during the Wars of the Roses. Ownership was finally restored in 1750 when Yorkshire squire Sir Hugh Smithson married Lady Elizabeth Percy and became Hugh Percy, First Duke of Northumberland, but by then Alnwick Castle was the main family home.

Warkworth Castle is now in ruins, but its position at the top of the hill, with its magnificent keep and sweeping curtain walls rising above the main street, lends an appearance of great feudal strength. The main entrance is now via the postern gate, but originally visitors would have used the gatehouse leading directly into the courtyard. The most prominent structure of the whole fortification is the keep, elevated by being built on an artificial mound; this is possibly older than the keep itself and was probably the site of the original wooden structure. The plan of the keep is unusual in that it is square in shape, with a hexagonal tower on each side, and surmounted by a high exploratory turret. It provides an excellent example of the transition of use from a purely military castle to a fortified house; the keep is lofty and well-lit, and yet it is laid out to the best possible plan for the efficient running of a large domestic establishment.

To the south-west is the Lion Tower, built in around 1480 by Henry Percy, the Fourth Earl of Northumberland, and so-named because of a weathered sculpture of a strange lion above the entrance. West of the gatehouse are the remains of an old chapel from which a stairway leads to the great chamber, or sitting room, and from there to a tower topped by spire, known as the Carrickfergus Tower. Incorporated into the eastern wall are the Grey Mare's Tail Tower, which dates from the 1290s, and the Amble, or Montagu Tower, built in the 15th century. The

NORTHUMBERLAND COAST

Norman Bridge, Warkworth

Gatehouse, Norman Bridge, Warkworth

Collegiate Church divides the outer from the inner ward. It was the intention of the Fourth Earl to found a college of secular priests, but, following his death at the hands of a mob in 1489, this building was never completed.

An old folktale tells of a strange blue stone seen in the courtyard of Warkworth Castle. According to the story, many years ago a custodian had the same dream three nights in succession – that a vast number of gold coins lay buried in a large kettle beneath a blue stone in a remote part of the castle. Extremely disturbed by this, he told a neighbour about his experiences. A few days after the last of these dreams, the custodian decided to investigate and went secretly to the place in question. To his utter surprise, he found a blue stone on the edge of a huge hole – clearly he had been beaten to it! Strangely, his neighbours suddenly became very rich; it is also said that a few weeks later a large kettle was found, weighted down, in the middle of the river behind their home.

About half a mile along the Coquet to the west of the town, and only reachable by a small ferry, is the Hermitage. This remarkable little chantry cut from the solid rock face is unique in England. A building approximately 18ft square stands against the cliff near to the landing point; this is believed to have been the kitchen of the chantry priest who lived here in the 15th century. A nearby doorway gives access to a seat overlooking the river, and a flight of 17 stone steps leads up to the Hermitage itself. A little porch with a stone seat on either side of it forms the entrance. On the inner wall, above the entrance, is a worn inscription in Old English: *"Fuerunt mihi lachrymae meæ panes die ac nota"*, which translates as "My tears have been my meat, day and night".

The three rooms of the Hermitage are known as the chapel, the confessional and the dormitory. The chapel is the largest of these at around 20ft long by 8ft wide and 8ft high. At its eastern end is a stone altar and, beside this, the recumbent effigy of a lady resting her feet on what some historians believe to be the carving of a bull's head – the crest of the local Widdrington family – but others think is a dog, the symbol of fidelity. At the foot of this monument, the stone figure of a hermit kneels in an attitude of sorrow or penitence, his left hand on his breast and his right hand supporting his forehead.

The confessional is only 5ft wide, and is so-named because of a simple stone seat carved from the altar on the far wall. The third room, the dormitory, has three openings – reminiscent of a small window – in the wall looking into the chapel, and a window in the south wall overlooking the Coquet. Outside, there would have been a small cloister, but unfortunately this has been destroyed by rockfall. Precarious winding steps from here to the top of the cliff would have led to the hermit's garden, but all this has now disappeared in the tangled undergrowth. Two marks on the inner wall of the kitchen commemorate the depth of flood

Hermitage Chapel window

The Hermitage, Warkworth

water on 9th February 1831 – the highest it had reached up to that date – and of a great flood almost a century later on 27th October 1900.

The Hermitage is traditionally linked to a well-known Northumbrian ballad or folktale – that of the love between Sir Bertram, Lord of Bothal Castle, and Isabel, the daughter of the neighbouring Lord Widdrington. Although Isabel was deeply in love with Bertram, she wanted him to prove his devotion beyond all doubt. While he was attending a feast held by Lord Percy at Alnwick, her maid delivered a splendid war helmet to Bertram as a gift, with a message that if he were to put it to the test in battle and it withstood "the sharpest blows", Isabel would agree to be his bride.

Lord Percy immediately decided to carry out a raid into Scotland, and young Bertram rode with him to engage the old enemy. In a desperate and bloody encounter with the Scots, Bertram fought valiantly, but took a dreadful head wound from a Scottish battleaxe. The lord was saved by his friends and taken to Wark Castle to receive attention. Isabel was extremely distressed and, blaming herself for Bertram's awful wound, vowed to make up for her foolish pride by nursing him back to health. She set off on her journey accompanied by two strong yeomen, but they were killed, and she was captured near the Cheviots by a Scottish chieftain who carried her off to his stronghold, intent on marrying her.

Bertram eventually recovered from his wound and, with his brother, decided to search for Isabel. One brother went north, the other west, and when Bertram finally found where she was being held captive, he hid nearby, waiting for an opportunity to rescue her. In the dark, Bertram saw his lady descending a rope ladder with a young man in Scottish dress. Blind with rage and jealousy, he followed them and, when the chance arose, drew his sword and attacked the stranger, shouting, "Vile traitor! Yield up that lady!"

Isabel recognised Bertram's voice and tried to stop him, shouting that she had been rescued by his brother, but it was too late, the fatal blow had been struck. In the confusion, she had tried to get between them, and she too suffered a mortal wound. From Isabel's dying lips, Bertram learnt the story of her capture, and of her rescue by his brother. Filled with remorse and anguish, he gave all his possessions to the poor and, after hewing the hermitage out of the solid rock, withdrew from the world to spend the rest of his life in penitence before the effigy of his lost love.

EXPLORING NORTHUMBERLAND HISTORY:
LINDISFARNE

Lindisfarne Castle and Harbour

LINDISFARNE

Lindisfarne Causeway

LINDISFARNE

The Holy Island of Lindisfarne is a small tidal island just off the coast close to Bamburgh. It is about 2½ miles long by about 1½ miles wide at its broadest point. Covering an area of about 1000 acres, it is reached by a paved, metalled causeway three miles long, although for the last two miles it curves around the lee of the island. The drive across to the island is quite easy, but every year, in spite of warnings, motorists are stranded by the incoming tide. There are small, elevated refuge stations for people thus embarrassed – a local story says there is a bottle of whisky in each, in case of such emergencies! However, this modern causeway is vastly different from the series of stepping stones that marked the 11th century Pilgrims' Way, the line of which is still visible, marked by a line of stakes.

A wide expanse of tidal flats opens out on each side of the causeway, forming a naturally enclosed basin that abounds in ducks, geese and wading birds, especially during the winter months. The curious geological formation known as the Great Whin Sill, which has given rise to islands such as Lindisfarne, traces its way across Northumberland from east to west. Created by volcanic intrusions of dark dolerite through limestone, it is visible on Lindisfarne as an outcrop on which the castle is built, and as the mound on which the priory is built. Other examples can be seen on the Farne Islands, at Bamburgh and Dunstanburgh castles, and, of course, on the line of Hadrian's Wall.

The history of Lindisfarne really begins with St Aidan and the growth of Celtic Christianity in the Kingdom of Northumbria. In AD 634, King Oswald, who had been educated and raised as a Christian on the island of Iona, defeated the army of Cadwallon of Gwynedd to re-establish a foothold for Christianity in the North. He sent to Iona for a bishop, but we are told in the writings of the Venerable Bede that he "was beaten by the intractable nature of the people he had come to teach". The next bishop who came was the wise and gentle Aidan, and with the help of the king, he soon established a new monastery on Lindisfarne. His Christian teaching was to reach out across Northumbria. Aidan not only taught people in church, he also went out into the villages and

Upturned fishing boats as sheds, Lindisfarne

Pilgrimage on Lindisfarne

Pilgrim's Causeway Lindisfarne at sunset

countryside to spread the word, and, indeed, is said to have been so successful in his efforts that he once baptised 15,000 people in the space of a week. Oswald ruled for nine years before he was killed in battle at Maserfield (modern-day Oswestry). His head was returned to Lindisfarne and one of his arms to Bamburgh, where they became sacred relics.

He was succeeded by his half-brother Oswiu, who ruled the more northerly kingdom of Bernicia, but who was rejected by the people of Deira to the south, who recognised his distant cousin Oswin as their king; Oswin became a close friend and confidant of Aidan.

After 16 years in his episcopate, Aidan died on 31st August, AD 651, and his body was taken to Lindisfarne for burial. It was Finan, a Scot from Iona, who succeeded Aidan just at a time when the differences between the Celtic (or Ionan) and Roman forms of Christianity were about to come to a head. King Oswiu was a follower of Celtic Christianity, but his son Alhfrith, who was a pupil and friend of the monk Wilfrid, preferred the Roman way. Following the death of Finan, his successor Colmán attended the famous Synod of Whitby, called by the king in AD 664 to finalise the matter once and for all. Colmán and Wilfrid were the main speakers, but it was the latter, who had been to Rome and travelled widely on the continent, who prevailed, and the king made the final decision to accept the Roman ways.

For a time, there was a lot of interplay between the two sides, and Northumbria came to represent the dividing line between the teachings of St Columba of Iona in AD 565 and the work of St Augustine of Canterbury in AD 597. Almost overnight, the importance of Lindisfarne changed, and Bishop Colman and many of his followers returned to Iona, taking with them some of the relics of St Aidan. Under Wilfrid's leadership, Hexham grew in importance while the episcopate of Lindisfarne diminished in size and eventually came under the influence of the monastery at Melrose – it was from here that many of the succeeding bishops came, the most important being Cuthbert.

It is said that a vision of St Aidan's body being taken to heaven by a host of angels was what finally persuaded Cuthbert to become a monk, although it seems that right from childhood he moved with ease and grace towards a religious life. Cuthbert entered the monastery at Melrose because he had been attracted by the stories he had heard of the prior, Boisil. The prior received Cuthbert with kindness, and when Eata, the abbot of Melrose, returned from a journey he obtained permission for the boy to receive the tonsure and join the brethren. After six or seven years, Cuthbert moved to Ripon with some of the brethren; this was a new monastery, but still under the control of Eata. Here, Cuthbert held the position of guestmaster, an important role that brought the monastery into contact with the outside world.

Following the Synod of Whitby, the king issued an ultimatum to the community: either accept Roman Christianity or depart. The monks promptly returned to Melrose where the Celtic ways predominated. Not long after Cuthbert's return to Melrose, a plague epidemic ravaged the monastery in AD 664 and both Boisil and Cuthbert were struck down. Cuthbert recovered, but Boisil died, and it was during these last few days they spent together that Boisil foretold Cuthbert's future life for him, including a prophecy that he would be made bishop. After Boisil's death, Cuthbert was made prior of Melrose, and it was while he held this post that Cuthbert spent much of his time covering great distances, mostly on foot, in the high, wild Northumbrian hills to preach the gospel.

When Cuthbert was around 30 years old, he was transferred by Eata to the monastery on Lindisfarne. It fell to Cuthbert to persuade the monks of Lindisfarne to accept the decision taken at the Synod of Whitby, which he did with patience, good humour and diligence in the face of heated debate fuelled by fury and anger. Cuthbert also travelled far and wide from Lindisfarne to spread the word of Christianity and soon became as famous for this as he had been at Melrose.

After he had served as prior for 12 years, Cuthbert felt that he was ready to "rise to the repose of divine contemplation" that is to become a hermit. His withdrawal was gradual: at first, he retired to a rocky island only 100 yards to the southwest of the priory, surrounded by water at high tide but approachable by a ridge of slippery stones at low tide – the ruins of an ancient chapel mark the spot, which is known as 'St Cuthbert's Isle'. After a while, he sought a place of retreat further away and more remote – he chose Inner Farne, the largest and closest to the mainland of the Farne Islands.

Cuthbert's withdrawal from active life at the monastery did not mean he was forgotten: his little realm became known all over England, and many people, attracted by his famous miracles, came to visit him from every corner of the country. He only left Inner Farne once during the first three years he spent there and that was to visit King Oswiu's daughter Ælflæd, Abbess of Whitby, on Coquet Island; this was judged to be the halfway point and a suitable place for their meeting.

St Aidan

While Cuthbert was living peacefully on his island, rivalries and quarrels had been dividing the Northumbrian church. Wilfrid had been active in his position as Bishop of York since AD 669 and had built grand churches, such as those at Hexham and Ripon, with great enthusiasm. His fame and wealth increased to such a level that Ecgfrith – son of Oswiu, and now king – saw him as a rival. The king was pleased, therefore, when a suggestion was put forward by Archbishop Theodore of Canterbury that the vast Northumbrian diocese should be divided into three: Bernicia (with its see at Lindisfarne or Hexham), Deira (with its see at York) and Lindsey in Mercia. Wilfrid didn't like this idea and promptly left for Rome to complain to the Pope. While he was away, three bishops were appointed, and they were already performing their duties when Wilfrid returned with a decision favourable to himself. Ecgfrith refused to accept this and put Wilfrid in prison for a year and thence into exile. He divided the diocese even further in AD 681, by consecrating two separate bishops of Lindisfarne and Hexham. Bishop of Lindisfarne was Cuthbert's abbot, Eata, but a vacancy soon arose for the position in Hexham when Tunbert was deposed in AD 684.

It was then decided unanimously, by synod, that Cuthbert should be consecrated Bishop of Hexham, and messengers and letters were sent asking him to accept the office. Cuthbert was not eager to take the post and he demurred and delayed until he eventually had no choice. The

King of Northumbria and Bishop Trumwine of the Picts, accompanied by a great number of other ecclesiastics and nobles, came to Inner Farne and begged him to accompany them to the synod at which Archbishop Theodore was still presiding. Cuthbert knew then that he could no longer refuse and sailed with them, away from his beloved island. Eata made a great concession to him by offering to exchange his own bishopric for Cuthbert's new bishopric of Hexham so that the latter did not have to leave the monastery he loved and could carry on his episcopal duties as Bishop of Lindisfarne.

Although Cuthbert had to forfeit his solitude, he was still able, in many ways, to continue the way of life that he had followed for 30 years. It is said that *"he maintained the dignity of a bishop without abandoning the ideal of a monk"*. He did not neglect his flock and regularly set out on pastoral visits, only now they extended as far west as Carlisle and, in addition to evangelisation, they included confirmations and the ordinations of priests.

During Cuthbert's first year of office, in AD 685, King Ecgfrith's army was ravaging the Pictish kingdom with great ferocity. While Cuthbert was in Carlisle, awaiting the outcome of the battle, he had a vision that the king would be killed and his army defeated, so he warned Queen Erminburgh, who was also in Carlisle, to return to Bamburgh for safety. A messenger arrived from the battlefield and confirmed the defeat had taken place at the very time Cuthbert had seen the vision. It was after this fateful event that Northumbria finally lost its supremacy north of the Firth of Forth.

Cuthbert continued to preach and heal throughout his episcopate. The plague was rampant in Northumbria during the second half of the 7th century and many villages were almost depopulated by its ravages. Cuthbert was keen to visit the survivors of an epidemic in any region, however remote, to offer them comfort with his prayers and readings from the gospel. However, his visions and prophecies appear to have impressed his contemporaries even more than his power to heal diseases, because it was these visions and prophecies that were considered to be evidence of saintliness.

It is interesting that although Cuthbert was later attributed with being a woman-hater, his last two visits before resigning the bishopric were to women friends. After a further meeting with Ælflæd of Whitby, he stayed at St Hilda's in South Shields – a *"monastery of virgins"* – where, Bede reports, Cuthbert was magnificently received by the Abbess Verca. It was here that he had a drink of water in preference to the beer or wine he was offered. Cuthbert then handed the half-full cup to his priest. The priest passed it to a steward, who asked if he could drink from the cup. The bishop's friendly answer was that he could, and the servant found that the water had taken on the taste of wine. Although the miracle was great in itself, it was Cuthbert's friendly simplicity that endeared him to all he met.

Cuthbert had held the office of Bishop of Lindisfarne for only two years when his prophetic spirit told him that he was soon to end his earthly life. His earlier austerities had severely weakened his physical strength, even though his mental powers were unimpaired; he was only 51 years old. It was with considerable relief and thankfulness that he resigned his office. Just after Christmas AD 686, he was preparing to row one final time across the seven miles of sea that separated Lindisfarne from his island retreat. As the little boat was made ready at the monastery landing stage, a crowd of

"The Journey" by Fenwick Lawson

brethren stood sadly, waiting to say goodbye, when an elder monk asked, "Tell us, Lord Bishop, when may we hope for your return?" Bede writes that Cuthbert answered, *"When you shall bring my body back here."*

Cuthbert did not resume his former life of strict isolation on Inner Farne, but made a custom of emerging frequently from his dwelling to talk with the brethren who came to visit. He had only enjoyed two months of his recovered quiet and solitude when he became ill with the disease that was to cause his death. The monk Herefrith, later Abbot of Lindisfarne, was able to give Bede a personal account of the hermit's last days as he was staying on Inner Farne with three other monks when Cuthbert fell ill. Herefrith and his companions were about to return to Lindisfarne and approached Cuthbert for a blessing. He granted it, but the monks noticed his condition was considerably worse and begged to stay with him. Cuthbert told them to board their vessel and go, but also, rather strangely, informed the monks that he wanted to be buried near his oratory on Inner Farne – furthermore, his coffin was to be hidden beneath the turf on the north side of the chapel. In the coffin, he said, they would find a fine cloth given to him by the Abbess Verca, which, out of affection for this deeply religious woman, he had kept for the wrapping of his dead body. Herefrith begged Cuthbert to allow some of the brethren to stay and look after him, but he replied, *"Go now, but return at the proper time."* Herefrith asked when they should come back, to which Cuthbert answered, *"When God so wills it, and when He Himself shall direct you."*

On his return to Lindisfarne, Herefrith immediately called all the monks to the church and commanded that unceasing prayer be offered for their beloved bishop. Herefrith waited five days for a fierce storm to abate before making the crossing to Inner Farne. When he reached the island, he found Cuthbert dreadfully weak from pain and a lack of food. The bishop told Herefrith that he had been unable to move from his bed for the last five days and nights. When Herefrith asked how he had been able to go so long without food, Cuthbert revealed five onions he had concealed among his bedding. "This has been my food for five days," he said. *"For whenever my throat became too dry and parched with thirst, I cooled and refreshed myself by tasting these."* But little more than half of one of the onions appeared to have been eaten.

Herefrith returned to Lindisfarne and explained to the monks that Cuthbert wished to be buried on his own island. However, they all agreed that it would be much easier to give his body the honour it deserved if they were allowed to bring it to the Lindisfarne church to be buried. Their feeling was so strong that Herefrith asked Cuthbert again. The bishop replied that he wanted his body to rest on Inner Farne where he had "fought his battle for the Lord", and also that he foresaw fugitives and wicked men seeking sanctuary near his body – an inconvenience that he did not want the monks to suffer. But when they refused to accept this argument, Cuthbert capitulated, asking only that his body be buried inside the church on Lindisfarne; this way, the monks alone would have access to the tomb, and they could still exclude others if necessary.

At last, Cuthbert realised his end was near, and Herefrith approached him for some final words for the brethren. He told them always to keep peace and divine charity among themselves; to be unanimous in their counsels; to be hospitable, kind and humble; and to keep the monastic rule he had taught them. *"Know and remember,"* he said, *"that if of two evils you are compelled to choose one, I would rather that you should take up my bones and leave these places, to reside wherever God may send you, than consent in any way to the wickedness of schismatics and so place a yoke upon your necks."* Perhaps Cuthbert had a vision of the cruel Norsemen invading Northumbria a hundred years later, but his followers had their instructions, which would be passed from generation to generation so that when the heathen hoards approached, the coffin would be carefully retrieved from its quiet island retreat to begin its wanderings all over the north of England.

Cuthbert lasted another day and night, after which he received communion from the faithful Herefrith. And then, as he raised his eyes and hands to heaven in an act of praise, his spirit left forever the sea-guarded rock that had been his home for 10 years. When Herefrith joined the waiting brethren outside, he found them singing the 59th psalm. Immediately, one of them lit two torches, an agreed signal that a monk watching on Lindisfarne would see across the seven miles of water. This monk ran quickly to the monastery church, where the assembled brotherhood were also singing the 59th psalm: *"O God thou hast cast us off and broken us down."* Bede suggests that this coincidence was prophetic in view of the severe troubles that were shortly to befall the Northumbrian church. Cuthbert's body was prepared for burial and met on Lindisfarne by a large assembly of monks. It was placed in a stone coffin beneath the floor of the church, to the right of the altar. He was buried on the day of his death – 20th March,

Celtic Cross

AD 687 – and ever since this date has been kept as his festival.

Miracles of healing are recorded as having taken place soon after Cuthbert's death. A youth 'possessed by a devil' was said to have been cured when he drank water mixed with some dirt from the spot where the water that had washed Cuthbert's body had been poured away. Bishop Willibrord, Apostle to the Fresians, was cured of a painful illness by kneeling at Cuthbert's tomb.

It was the custom at that time to open the coffins of holy people between 10 and 20 years after their death and wash the bones with great reverence before wrapping them in silk or linen and placing them into a chest in the interior of the church, where these relics would become an object of veneration. Eleven years after Cuthbert's death, the monks of Lindisfarne asked permission from Bishop Eadberht to perform this ceremony. He readily agreed but stipulated that it should be carried out on the anniversary of his burial. Eadberht was not present when the coffin was opened on 20th March, AD 698, because he traditionally spent the season of Lent on St Cuthbert's Isle. He was amazed when some of the monks burst into his retreat in a state of extreme excitement and terror. They explained that when they opened the stone coffin, they found Cuthbert's body intact and incorrupt, lying as if asleep, his skin soft and pliable, joints flexible and garments looking like new.

The monks brought the chasuble from the corpse to show to the bishop, who received it with delight and told them to replace the vestment with a new one. Before the sacred body was placed in a new wooden coffin, the shoes and head cloth were also replaced. This story was verified by Bede, who would have had a number of first-hand accounts from the monks directly involved. The fame of St Cuthbert, already widespread, increased dramatically as this extraordinary event became known, and more and more pilgrims visited the simple shrine of the humble hermit of the Farnes.

A hundred years later in AD 793, a raiding party of Vikings landed on the coast of Northumbria; churches were plundered, and Lindisfarne was robbed of most of its treasures. Those monks who escaped death fled inland, and when they were able to return they found that the tomb of St Cuthbert had miraculously escaped damage.

Monastery life was resumed and continued in reasonable peace and quiet for another 80 years. And then a second raid took place, this time stronger and more determined. Tynemouth Priory was sacked and then the strong and fierce army of Vikings turned their attention towards Lindisfarne. The bishop and the abbot remembered Cuthbert's dying instructions, so, after a brief discussion, they ordered the saint's body to be taken from its resting place. Other relics were also placed in the coffin, such as the head of Oswald and the bones of Aidan and Eata. The monks left their beloved island retreat for the mainland in sorrowful procession. They were to wander for seven years among ruined churches and monasteries on both sides of the border. The feared inevitable Viking raid ravaged Lindisfarne and its monastery, with the full horror perhaps best described by the monk Symeon of Durham in his 12th century account: *"In the same year [AD 793], the pagans from the northern regions came with a fleet of ships to Britain like stinging hornets and spread on all sides like fearful wolves, robbed, tore and slaughtered not only beasts of burden, sheep and oxen, but even priests and deacons, and companies of monks and nuns.*

"And they came to the church of Lindisfarne, laid everything waste with grievous plundering, trampled the holy places with polluted feet, dug up the altars and seized all the treasures of the holy church. They killed some of the brothers, took some away with them in fetters, many they drove out, naked and loaded with insults, some they drowned in the sea..."

The wanderings were a time of great danger and privation. The coffin of St Cuthbert was carefully guarded throughout this time by seven men specially chosen for this sacred task. Wherever the company went, the greatest respect and affection were shown for their precious burden, and many fine gifts were showered upon them; they received food from poorer folk, while wealthier individuals, the nobility and even royalty gave jewellery, money, and clothing of fine silk and wool. In AD 883, the monks settled at Chester-le-Street, where they remained undisturbed for more than a hundred years.

The move from Chester-le-Street came in AD 995 with the threat of another large Viking incursion. This time, the huge company moved south to Ripon. They had spent just four months with the religious community there when it looked as if peace had returned, so the monks turned north again, intending to go back to their former site. However, they did not reach Chester-le-Street. According to tradition, the monks were still several miles away when the cart carrying the coffin stuck fast and no amount of determined effort could persuade it to move. The company fasted and prayed, hoping for guidance. After six days, St Cuthbert appeared in a vision and told them that he wanted his body taken to a resting place on 'the Dunholm'. The monks did not know of the place he referred to, but they were pleased that at last the cart could be moved easily and they could begin their search for this mystery location. During their travels, they encountered two dairymaids discussing a lost cow and heard one of them say she had seen it on the Dunholm. The monks, of course, quickly asked directions and were guided onto the Dunholm – or 'Hill Island' – a place with thick, deep woods and dense undergrowth, where the river almost turned back on itself in a tight loop, forming steep banks and a naturally defendable peninsula. They had found the final resting place for St Cuthbert.

The first shrine was a rough shelter of boughs and branches, but by AD 999 a stone building of considerable size, known as the 'White Church', was ready for the saint's body. This church was finished in 1017, but by then the see of the Bishop of Durham was established and a steady stream of pilgrims began to flow to the shrine. Eventually, a cult following developed, which provided an excellent source of income for the people of Durham.

The North was slow to accept the Norman Conquest, and in 1067 the first Norman Earl of Northumberland was tried for treason and beheaded. And, just to compound their displeasure, the First Norman Bishop of Durham, Walcher of Lorraine, was murdered by an angry mob in Gateshead in 1080.

William the Conqueror sent an army to deal with the rebellion, but it was turned back by a thick mist that, it was said, had been sent by St Cuthbert for the protection of his people. This spurred the king to wage a more savage form of retribution – the infamous 'Harrying of the North'.

The terrified monks of Durham decided to return to Lindisfarne for refuge, taking the body of their saint with them. After an 80-mile journey, they reached the shore opposite the island just after nightfall, but a storm was raging, and their way was blocked because the sea had covered the causeway. Tired and scared, the monks were in fear of their safety, when, miraculously, the sea parted and the path onto the island lay before them. They had been away so long they had forgotten that at high tide the island is cut off from the mainland; when the tide went out, they thought the way had been specially opened for them by St Cuthbert. The monks did not stay long at Lindisfarne and were back in Durham by the beginning of Lent in 1070.

The Normans solved their difficulties in the North – to a certain degree at least – with the reorganisation of the Durham monastery and the building of a new cathedral to house the shrine of St Cuthbert.

The foundation stone of Durham Cathedral was laid in 1093 by Bishop William de St Carileph and Prior Turgot of Durham, and St Cuthbert was moved into the building in September 1104. Four centuries later, in 1538, three of King Henry VIII's commissioners visited Durham to examine its treasures prior to the dissolution of the monastery. They discovered that stories of the saint's valuables had not been exaggerated and they fully expected to find even more inside the coffin. The king's men broke it open and were astonished to find the body of the saint whole and incorrupt. The garments on his body were fresh and intact and there was absolutely no sign of decay to be found. The prior and the monks reburied the coffin in the ground directly beneath the famous shrine behind the high altar.

When the coffin was opened again in 1827, skeletal remains were revealed. However, there is a story that suggests St Cuthbert's body was removed to a safer resting place at the time of the Dissolution and even now lies uncorrupted in a secret location known only to three Benedictine monks. Perhaps the best and most fitting memorial to this much-loved Northumbrian saint is the mighty Durham Cathedral itself, a symbol and a shrine to this humble pioneer of Christianity in the North.

Lindisfarne Castle from the west

LINDISFARNE CASTLE (National Trust)

Strategically sited on a rocky outcrop of the Great Whin Sill known as Beblowe Craig, Lindisfarne Castle was built in 1550 as a border fort to protect the island harbour and is now in the care of the National Trust. At the outbreak of the Civil War, the castle was garrisoned for the king, but in 1646 the Parliamentarians took control; the islanders were such staunch supporters of the Commonwealth that Lindisfarne was one of the last places in England to accept Charles II after the Restoration.

Perhaps the most interesting event in the castle's history took place during the first Jacobite Rebellion of 1715 when a master mariner named Lancelot Errington and his nephew Mark successfully carried out an audacious plan to capture the fortress for the Pretender. The Erringtons sailed their ship into the harbour and invited aboard the sergeant in charge of the castle and all those men not on duty. The drink flowed freely, then, when the military guests were completely drunk, the Erringtons made for the castle, overpowered the few defenders remaining, and closed the gates behind them. The Jacobite flag was then run up the pole and James III proclaimed King of Lindisfarne! Their success was short-lived: the next morning, a detachment of royal troops arrived from Berwick and the unfortunate Erringtons had to surrender; they were taken away and imprisoned in Berwick Gaol. However, they were not to be beaten and made their escape by tunnelling beneath the walls, hiding the excavated soil in an old oven. Lancelot Errington went on to take ownership of the Salutation Inn in Newcastle's Flesh Market (later Cloth Market), although he is said to have died in great distress on hearing that Jacobite hopes had been dashed for good at Culloden in 1746.

In 1901, Edward Hudson, the owner and founder of *Country Life* magazine, was on holiday in Northumberland with his editor Peter Anderson Graham when they came upon the derelict castle and scaled the walls. Although it was in a neglected state, Hudson saw the potential of these romantically situated ruins. Thus inspired, he bought the castle from the crown and almost immediately asked his friend, the rising young architect Edwin Lutyens, to inspect the building. Hudson and Lutyens were firm friends and shared a great understanding of the English country house and all it represented, so the opportunity to rebuild this derelict castle as a fine stately home fired their imaginations.

Lindisfarne Castle is approached by a road that winds its way around the edge of the cliff, and Lutyens removed the balustrade, making the entry even more dramatic. Cobbles were laid in his favourite herringbone pattern, and steps lead from the portcullis up to the lower battery and the entrance hall. Throughout the building, there is evidence of Lutyens' eye for detail, and of his ability to create a style in keeping with the elemental quality of the castle. The architect skillfully designed the interior using some of its original construction. The fine vaulted dining room and ship room are almost as originally presented, but the ingenious impression of passages hewn in the rock, as well as large vaulted chambers, short circular pillars, low arches and beamed ceilings, combine to create a romantic and comfortable country home; a wonderful collection of Dutch paintings and Flemish and English oak furniture enhance this effect.

The castle had batteries for gun emplacements on two levels and was occupied as a garrison until 1819, although towards the end of the century it was taken over and used as a coastguard station. There are excellent views from the upper battery across the sea to the Farne Islands and Bamburgh Castle, and across the island to the dramatic ruins of Lindisfarne Priory. The jetty, the remains of which can be seen below the castle, was where lime from the nearby kilns was loaded onto boats. The Castle Point Lime Kilns, among the largest of their kind in the whole of the country, were established on the island in 1860 and continued in use until 1900 when they were fired for the final time. In recent times, however, careful work by the National Trust has restored the structures to their former glory.

In 1911, Hudson engaged garden designer, writer and artist Gertrude Jekyll to create the small walled garden a short walk away over the fields to the north of the castle. The garden is sufficiently sheltered from the strong local winds to allow an excellent selection of colourful plants, and the rediscovery in the early 80s of Jekyll's plans enabled the replanting of more than 50 species she had originally selected.

Lindisfarne Castle from the east

Lindisfarne Castle and Lime Kilns

LINDISFARNE PRIORY (English Heritage)

Following the monks' eventual flight from Lindisfarne in AD 875 – taking with them the beautiful Lindisfarne Gospels and the body of their beloved St Cuthbert – fearsome Viking raiders reduced the island's priory to rubble. For more than two centuries, the 'Cradle of Christianity' was no more than a pile of broken stones and crumbled masonry.

However, in 1082, a new phase of life began. Bishop William de St Carileph granted a group of Benedictine monks permission to live on Holy Island – as it had become known – and to begin the rebuilding of the ruined church and monastery. A Durham monk named Edward was the architect, and in 1093 the foundation of the new priory, based on the design of Durham Cathedral, was laid. The red sandstone used was quarried at Goswick on the mainland, and the huge blocks were carried across the sands at low tide. This soft stone was not really suitable for such an exposed site, and, although the ruins today appear very attractive, there is no doubt that weathering has largely contributed to their decay over the centuries.

Following the completion of the new Benedictine priory in 1120, life for the Lindisfarne community was mostly peaceful, bar a disturbance in 1326 when William de Prendergast and a party of Scots raiders descended upon the island; fortunately, they left the treasures of the priory alone and concentrated their efforts wholly on the bakehouse and brewhouse.

Sadly, the priory never again flourished as it had in the days before the Viking invasions. At the time of the Dissolution, its total wealth was assessed at less than £50, and it was demolished along with other minor houses in 1541 when Thomas Sparke was prior. Twenty years later, the remaining buildings were used as storehouses by the Crown, and by 1613 then owner Lord Walden had demolished the roofs of the main buildings and took away the lead and the bells by ship, which unfortunately sank just off the coast with the loss of all crew and passengers.

Today, the priory ruins are in the care of English Heritage. The priory church dates from the early to mid-12th century and is believed to stand on the same site as the small 7th century church that housed the shrine of St Cuthbert. It is entered by the west door, an excellent example of the Norman style with a chevron-moulded arch supported by triple shafts on either side.

The northwest and south-west piers of the crossing can still be seen, but all that remains of the tower is the graceful 'Rainbow Arch'. A considerable part of the choir is still complete, along with the frame of the large east window, which dates from about 1140. From the south transept, the way leads through to the cloister garth, although most of the buildings here were completed after the church, dating from the 13th century. It is here along the eastern side that the remains of the sacristy, the chapter house and the prior's lodging with its impressive chimney stack can still be seen. The kitchens, larder and cellars are visible on the western side, together with the later 14th and 15th century remains of the bakehouse and brewhouse. However, the 13th century refectory, which stood on the south side of the cloister garth, is no longer clearly recognisable. Also once situated here was a porch where a porter would have kept out any unauthorised visitors.

In the 14th century, a defensive barbican was added – a reminder of the danger to which the monastery was exposed at that time. At the same time, an outer court was added to the south of the existing buildings. The buildings here would have had various purposes; there was guest accommodation, stables, a room with a small kiln, another housing a well, and a further chamber with a small vat, probably used for brewing or tanning. The priory would have needed to be self-sufficient as far as possible, and additional buildings in the outer court would have been used for the storage of cereals, fodder and logs. Another would, perhaps, house a small smithy, while others would provide shelter for cows, pigs, goats and fowl. The site of the outer gatehouse is in the northwest corner of the outer court and would have been the main entrance to the monastery in the Middle Ages.

Sir Walter Scott used the location of the priory as the setting for one of the more poignant scenes in his 1808 historical narrative poem *Marmion: A Tale of Flodden Field* – particularly the ghastly trial of Constance de Beverley, which followed her imprisonment in the barbican. It has been suggested that a stone coffin near to the barbican could have some connection with the wretched Constance, but scholars and experts are unanimously agreed that the story is purely a product of poetic licence!

A modern statue of St Aidan stands within the grounds of the priory, and close to the entrance of the ruins is the pedestal of St Cuthbert's Cross, originally erected by Bishop Ethelwold. The current cross is a stone copy of the original, installed by Henry Collingwood Selby, lord of the manor of Lindisfarne, in the early 19th century. The ancient pedestal is known as 'the Petting Stone', and local legend dictates that a new bride must loup (leap) over the stone for the marriage to be blessed with good luck.

Lindisfarne Priory

Church of St Mary the Virgin, Lindisfarne

ST MARY THE VIRGIN

The Parish Church of St Mary the Virgin is largely 13th century, but contains fragments of older, possibly 11th century masonry and may be built on the site of another church that was part of the Anglo-Saxon monastery. St Mary's was restored between 1861 and 1862, when any of the original structure that might have remained was plastered over. Parts of the west front are probably original, and the exceptionally stout buttress constructed in the form of an arch and designed to carry the 18th century bell turret is most unusual.

The interior is mainly late 12th or 13th century in origin, and the piers of the north arcade are ornamented with alternate layers of red and white sandstone, an unusual feature in England. In the south aisle is a large trefoiled piscina (a basin for washing vessels for communion or mass) and an aumbry (a recess to store the same). A closed recess in the wall of the aisle indicates the probable site of a former chantry chapel. In the wall of the aisle, there is an arched doorway mostly below ground level, which could possibly have led down to a crypt.

The church is rich in architectural mysteries and is certainly worth close exploration. Another unusual feature is what looks like a little north porch with a blocked door; this was added in the 19th century as a mortuary for shipwreck victims. Many of the tombstones in the churchyard are curious: some carry inscriptions recording deaths by shipwreck, others are merely memorials to those whose bodies were never found for burial.

Altar – Church of St Mary the Virgin, Lindisfarne

St Cuthbert's Isle or Hobthrush Island

ST CUTHBERT'S ISLE

A small island lying a quarter of a mile to the southwest of the priory ruins, St Cuthbert's Isle – also known Hobthrush Isle – is only accessible at low tide. Originally there was a 7th century monastic cell on the isle; however, the low remains visible today are those of a medieval chapel. A wooden cross serves as a poignant reminder of the deep religious significance of this tiny island where St Cuthbert and subsequent ecclesiastical occupants of the Holy Island of Lindisfarne spent their time in solitude, prayer and contemplation.

EXPLORING NORTHUMBERLAND HISTORY:
TYNE VALLEY

ACOMB, St John of Beverley

Acomb is a former lead-mining village with several fine buildings dating from the 15th and 16th centuries. Half a mile south of the village is the Church of St John of Beverley – formerly the Church of St John Lee – which stands, it is thought, on the site of a chantry erected by St Wilfred and dedicated to St Michael the Archangel. The church was built in 1818 by noted Newcastle architect John Dobson, in the style of the 14th century. There is evidence to suggest a church has stood on this site since that time, but, apart from the original tower, the building we see today dates mostly from modifications in 1886 by another local architect, WS Hicks. St John's has some wonderful stained-glass windows depicting early Northumbrian ecclesiastical history, as well as fine examples of cup-and-ring markings on a stone in its entrance.

It was here, in 1765, that a wedding took place between Robert Scott, a 90-year-old man, and Jean Middlemass, aged just 25. The groom was well known for his skill and ability on the Northumbrian pipes, and for almost 25 years he had performed all over the north, despite being dependent on crutches. However, on the day of the wedding, Scott tossed aside his crutches and walked from his home in Wall, three miles away, and back again after the ceremony, completely unaided. A remarkable recovery indeed! All those who took part in the wedding were either pipers or had some direct connection with the instrument.

Horse trough and drinking fountain, Acomb

Church of St John of Beverley formerly known as Church of St John Lee, Acomb

ALLENDALE

Like Haltwhistle, about 10 miles to its north-west, Allendale Town once laid claim to be the geographical centre of Britain. This assertion is supported by an inscription on a sundial on the south wall of the Church of St Cuthbert, which records the town's coordinates as "HORA FUGIT 1842 LAT 54 50". The church also boasts a window mosaic depicting the Last Supper, and a beautifully carved lychgate.

Allendale is an attractive, sleepy sort of place with a large market square, unusual in that it has two islands of houses in its centre. It is nevertheless well served with hotels, pubs, shops, and plenty of opportunities to enjoy a cup of tea or coffee. Life here moves at a tranquil pace, and Allendale is a wonderful location for a quiet holiday with gentle walks and clean country air.

However, it was not always like this: for centuries, Allendale was where the agricultural hirings took place. Held twice a year in May and November, these were major events where labour was bought and sold.

Guisers – Allendale Fire Festival

The town would be alive with activity; there would be fairs, livestock for sale, stalls selling produce, and tinkers, pedlars and traders would be attracted from all over the north. Here was a truly festive occasion with singing, dancing and merrymaking.

These fairs are no longer held, but Allendale still hosts what is possibly one of the most spectacular folk festivals in all of Britain, perhaps even all of Europe: the Allendale Fire Festival, or "Tar Barlin' Ceremony". Every New Year's Eve, with bars and hotels packed to capacity, a large crowd of locals and visitors assembles in the square, gripped by anticipation and growing excitement. Then, just before midnight, accompanied by the town's band, a column of men in fancy dress, or 'guisers', strides purposefully into view. On each of the guisers' heads is a barrel of blazing fire, the flames leaping more than 6ft into the cold night air – a truly wonderful sight. The men proceed at a rapid pace around the perimeter of the market square, which is a highly dangerous operation, for the sawn-off tar barrels are filled with wood shavings, sticks and paraffin. The 40 guisers are all Allendale born and bred; indeed, there is no greater honour for a local man. However, a fair degree of fitness and stamina is required to bear these dangerous loads: after being lit and then lifted onto the head by two men, and has to be carried for more than half an hour, and should a guiser drop his barrel, he forfeits the privilege to take part the following year. The strange procession quickly winds its way back to the centre of the square, where there is a huge bonfire of wood. One after another, the guisers tip their flaming load onto the bonfire, and, as the church bell signals midnight, this great fire instantly sends huge sheets of flame and sparks up into the night sky, while the crowd links hands, sings Auld Lang Syne, and joyously welcomes in the new year. The guisers then "first-foot" around the town, carrying embers of the fire – legend has it that as long as there is a fire in Allendale, the community will not die.

Some of the guisers have been a part of the ceremony for more than forty years. These stalwarts form the fire committee, which meets twice a year – in February and October – to organise the building of the fire and the appointment of new guisers. It is a much sought-after position, and there is always a waiting list of between eight and ten men eager to join. This is not a task to be undertaken lightly, however: filled with a mixture of sawdust and shavings soaked in paraffin, the sawn-off whiskey barrels can weigh as much as 35lb.

The origin of tar bar'lin' is not known, but it is believed to be linked to a range of fire festivals that have taken place all over Europe since Celtic times. These are reputedly connected to the death of Balder, a Norse god associated with agriculture, and the symbolic burning of old and dying vegetation to promote new, healthy growth. The fire itself is said to signal the upward turning of the Sun from its lowest seasonal point in the heavens. The midwinter fire festival is a deep-seated, enigmatic community tradition meant to reforge the ancient and mystical bond between man and nature.

ALLENHEADS

Located around seven miles south of Allendale Town, Allenheads owes its existence to the lead-mining boom of the 19th century, and at one time was producing over 70% of all the ore mined in Great Britain. All around the village are sites and relics of this once prosperous industry. A footpath leading west over Killhope Law follows the old packhorse route that once linked Allenheads Smelt Mill with Killhope Lead Mine in Weardale. 'Carriers Way', as it is known, is a splendid walk – especially in summer – but should not be tackled without a good map and the proper equipment. The walk is not for the faint-hearted, but the superb views over the tops of the North Pennines on a clear day are a suitable reward.

The main industry in Allenheads today is farming, although it is also a great attraction for walkers, cyclists and tourists. There is an excellent heritage centre that recalls the village's past, and outside the nearby inn is a display of industrial artefacts, while the interior is crammed full of antiques and other fascinating and unusual items collected by the landlord on his travels.

The Allendale washing floors are absolutely fascinating and, during the height of lead mining, must have been among the busiest places in the village. Tubs of mineral, or 'bouse', were pulled by ponies to the 'bouse teems' where men worked crushing machines and operated jiggers and buddles to separate the lead ore from the waste. For their first year of employment, boys as young as nine picked out the biggest pieces of ore by hand; then, in their second year, they graduated to heavier work. By the time the boys were 15, they worked the jiggers and buddles. After seven years, they had gained enough experience to become mastermen washers or even to join a partnership and work in the mines.

All the machinery was driven by water power – it drove the crushing machine, and powered engines and waterwheels in the mines, workshops and smelting mill. The reservoirs in the area held around 60 million gallons of water, and a network of overground water channels, or leats, led from the reservoirs around the village to the washing floors. Thomas Sopwith was the chief agent for the Allenheads mine owners, the Beaumont family. He ensured his workers enjoyed good conditions; this included improvements to housing and the building of schools for their children. Sopwith was a strict timekeeper and demanded punctuality both at school and the mine. He was a friend of the great Lord Armstrong, the famous engineer and millionaire businessman, and together they developed modern machinery to speed up production.

The Gin Hill Mine Shaft – just across the road from what was the mine office – has a vertical drop of 240ft and once provided access to five different levels.

Mine trucks, Allenheads

The washing floor and Bouseteams, Allenheads

This underground system meant men could easily get to the seam; it also transported equipment, ore and spoil. The men climbed down a series of ladders to their work, but their ponies were able to use a gentler entrance about 50 yards away. The miners dug upwards and, as the waste piled up below them, stood on it to be able to reach further up into the narrow columns – with a complete disregard for health and safety – to chop out more lead ore.

There's a disturbing tale connected to Allenheads that dates from the early 20th century and is still told by some of the older folk in the dale. In the winter of 1904, the local newspaper reported that a ferocious animal was slaughtering livestock in the area. For days, news of this elusive creature gave rise to fear and speculation. Fleeting sightings and signs left behind after the killings soon made it obvious that a wolf was at large in the wilds of Allendale. Eventually, it was suggested that this was a beast that had escaped months earlier from the grounds of its owner, one Captain Bain of Shotley Bridge.

Foxhounds were brought in, and farmers organised shooting parties – a big-game hunter even came to match his wits against the wolf – but the fierce killer continued its dreadful devastation. The end to the slaughter, however, was sudden. One night, following a particularly savage attack on sheep just over the border near Alston, news came that a wolf had been hit and killed by an express train. At first, no one believed that this was the same creature, but the attacks indeed stopped, quashing doubts that the killer was dead.

An interesting footnote to the story describes the wolf hit by the train as more than 5ft long and 80lb in weight, while Captain Bain's animal was only a year-old cub. This suggests the possibility that the true identity of the savage killer was never discovered.

Thorgreen Lime Kilns, Allenheads

Aydon Castle, Corbridge

AYDON CASTLE, CORBRIDGE (English Heritage)

Aydon Castle, or 'Aydon Halle' as it was called in the 13th and 14th centuries, occupies a fine position above the well-wooded dene of the Cor Burn. As early as the 1200s, a timber-framed hall stood on this site, and this was replaced by a more impressive manor house at the end of the century; permission to crenellate was granted to then owner Robert de Reymes, an active knight, in 1305. To this day, Aydon Castle remains one of the most interesting examples of a fortified manor house in all of Northumberland.

In 1346, the Scots, on their way to the Battle of Neville's Cross near Durham, attacked the castle and negotiated a surrender, the condition being that the defenders escaped with their lives. The fortification has four large towers, very thick walls and defendable courtyards that convey the impression of great strength. It would appear that although timber was used in the construction, this was kept to a minimum, making it not so easily burned by Scottish raiders.

A local legend tells the story of a small group of reivers who had been captured by the English lord Sir Robert Clavering and were condemned to die. Their dreadful sentence was to be thrown from the roof of Aydon Castle into the stream far below. One of the Scotsmen, the only one to survive, escaped his terrible fate with a superhuman leap onto a huge rock across the burn; this place has henceforth been known as 'Jock's Leap'.

BELLINGHAM

Bellingham is a small market town pleasantly situated on the north bank of the North Tyne. A typical border centre, for many years up until 2004 it attracted farmers from both Northumberland and Scotland to its sheep sales. Bellingham was once on the direct route used by the reivers from the valleys of Tynedale, Redesdale and Liddesdale when riding south on their frequent forays. It would appear that the name of the town was originally spelt *Bellinjham* – perhaps it was from this that the modern pronunciation of 'Belling-jum' is derived?

This was the home of the powerful de Bellingham family, who were granted the lands here during the reign of William the Conqueror. The site of their castle is now visible as an artificial mound, not far from the mill they rented from the Scottish king in 1263 at the sum of ten pounds per year.

Bellingham is regarded as the capital of North Tynedale, because it is one of the few towns of any size for many miles around. Visitors see it as a centre for access to the fine countryside, being a gateway to both the Kielder Forest Park and the Northumberland National Park; also, the Bellingham Show and Country Festival is held here every August. Industry in Bellingham was centered mainly around the ironworks which operated from 1838 until 1848; there were several blast furnaces, 24 kilns and 70 coke ovens. There was also a dam, 20 feet high and 31 feet wide, the only visible remnant of this brief industry.

The town's church is dedicated to St Cuthbert, marking the temporary resting place of the saint's body on its epic journey around Northumbria before its final interment in Durham.

Behind the churchyard a pathway leads to St Cuthbert's Well, or Cuddy's Well, as it is locally known, its waters are said to have great healing powers and are still used in baptisms today.

Built in the late 12th century, the church was designed in the early Norman style. It is also one of the few in England with a massive stone roof – this dates from the early 17th century, after the original wooden roof was twice burned by the Scots during the border wars. The extremely narrow windows of the nave, with their emphasis on defence, are another feature that recalls these turbulent times. According to the records of the Dean and Chapter of Durham in 1607, the church was not very well supported by the local people, and communion was only held once a year! Also, the font was badly damaged; the Bible, the Prayer Book and Psalters were missing; and the clerk could neither read nor write.

A strange kind of justice was dispensed in 1711 to one William Charlton of the Bower – or 'Bowrie' as he was known – after he had killed Henry Widdrington of Buteland in a quarrel. The victim was buried in the entrance to the Charltons' pew at St Cuthbert's, and consequently, it is said, William Charlton

St Cuthbert's Church, Bellingham and the "Long Pack"

St Cuthbert's Well, Bellingham

would never take his seat in the building again.

In the churchyard, there is a curious gravestone shaped like a long peddler's pack of the kind used in the early 18th century. It recalls a well-known local tale, 'The Legend of the Lang Pack', as told by James Hogg (also known as 'the Ettrick Shepherd'), a poet and friend of Sir Walter Scott, by whom many border ballads have been preserved. The story concerns a peddler who called at one of the great houses in the Bellingham area, Lee Hall. He found there was no one at home but a young maid, so the man asked if he could leave his pack for safekeeping while he went into the village to look for shelter, and then return for it later that evening.

The maid agreed, but suspicions were aroused when the other servants arrived home and one of them noticed a movement inside the pack. An old shotgun was brought down to the kitchen, and several shots were fired into the eerily moving bag. They opened it and found a young man dying of his wounds; with his last breath, he told the servants that he had planned to let his accomplices into the house after dark.

So, an armed welcoming committee was formed, and the agreed signal given. The intruders were met with a hostile reception and a fusillade of shots. It is said that several local robbers were never seen again after this terrible incident. The young man was buried in the churchyard, although it is said that his body was removed by unknown persons at a later date.

Mounted on a plinth in front of Bellingham Town Hall is an unusual relic from the turn of the 20th century: a musket, or gingall. The old weapon, which looks rather like a harpoon gun, was brought to Britain by a member of the Charlton family who served in the Royal Navy; it was captured in 1900 during the suppression of the Boxer Rebellion in China.

Just to the north of Bellingham is Hareshaw Burn, which flows south into the North Tyne. There is a walk of about a mile and a half up the dene to Hareshaw Linn, where this attractive waterfall drops about 30ft into the shady, wooded valley. This is reputed to be the secret place where St Cuthbert's coffin was kept safe during its brief stay in the area.

St Cuthbert window detail, Beltingham

BELTINGHAM, St Cuthbert's Church

St Cuthbert's Church in Beltingham enjoys a beautiful, peaceful setting above the ravine of the Beltingham Burn to one side and close to the South Tyne on the other. The building dates back to the late 15th century, although the remains of a seventh-century Saxon cross and a second-century Roman altar in its grounds have led historians to believe that an older church constructed of wood once stood on the site. And, indeed, is believed to have once been the stronghold of a Viking Chief called Boltr, from which the village name is derived.

It is said that St Cuthbert preached beneath one of the churchyard's three massive yew trees – believed by some to be around 2,000 years old – during his visits to the more remote parts of Saxon Northumberland; Beltingham is also thought to have acted as a safe temporary resting place for his body when monks fled Lindisfarne in fear of Norse invaders. The church's deep connection to Cuthbert is commemorated by a beautiful stained-glass window created by Welsh artist Leonard Evetts in the early 1980s, illustrating significant events in the saint's life, and is dedicated to Douglas Smith OBE. JP, churchwarden and benefactor of the parish. The grated squint in the chancel is thought to have been for the use of lepers, or possibly by an anchorite in an adjoining cell.

In common with most of Tynedale, St Cuthbert's suffered the border wars and reiver raids: its vicar

Lepers' Squint, Beltingham

The famous Yew tree, Beltingham

was carried off by invading Scots in 1311 and his house let to raise the ransom. Unfortunately, the ransom was not paid, and the Scots returned in 1314, burned the village and wiped out the inhabitants. The legacy of these unstable times can still be witnessed: deep incisions scar the church's exterior walls where archers sharpened their arrow points; archery was compulsory at the time, and practice took place after services.

St Cuthbert's Church enjoys a long association with the Bowes-Lyon family, who once owned the nearby Ridley Hall, and the churchyard has a separate plot for the family graves.

The remarkable lychgate was donated by the Hon Francis Bowes-Lyon in 1904.

Lychgate, St Cuthbert's Church, Beltingham

BLACK MIDDENS BASTLE

Black Middens Bastle is situated near the confluence of the Tarset Burn and the Black Burn, around seven miles north-west of Bellingham. From the time of Edward I up until the beginning of the reign of James I, the border regions were in a state of turmoil, with reiving, ambushes and skirmishes an everyday occurrence. Almost every family living within 20 or 30 miles of the border was under the constant threat of attack by invading armies, and, consequently, most of the dwellings within this narrow strip of land were constructed with the emphasis very much on defence.

The most common of these was the fortified farmhouse known as a bastle, which took its name from the French word bastille, meaning fortified tower. The bastle was an extremely strong, two-storied, stone-built construction about 20ft high with walls almost 4ft thick. Usually, the farmer and his family lived on the upper floor, which was only accessible by a ladder from the outside or a trapdoor from the basement; either way, it could be made very secure. A small door at ground level allowed access to the basement, where livestock could be sheltered during times of trouble. Bastles had few windows, and these were set high up in the walls; the floors were stone-flagged and the roof stone-tiled, both to minimise the risk from fire.

Black Middens Bastle

There were three bastle houses fairly close together in this area, and towards the end of the 17th century one of them was occupied by a powerful member of the Milburn clan, one of the dominant families in Tynedale at the time. The man, known as 'Barty o' the Combe', was a farmer, but supplemented his income with a bit of reiving. One morning, he awoke to find he had been the victim of a stealthy raid; his sheep had been driven off by a party of marauding Scots. He quickly summoned a faithful ally and fellow reiver named Corbit Jack, who lived a little further along the Black Burn, and the pair set off in quick pursuit, but unfortunately they lost the trail north of Carter Fell.

Barty didn't like the idea of returning home empty-handed, so he and his associate decided they would round up and bring back some Letham sheep to make the journey worthwhile. They had got as far as the waterfall known as Chattlehope Spout when they were overtaken by two burly Scots who were the rightful owners of the sheep. A desperate hand-to-hand fight ensued in the long heather above the fall, during which Corbit Jack was killed. Barty was wounded in the thigh, but, with a superhuman effort, he swung his sword at his companion's slayer and caught him in the neck; it is written that his enemy's head "sprang alang the heither like an inion". The other assailant tried to make off, but he too was cut down before he had gone many yards.

Barty took both their swords and lifted his dead companion onto his back. In spite of the dreadful wound he had suffered, he drove the captured sheep safely back, leaving Corbit Jack's body at his own door, on his way home. These were the sort of hard men who lived in the border country at that time, brought up in a war of attrition and accustomed to a life of raid and reprisal that was the accepted way of life.

BLANCHLAND

Blanchland Abbey

Gatehouse, Blanchland

Blanchland is a remote but attractive settlement that nestles on the northern bank of the River Derwent, right on the border between Northumberland and County Durham. The village grew up around a religious community of Premonstratensian monks – an order originally from the north-eastern France – who founded the abbey here in 1165, and its name is derived from the blanched habits worn by these 'white canons'.

With their monastery snugly sited in a little wooded hollow, it would seem to these monks that they would be able to proceed with their devotions completely unmolested. However, this was not to be, for in 1327 King Edward III led an army of 60,000 men in a hunt for the Scots who were continually ravaging the northern part of his realm. They searched across the Tyne Valley to no avail, but then word came that the Scots had been sighted. It was on his way to a confrontation with the army of Sir James Douglas that the king and his troops stopped in Blanchland. Edward was received by the abbot, who took him into the church, heard his confession and ordered masses to be said.

Almost two decades later, in 1346, there was a most unfortunate and disastrous raid by a party of Scots who had ridden down from the border to attack the monastery. The robbers had lost their way on the remote moorland in a thick mist and had just begun the long journey home when they heard the monastery bell ringing nearby. Overjoyed to see the Scots leaving, the monks had prematurely sounded the bell to summon the brethren to a Te Deum to give thanks. The sound of the bell guided the robbers to their target, where they broke through the gates, murdering all the monks and setting fire to buildings before riding swiftly away with the spoils of their raid.

Parts of the church were never rebuilt, and, by the time of the Dissolution in 1539, annual revenues had dwindled so much – to as little as £45 – that the property was given by the Crown to various lay owners. In the early 17th century, the Forster family, owners of Bamburgh, took control of the estate; however, following the involvement of General Tom Forster in the Jacobite uprising of 1715, their land was forfeited to the Crown. It was Nathaniel Lord Crewe, Prince Bishop of Durham and the uncle of the unlucky Tom, who purchased the estates. On the bishop's death in 1721, these passed into the ownership of the Lord Crewe Trust, a body set up to ensure that any income was donated to various charitable and educational causes; the trust still manages the estates.

Perhaps the most charming aspect of the village is its quadrangle of stone cottages, which contain a number of secret cupboards, chambers and stairs. These cottages were built for lead miners who worked in the district – there are numerous sites of lead-mining remains in the surrounding hills – and the square around which they are grouped is broadly L-shaped. The main building is the renowned Lord Crewe Arms, which is mostly Georgian but incorporates fragments of the earlier monastic buildings – this is where the guestmaster of the abbey would have entertained visitors. The hotel sign shows the distinctive coat of arms of Lord Crewe accompanied by a crossed sword and crosier, denoting his position as a prince bishop.

Dating from the 15th century, the abbey's gatehouse forms the northern entrance to the square, but very little of the original 13th century fabric of the abbey remains, apart from the square tower and the north transept.

Methodist leader John Wesley preached to a large gathering of lead miners and their families in the churchyard here on 24th March 1747.

Methodism developed a great following among the miners and its simple, uncomplicated, doctrine had enormous appeal for the people who came from miles around to share words and prayers.

St Peter's Church, Bywell

BYWELL

Bywell has been occupied since Roman times, they had a bridge over the river here, the remains of which were visible in the middle of the river right up to the mid 1800s until they were blown up when the building of the present bridge was begun.

Bywell has not one but two parish churches, which is unusual for a village as small as this. Legend has it that St Andrew's and St Peter's were conceived by two sisters who were unable to agree on the type of building they wished to erect as a church, so each built their own. St Andrew's is referred to as 'the white church' and was most likely founded by the white-robed Premonstratensian canons of Blanchland; St Peter's – 'the black church' – was, in all probability, established by the black-habited Benedictine monks of Durham.

St Andrew's stands on the site of an earlier building erected by St Wilfrid and has a tower that incorporates early Saxon work. Following extensive restoration work in 1857, little else of the Saxon architecture of St Andrew's remains; however, some fine examples can still be seen in the form of the three-light window of the chancel, and the squint on the right-hand side of the chancel arch. The chancel itself is quite unusual in that it is 2ft longer than the nave.

Although the St Peter's we see today is built in the early Norman style, there is evidence of a Saxon church on the site. Indeed, it is believed that this ancient church was where, according to the chronicler Symeon of Durham, the 12th Bishop of Lindisfarne, Egbert, was consecrated on 11th June AD 803. The low, square embattled tower contains two very old bells with Latin inscriptions, one of which amusingly translates as, "I proclaim the hour for people rising, and summon those still in bed."

One very interesting relic from medieval times is the leper window on the south side of the chancel, through which the sacrament was administered to lepers or sick persons during the plague.

After the Norman Conquest, the barony of Bywell was given to Guy de Balliol, "for good and faithful service"; however, the family lost it during the reign of Edward I for disloyalty to the Crown. By the time of Richard II, it was in the possession of the Nevilles, who were the Lords of Raby and Earls of Westmorland. They lost the estate during the reign of Elizabeth I, when they forfeited all their possessions for their part in the 'Rising of the North', a plan that also involved the Duke of Northumberland and other northern lords in a bid to restore the Catholic religion and put Mary, Queen of Scots, on the English throne. The estate was held for a short time by the queen, before being sold to the Fenwicks, a family well-known for their reiving.

Standing on private property in the village, but visible from the road, is the dramatic tower known as Bywell Castle. This massive, three-story gatehouse with turrets at each of its corners was built in the 15th century by the Neville family as part of a larger fortification that was never completed.

To the east of St Andrew's church stands Bywell's Grade II-listed village cross, which dates from the 13th century. After suffering extensive damage over subsequent years, the landmark was restored and altered in the 18th century, when a stone ball was added to the top of the remaining column.

Written around the time of 'the Rising of The North' in 1569-70, the Royal Commission's report gives an excellent indication of the awful uncertainty of living under the threat of the Border Reivers: *"The town of Bywell is builded in length of one street upon the river or water of Tyne, on the north and west part of same; and is divided into two several parishes, and*

St Andrew's Church, Bywell

inhabited with handicraftsmen, whose trade is all in iron-work for the horsemen and Borderers of that country, as in making bits, stirrups, buckles and such others, wherein they are expert and cunning; and are subject to the incursions of the thieves of Tynedale, and compelled winter and summer to bring all their cattle and sheep into the street in the night season, and watch both ends of the street; and when the enemy approacheth, to raise hue and cry, whereupon all the town prepareth for rescue of their goods; which is very populous, by reason of their trade, and stout and hardy by continual practice against the enemy."

Bywell did not escape the Great Flood of November 1771. In a desperate bid to save some of the village's most valuable horses, their owners drove them into church for safety, but the situation was so treacherous that the men narrowly escaped drowning by hanging onto the pews, and one horse was only saved by mounting the altar. Both churches were severely damaged in the flood and their churchyards almost completely destroyed. Worst of all, 10 houses were swept away in the dreadful deluge, and six people died.

Bywell Village Cross

CHERRYBURN, MICKLEY
(National Trust)

Cherryburn is a small stone cottage in the village of Mickley on the banks of the River Tyne, and the birthplace of Thomas Bewick. The wood engraver and naturalist, who was greatly inspired by the countryside surrounding his home, is arguably Northumberland's best known and most highly respected artist.

Bewick was born on 11th August 1753 at Cherryburn and grew up in the cottage with his parents, who were tenant farmers, and seven brothers and sisters. When part of the original cottage was knocked down, Thomas's brother and his family built the nearby farmhouse, which now houses artefacts and displays telling the artist's life story. In his day, Thomas Bewick was very popular and immensely influential, both for his engravings and for his books on natural history. At the age of 14, he was apprenticed to Newcastle engraver Ralph Beilby and showed so much talent that eventually he became a partner in Beilby's business.

Thomas Bewick's Cottage, Cherryburn

Apprentices trained by Bewick include John Anderson, Luke Clennell and William Harvey, who went on to enjoy successful careers as painters and engravers. In his early career, Bewick made woodcuts for advertisements and for use as illustrations in children's books, but in time he began to create his own works, writing, illustrating and publishing titles on natural history. In 1786, when he was financially secure, he married Isabella Elliott from Ovingham, a friend since childhood. They had four children: Robert, Jane, Isabella and Elizabeth (the daughters worked on their father's memoir after his death). At this period in his life, Bewick was described by the Newcastle artist Thomas Sword Good as *"a man of athletic make, nearly six feet high and proportionally stout. He possessed great personal courage and in his younger years was not slow to repay an insult with personal chastisement. On one occasion, being assaulted by two pitmen on returning from a visit to Cherryburn, he resolutely turned upon the aggressors and, as he said, 'paid them both well'"*.

Bewick's first popular book was A History of Quadrupeds (1790), but he is probably best known for *A History of British Birds*. Given his detailed knowledge of the birds of Northumberland, Bewick prepared the illustrations, so Beilby was tasked with assembling the text, which he struggled to do. Bewick ended up writing most of the text, which led to a dispute over authorship; Bewick refused to have Beilby named as the author, and as a consequence only Bewick's name appeared on the title page, along with a paragraph of explanation at the end of the preface. The book was an immediate success when published by Beilby and Bewick in 1797; just prior to this, Bewick had published an anthology in 1795, titled *Characters of*

Printing press, Cherryburn

Thomas Bewick drawing - Chillingham Bull

the Kings and Queens of England. Given the success of his first volume of bird illustrations, Bewick started work at once on a second, devoted to water birds, but the disagreement over authorship led to a final split with Beilby. Bewick was unable to control his feelings and resolve issues quietly, so the partnership ended turbulently and expensively. Bewick was left with his own workshop, for which he had to pay £20 – equivalent to around £25,000 today – in lawyer's fees and more than £21 for Beilby's share of the equipment.

With the assistance of his apprentices, Bewick brought out *A History of British Birds: Volume II* in 1804, as the sole author. He found the task of managing the printers troublesome, but the book met with as much success as the first volume.

Bewick is credited with adopting and popularising publishing innovations that increased the quality of printed illustrations at low cost. By utilising tools normally used by metal engravers and cutting hard boxwood across the grain, he created printing blocks that were more durable and detailed than traditional woodcuts and could also be integrated with metal type.

Even his most serious works of natural history were often illustrated with humorous 'tail-pieces' – small drawings at the end of chapters – frequently depicting scenes from Aesop's Fables. Bewick was a staunch advocate for the ethical treatment of animals, and he possessed a strong sense of moral justice, as his illustrations often show. His final (unfinished) wood engraving, *Waiting for Death*, shows an old workhorse standing beside a tree stump, looking forlorn and neglected.

Bewick died at home on 8th November 1828, following a brief illness, and was buried beside his wife Isabella, and close to his parents and his brother John, in the churchyard of St Mary the Virgin, Ovingham. Posthumously, in 1830, Bewick's swan was named after the artist.

The King's Oven, Corbridge

The Vicar's Pele, Corbridge

CORBRIDGE

The ancient town of Corbridge has played an important role in the history of Northumberland. The Romans first came here in AD 81 and established a strategic crossing point on the River Tyne, and by the third century it had evolved into a civilian town.

In Saxon times, Corbridge was considered to be a place of great importance; some historians believe it was a royal residence. As far back as AD 771, the town had a flourishing monastery, most probably founded by St Wilfrid when he was presiding over the See of Hexham. In AD 918, the Battle of Corbridge was fought between the Norse army of Ragnall and a Scottish army under Constantine II allied with the forces of Ealdred I of Bamburgh. The engagement turned out to be indecisive, although it did allow Ragnall to further establish himself in Northumbria, and by the end of AD 919 he had taken York and proclaimed himself king.

In 1138, there was another nasty brush with the Scots when King David I and his army camped near Corbridge and *"committed the most horrid barbarities throughout the whole neighbourhood"*. In 1201, when King John was in the North, he instigated a huge search for hidden treasure, convinced that the inhabitants had hidden their wealth from the regular incursions of the Scots. The search, of course, proved fruitless.

Within the space of 50 years, Corbridge suffered three dreadful raids: it was burnt by William Wallace in 1296, and again by Robert the Bruce in 1312, and yet again by King David II in 1346 on his way to his encounter and, indeed, resounding defeat by Lord Neville and the English at Neville's Cross, near Durham.

Towards the end of the 13th century, Corbridge was at the height of its prosperity. A weekly market was held, and the town was one of only three in Northumberland that enjoyed the privilege of sending representatives to Parliament, though they soon gave this up to escape the burden of the members' expenses!

In the Middle Ages, the plague raged here with such ferocity that more than half of the population of Corbridge died. The only survivors were those who had camped on the north side of the town, in a field called the Leazes. However, it is said that when they returned to the town, the streets were overgrown with grass.

In 1644, a battle took place in Corbridge between a regiment of royalist troops led by Sir Marmaduke Langdale and two regiments of Scottish troops, which were completely routed.

It would seem that in the middle of the 19th century Corbridge was not considered to be the pleasant and attractive place it is today. The eminent historian John Hodgson, who visited the town in 1830, said, *"The town is dirty and, in all the streets except that through which the Newcastle and Carlisle road passes, is filthy with middens and pig sties with railings before them of split board. The population seem half-fed; the women sallow, thin-armed, and the men flabby, pot-bellied and tender-footed; but still the place bears the appearance of being ancient."* An unflattering picture that would certainly not endear him to the residents!

St Andrew's Church is, along with the crypt at Hexham Abbey, the most important Saxon religious site still in existence in Northumberland, and is the only survivor of four Saxon churches that once stood in Corbridge. The lower part of the tower dates from before AD 786, and judging by the remaining window there was also a porch here. The upper part of the tower is from the 11th century, the battlements having been added at a later date.

The most impressive feature of the interior is the round-headed tower arch, a former Roman gateway with huge square stones, transferred intact from Corstopitum. The rest of the interior is mainly 13th century, although the remains of some Saxon work is visible in the two window heads of the nave. The north arcade dates from around 1200, while some Norman zigzag work can be seen around the south doorway.

In the southern corner of the churchyard is what is known as 'the Vicar's Pele', an excellent example of a tower house, built in 1318 using Roman stones. With its overhanging parapet, the tower stands as a grim reminder of the days of the Border Reivers, when dwellings had to be constructed with the emphasis firmly on defence in order to withstand frequent vicious raids.

Corbridge Bridge, which crosses the Tyne at the southern entrance to the town, was built in 1674 and was the only bridge on the river to survive the tremendous flood of 1771. It is said that the Tyne rose to such a height on that occasion that some of the town's inhabitants were able to lean over the parapet and wash their hands.

It was near this bridge, in 1735, that the famous Corbridge Lanx was found. The Roman silver dish, which weighed over 11lb, was originally bought by a Newcastle goldsmith but later recovered by the Crown as "treasure trove".

Corbridge Bridge

Corstopitum with Corbridge in the distance

CORSTOPITUM (English Heritage)

The Roman station of Corstopitum lies only a short distance from the town of Corbridge. This great camp has been described as the true foundation stone for much of this part of Tynedale, and for many years after the departure of the Romans it was used as an unprotected quarry, proving a valuable source of ready-dressed stone for the builders of churches, manor houses and castles.

Corstopitum stood at the junction of the two main Roman roads in the north: the Stanegate, which linked a line of forts along the Tyne Valley, and Dere Street, which, on its way from the south, connected settlements at Piercebridge, Lanchester, Binchester and Ebchester. Its main function was to guard the river crossing at this point and, of course, to act as a military town and supply base.

The fort dates from around AD 86. Roman occupation began here after the withdrawal from Scotland north of the Clyde-Forth line, a move that was completed by AD 90. There was a series of three successive timber-built constructions on the site initially, but, as the importance of Dere Street increased, a fort built mainly of stone was established in around AD 138. Early in the AD 160s, there was a further retreat from Scotland, which reduced the military value of Corstopitum and saw it begin to develop as a town.

It is clear that Corstopitum was built well before Hadrian's Wall a few miles to the north, and, although it has become customary to link the two, the Roman camp was merely one of a line of forts built originally by the governor Agricola to defend against attacks from the north; it did eventually become one of the chief store depots for the Wall itself, however. The settlement covered around 20 acres and was not only of significant military importance at its peak but also rose to a position of considerable magnificence and became one of the most splendid Roman establishments north of York.

About half of the town has been excavated. The main buildings include two buttressed granaries with under-floor air circulation to keep the grain dry; the remains of a water tank fed by an aqueduct; a huge, uncompleted storehouse with a large central courtyard; a group of small temples; and two military compounds, one of which has been described as a workshop. The modern museum has an excellent collection of Romano-British sculptures, particularly the Corbridge Lion. This rugged artefact depicts a lion killing a sheep or a goat and, although the scale is not quite right, is one of the most impressive pieces of sculpture found in the area. The work was originally made to go on top of a mausoleum, but it was subsequently used as a fountain head, with the lion's teeth cut out to form a hole for a pipe.

An aqueduct brought water from the north to feed an ornamental fountain set into a large basin sited in the fountain house; from here, water flowed through stone pipes to various parts of the site.

On the western side of Corstopitum, a section of the Stanegate lies untouched, just as it was used 1,700 years ago.

Corstopitum

Corbridge Lion

FALSTONE

There are two theories on how the village of Falstone got its name. One train of thought suggests it is a corruption of the Anglo-Saxon word *Faeston*, meaning a stronghold for livestock; others believe it comes from Old English and refers to a dull or speckled stone, possibly a marker of some kind.

The bridge leading into the village, crossing the North Tyne, was built in 1843 by Henry Welch; it originally carried a toll road constructed by Sir John Swinburne to transport the coal from his mine in Lewisburn, which is now submerged beneath Kielder Water. The road carried on westwards over the Scottish border, and its route is still marked – about eight miles from Falstone – by the Bloody Bush toll pillar, which carries a detailed inscription of the proprietors' names, plus toll rates and distances to towns and villages.

"The Stell" by Colin Wilbourn, Falstone

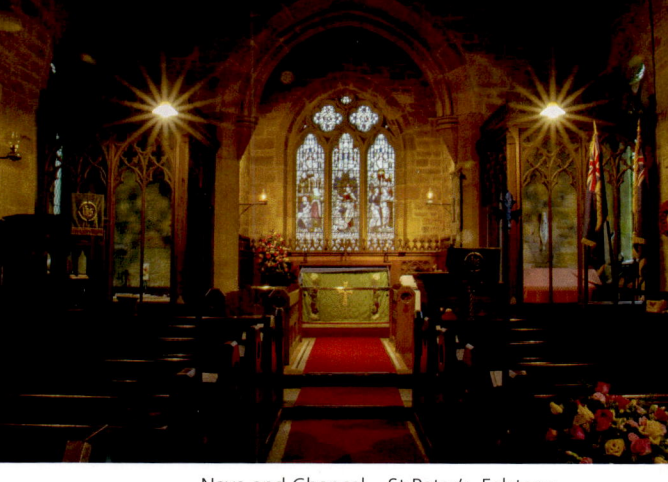

Nave and Chancel – St Peter's, Falstone

Falstone has two churches: St Peters' and the United Reformed and Methodist Church.

St Peter's Church was built in 1824, but was badly damaged by fire in 1890, resulting in extensive restoration. In the churchyard, a number of early 18th century gravestones can be seen, including one depicting a woman beside a skeleton. Established in 1807, possibly on the site of the village's original medieval church, the United Reformed and Methodist Church was formerly a Scottish Presbyterian kirk – one of the first built in England. To the south of the church is a farm that incorporates a bastle believed to date back to 1604.

In 1822, an Anglo-Saxon cross inscribed with runic characters was discovered in Falstone. The cross is thought to be inscribed on one side in Anglo-Saxon and on the other in Roman, making it a unique find; it is now in the antiquities collection of Newcastle's Great North Museum: Hancock. The cast-iron drinking fountain in the centre of the village was erected in 1897 and paid for by public subscription to commemorate Queen Victoria's Diamond Jubilee.

Church records dating back to medieval times include references to an ancient version of the family name Robson – one of the foremost names in this area of the country. Throughout the centuries of border turmoil, the Robsons often feuded with the Grahams and Armstrongs of Liddesdale. One North Tynedale tradition tells of a raid the Robsons once made into Liddesdale, returning with a flock of sheep belonging to the Grahams. Unfortunately, the animals had scab – a highly contagious disease caused by mites – which soon spread to the Robsons' own sheep. The Robsons were outraged and quickly made a second raid into Liddesdale, capturing seven of the most important Graham family members they could lay their hands on, and hanged them forthwith. They also left a note that warned: "The next time gentlemen came to take their sheep, they were not to be scabbed!" The Scotsmen did not appreciate the grim humour of the remark, and the incident only served to fuel the deadly feud.

A sculpture known as "The Stell" – a Northumbrian word for a sheepfold – can be found about three-quarters of a mile along the North Tyne to the west of Falstone. This architecture installation is the work of talented Sunderland-based artist Colin Wilbourn, who had the idea of "creating a homely place among rugged surroundings". The Stell successfully combines traditional dry-stone walling with modern steel-cutting techniques to make a place where people can meet and rest. The drawings on the steel antimacassars were done by locals, in cooperation with Wilbourn. The result is a wonderful piece of art that works on so many levels.

Ancient Gravestone – St Peter's, Falstone

"The Goatstones" (shot on black and white infra red film)

THE GOATSTONES

The Bronze Age monument known as the Goatstones stands close to Ravensheugh Crags, a couple of miles to the south-east of the village of Wark. The name is thought to be derived from the ancient Saxon words *'gyet stanes'*, meaning wayside stones. Though marked on maps as a stone circle, The Goatstones are, in fact, what is referred to as a 'four-poster' – four equally spaced stones set in a rectangle formation. One of the stones has thirteen cup markings and the remainder are decorated with grooves, which indicate a date of between 1600BC and 1000BC. These stones are the only recorded example of a four-poster stone circle with cup marks. The slightly raised centre suggests a cremation burial, but the grave has almost certainly been robbed.

Carving cup and ring markings into rock – whether on stone outcrops, solitary standing stones, or those forming a circle – was commonplace during the Bronze Age, and it is thought that the shapes were picked out with a stone or metal tool. The most commonly carved pattern comprises a cup-shaped hollow surrounded by concentric rings and sometimes intersected by radial lines or joined to other similar motifs. One widely held theory is that the markings were connected to fertility rites.

Northumberland can boast many fine examples of these enigmatic rock carvings.

HALTWHISTLE

Haltwhistle is a charming market town that, because of its geographical location, claims to be the very centre of Britain. It serves a wide area and has the distinction of being the closest town to Hadrian's Wall, which lies just a couple of miles to the north. In the medieval period, Haltwhistle grew as a trading centre; a market granted by royal charter in 1207 is still held today. The town was a centre for the wool industry as early as the 13th century and well into the 18th century, and local farmers would use the clean, clear waters of Haltwhistle Burn to wash their wares.

With the building of the Newcastle to Carlisle Railway in the 1830s, Haltwhistle was transformed into a busy industrial centre, and its population trebled after the junction for the branch line to Alston was opened here in 1851. The station is certainly worth exploring, with a collection of buildings of interest to both the railway enthusiast and the industrial archaeologist. The former station master's house, the ticket office and the waiting room are all of the Tudor style much loved by the Victorians. The water tank is made of cast iron, appropriately decorated with sea-horse motifs and supported on a stone base. There are also two water towers with decorated ball finials – quite a rarity nowadays – along with a cast-iron footbridge (as at Wylam) and a signal box in timber on a brick base.

The Alston Arches Viaduct, which can be seen about a quarter of a mile to the south-east of the town, was opened in 1852 to carry the Alston branch line across the South Tyne. It has six main arches – the four over the river are wide and skewed – and each of the piers has a large arched opening cut through it, obviously to accommodate the original pedestrian walkway. The viaduct was restored and reopened as a footpath in 2006.

Standing just off the south side of the marketplace in Haltwhistle is the Church of the Holy Cross, which dates from the 12th century and is a typical, well-preserved example of Northumbrian ecclesiastical design. The chancel has a recumbent effigy of a member of the Blenkinsopp family, possibly from the 14th century; there is also a tombstone bearing the coat of arms of the same family, decorated with a flowered crosier, a broken-hilted sword and staff and scrip, signifying that the person buried beneath had once visited the Holy Land. Holy Cross also has an unusual font, and a carved marble reredos representing the adoration of the Magi.

Nowadays, Haltwhistle is a quiet, peaceful town, but from 1300 up until the time of the Union of the Crowns in 1603, it was the scene of many a deadly conflict, being in the area targeted by bands of dangerous border raiders. The notorious Armstrongs of Liddesdale plundered Haltwhistle in 1598, when Sir Robert Carey – who was to become the Earl of Monmouth – was Warden of the Middle March on the English side. The Armstrongs were among the most notorious of border reivers and often carried out raids into the North Tyne Valley, but on this occasion Haltwhistle and the surrounding area seemed to have been singled out for particularly ferocious treatment, suffering what was to become known as 'the Fray of Hautwessel'.

Satisfaction for this attack was demanded from the King of Scotland, James VI (later James I of England). His immediate response was to disown the Armstrongs, and he further recommended that the English warden should exact his own revenge. This was done the following year when the English entered Liddesdale and ravaged the land of the Armstrongs. However, during the raid, an Armstrong named Sim of the Cathill was killed by one of the Ridleys of Haltwhistle. This, of course, led to another vicious attack on the town by the Scottish outlaws, who plundered and burned in revenge, losing one of their leaders in the fighting. The area gripped in fear, Sir Robert Carey took steps to destroy the power of the Armstrongs and bring them to order. In 1601, he marched into Liddesdale to rid the border of this menace once and for all, laying siege to the Armstrongs' hiding place, Tarras Moss, a large area of boggy moorland covered in low scrub. This didn't worry the reiver family, however; so confident were they in the safety of their stronghold that they sent a party into England and raided the warden's lands. What's more, they sent Carey one of his own cattle, accompanied by a note saying that as he might run out of food while away from home, they were providing him with a supply of English beef! But, eventually, with diligence and skilful strategy, Carey broke the gang and captured its leaders; never again were they to attain such great power or notoriety.

It is much safer to wander Haltwhistle today, of course, and one particularly interesting diversion is seeking out the sites of the old businesses that were once the heart of the town. Across the road from the old cycle shop and bakery is a street once known as 'Physic Lane', where there was a dispensary for all manner of remedies, cures, potions, lotions, unctions and ointments.

Just to the north and east of the town flows the Haltwhistle Burn, the banks of which were once the scene of intense industrial activity, but now offer a peaceful walk through beautiful, serene woodland.

Centre of Britain plaque, Haltwhistle

Haltwhistle Brick Works

Haltwhistle Burn

Roman Font, Church of the Holy Cross, Haltwhistle

Bellister Castle

HALTWHISTLE, BELLISTER CASTLE

Bellister is connected to an eerie legend. It tells of a wandering minstrel who came upon the house and requested protection and a night's rest, which was readily granted. However, dark suspicions began to form in the mind of the Lord of Bellister; he feared his guest was really a spy, sent by a nearby baron who was a bitter enemy. The traveller noticed the unease and distrust of the lord, and, fearing his safety, he decided to leave the castle rather than stay the night. This appeared to confirm the suspicions of the owner, who let loose his bloodhounds on the poor minstrel; they had caught and torn him to pieces before any of the handlers were able to stop the carnage. Now seized by remorse, the lord spent the rest of his life in a state of great fear, haunted by the ghost of the innocent minstrel. It is said that many visitors to the castle since then have seen or heard this spectre, known as 'the Grey Man of Bellister'.

HAYDON OLD CHURCH

Old Haydon can be found on a hill to the north of the modern village of Haydon Bridge. Its church, dedicated to St Cuthbert, was originally a chapel of ease and served as one of many convenient places of worship for those living in the large parish of Warden. It became known as Haydon Old Church following the consecration of a new St Cuthbert's Church in Haydon Bridge in 1796.

Approached via an arched avenue of beautiful yew trees, Haydon Old Church is an excellent example of a small, northern, early English country church. It is an extremely interesting building for the ecclesiologist; the structure is believed to date from 1190. Evidence for this can be seen in the eastern wall of the church, which has three stepped, round-headed lancet windows, although further improvements appear to have been incorporated in the two subsequent centuries. Local stone was used in its construction, and the builders also sourced ready-dressed material from the nearby Hadrian's Wall; the font is made from a recut Roman altar. There is a great deal of speculation about the foundation of the pre-12th century church that once occupied the site. However, it is generally agreed that if the bones of St Cuthbert rested here during their epic journey from Lindisfarne, the original church must have been in existence before AD 995, when the saint's remains were interred in Durham.

Roman Font – Old Haydon

Lectern – St Cuthbert's Old Haydon

Haydon Old Church is not without its folklore, and one of its most renowned but eccentric parishioners was Edward Coulson, born in 1754. 'Ned' was known to visit the church at midnight, dress in the minister's surplice, and, by candlelight, read aloud a chapter of the Bible from the pulpit. However, Coulson's greater claim to fame was the speed at which he could run, and the prodigious distances he was able to walk: he is said to have walked 50 miles one night, then the same distance back home the following morning, to deliver a message for his master. He once won a wager to outrun a rider on horseback, which, it is said, he did easily. Coulson beat the steed so convincingly that the rider said, "It must be the devil, as no man can keep pace with my horse!" Another of his favourite tricks was to easily outpace the local stagecoach, bidding the occupants a hearty "Good evening!" as he ran past. He would then hide out of sight and pass the coach again, offering another friendly greeting, which caused further consternation among the passengers. Another of Coulson's eccentricities was that he was able to play his fiddle behind his back while running up the bank at Page Croft – an exceptionally useful skill to possess, it has to be said…

HEAVENFIELD

Near Chollerford, at the top of Brunton Bank, an imposing wooden cross marks the site of the Battle of Heavenfield. This is where, in AD 634, King Oswald of Bernicia and Deira – later united as Northumbria – defeated the combined armies of Cadwallon of Gwynedd and Penda of Mercia to re-establish a foothold for Christianity in the north of England.

To understand the importance of the battle of Heavenfield, we have to go back to the reign of King Edwin. In AD 625, he married Æthelburga, daughter of Æthelburt of Kent, the first Christian king of Anglo-Saxon England, who had been converted to Christianity by missionaries from Rome in AD 597. When Æthelburga came north as Edwin's queen, she was accompanied by a mission led by Paulinus, an Italian bishop. She had also secured a guarantee of full religious freedom, and had a promise from her new husband that he would consider conversion to Christianity.

Edwin, however, was not easily persuaded to convert – at that time, there were no other Christian kings in England outside Kent, so his reluctance would seem understandable. Eventually, it took a series of events to convince him, namely the safe birth of his daughter Eanfled; his escape from an assassin's dagger; his victory over Wessex; and the eventual domination of most of Anglo-Saxon England. But, before he took the plunge and was finally baptised, Edwin still discussed the issue with his advisors. The council he summoned took place near York, and after some initial debate he received its full support; at Easter in AD 627, Edwin and a large number of his followers were baptised. Paulinus was made Bishop of York, and in the months that followed he performed baptisms across the North – it is said that one ceremony, at Yeavering, lasted 36 days.

In AD 633, Edwin was killed in the Battle of Hatfield Chase, during an uprising led by those who had not submitted to Rome under his guidance; these were men from Mercia and Wales, who followed Penda and Cadwallon (himself a follower of Celtic Christianity) respectively. With Edwin dead, Bernicia and Deira fell into what the Venerable Bede describes as paganism. Paulinus fled south with the queen, her children and the special royal treasures, including a large gold cross and a chalice. Meanwhile, two of Edwin's sons, Oswald and Oswiu, were in exile on the small island of Iona. When the news reached the island that Edwin was dead and Cadwallon was in power, Oswald returned with a small army. His forces met Cadwallon's men on the flat table of land above Chollerford, close to the Roman Wall. Prior to the battle, Oswald ordered a wooden cross to be made, which he helped erect in full view of his army, then he knelt with his followers to pray for divine assistance. After a monumental struggle, Cadwallon's combined forces were defeated and fled. The Welsh monarch was caught and killed at a place that has been identified as Rowley Burn, near Hexham.

Roadside Cross and St Oswald's Church, Heavenfield

Most of the conflict would appear to have taken place to the south of Oswald's cross, in a field called Mould's Close, which has yielded a number of skulls and fragments of weapons during ploughing. The location where Oswald – later venerated as a saint – raised the cross and offered up his prayers is said to have been the scene of many miraculous cures.

Set in glorious isolation on the northern edge of the battlefield is St Oswald's Church, which was built in 1737, then much repaired and altered in 1887. It was during this restoration that a large silver coin depicting St Oswald was found; on one side was a representation of the saint's head, on the reverse a cross. The artefact was, it is said, used for a while by the monastery at Durham as their common seal in honour of St Oswald.

The church's original sundial is still evident, and among the alterations made the following century are the south porch and an unusual bellcote. Inside St Oswald's is a decorated Roman altar that has been modified to serve as the socket for a cross – possibly the predecessor of the modern roadside cross seen today.

Following the successful outcome of the Battle of Heavenfield, Oswald sent to Iona for missionaries to re-convert the people of the North to Christianity. We are told by Bede that the first monks who arrived were beaten by the intractable nature of the people they had come to teach. The next monk, the wise and gentle Aidan, established a monastery on Lindisfarne with the help of Oswald, and began his work spreading the word of Christianity.

HEXHAM

Hexham is regarded to be the capital of Upper Tynedale and also, indeed, of the vast expanse of rolling moorland that extends south from the River Tyne to the border with County Durham. The fascinating fabric of its rich and turbulent history has been woven around the architecturally outstanding abbey, and this interesting story begins in Saxon England with a town named Halgustad, later Hextildesham.

The foundation of Hexham and its abbey – completed in AD 678 – are closely connected to the somewhat tempestuous life of St Wilfrid, the bishop and saint who was educated under the guidance of the abbot Cudda on Lindisfarne. In truth, Hexham was the result of a series of quarrels between Ecgfrith, King of Northumbria, and his wife Ætheldreda. In the end, it was Wilfrid, then Bishop of York, who found a way out of the difficulty by suggesting that the marriage should be dissolved, and that Ætheldreda should become a nun. As a parting gift, the king gave his former wife the small town of Halgustad, and she, intending to enter the religious community at Ely, bestowed it upon Wilfrid "for ecclesiastical purposes". He then began construction of his monastery; the Roman camp of Corstopitum was a convenient quarry, and many of the inscribed stones since found in Hexham were brought there by the abbey's builders.

Not long after this, following further disagreements with King Ecgfrith, Wilfrid was expelled from York and travelled to Rome in search of justice, spending many years away from Northumbria. The banished former bishop favoured Roman church practices over those of the Celtic tradition, and had been the main protagonist for this point of view at the Synod of Whitby in AD 664. Eventually, in AD 686, following the death of Ecgfrith, Wilfrid returned to Hexham by consent of the new king, Aldfrith.

The Night Stair, Hexham Abbey

Hexham Abbey became the North's greatest religious treasure, and the community that surrounded it prospered. Accompanied by vast tracts of land that became known as Hexhamshire, it became similar to the later Palatinate of Durham – a self-contained ecclesiastical kingdom with its own law courts and justice. This came to an end in AD 876, however, when the Norsemen sacked the town and severely damaged the church. Sadly, the see of Hexham ceased to exist and, unlike Ripon, was never revived.

It was not until the early 12th century that Augustinian canons re-established the old church, with plans to enlarge it. In 1150, a gatehouse was added, and this was followed by further improvements towards the end of the century, although the project attracted the attention of the Scots, who made it a favourite target of their frequent incursions. The church seen today is, in essence, the one begun in the mid 12th century.

In 1296, Hexham suffered a large-scale attack by Scottish raiders, during which many buildings were destroyed and the church severely damaged; the following year, William

High Altar and Frith Stool, Hexham Abbey

Wallace and his army descended on the town, equally bent on destruction.

It also played a part in the Wars of the Roses, and in 1463 and 1464 battles between the Yorkists and the Lancastrians were fought on the Hexham Levels, two miles south of the town.

A large number of Hexham's inhabitants took part in the 1536 rebellion known as the Pilgrimage of Grace, where many of the noblemen of the North protested about the actions of Thomas Cromwell, the Vicar General of King Henry VIII, against the monasteries. The insurgents, led by Robert Aske under a banner showing the Five Wounds of Christ, demanded the restoration of smaller monasteries and that the reforming bishops be thrown out and Cromwell banished. The king cunningly compromised until the rebels disbanded, then had the leaders arrested and hanged.

In 1761, the Riot Act was read in the marketplace at Hexham after a large number of local men and women – including lead miners, craftsmen and agricultural workers – protested against conscription. On 9th March, now known as 'Bloody Monday', troops opened fire on the crowd; it is estimated that at least 45 protestors were killed and more than 300 badly wounded.

Hexham's main attraction is, of course, the abbey, which is perhaps best viewed from the grounds to the rear. The earliest part of the building is the Saxon crypt – built mainly from Roman stones, it is widely considered to be the finest example of Saxon stonework in Northumberland. The tunnel vault of the relic chamber retains much of the original plasterwork; it lay hidden for many years before finally being rediscovered during building work in 1725.

Rising from the magnificent south transept on the west wall is the Night Stair, a wide, well-worn flight of 35 steps by which the monks could return to their dormitory along the rib-vaulted passage, or slype, that linked the two areas of the abbey. In the centre of the chancel is the Frith Stool, also known as St Wilfrid's Throne, which is around 1,300 years old and is thought to have originally stood in the Saxon church. The Anglo-Saxon word *'frith'* signified peace and security, and it was ordained that sanctuary could be claimed by sitting in the chair. The privileges of sanctuary were much curtailed during the reign of King Henry VIII, however, then finally abolished in 1624 during the reign of James I. Some historians believe that the Frith Stool was the 'cathedra' of the see of Hexham, where the bishops were consecrated and even some of the kings of Northumbria crowned.

The Moot Hall Court, Hexham

Constructed between 1330 and 1333 on the order of William Melton, then Archbishop of York, Hexham Old Gaol is said to be England's oldest purpose-built prison. The building originally housed prisoners from Hexhamshire, and two centuries later it was also used to detain those from the English Middle March who were awaiting trial at the nearby court, Moothall.

The Old Gaol is now a museum and houses a wonderful collection of 15th and 16th century arms and armour once used by the march wardens and the notorious border reivers. One macabre object of particular interest is a skull said to be that of Sir John Fenwick, who was slain at the Battle of Marston Moor on 2nd July 1644. According to the 19th century local historian MA Richardson, Fenwick's helmet was "fastened on a pillar in the church of Hexham, and his skull, which was broken in the same place with the helmet, is still kept at the Manor office there". According to folklore, the skull has a "favourite" room at the Old Gaol, and whenever it has been moved – even to a different floor – it has found its own way back to its original position….

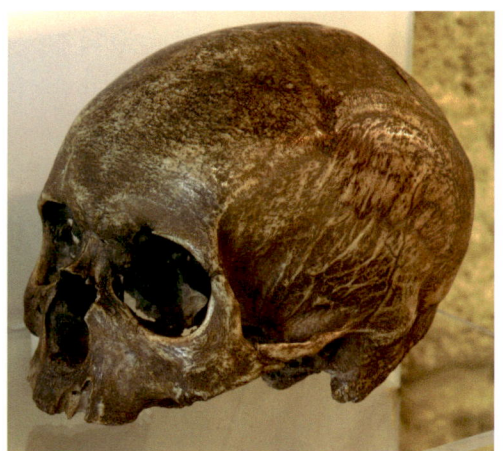

The Fenwick Skull, Hexham Old Gaol

Kielder Castle

KIELDER CASTLE

Kielder Castle is sited on a small hill known as 'Humphrey's Knowe', at the point where the Kielder Burn joins the North Tyne. It was built in 1775 by William Newton, in the Gothic Revival style, for the Duke of Northumberland as a shooting lodge in close proximity to his then far-stretching grouse moors. The castle, which was altered and improved by successive dukes, now houses a visitor centre.

Close by are traces of many ancient settlements and campsites that were inhabited by early man. Perhaps the easiest to reach is the Devil's Lapful, about a mile to the south-east. This long barrow and cairn, which consists of a mound of boulders and large stones, is believed to date from between 2000 and 1500 BC, though it was only given its eerie name in medieval times.

This region was one of the last to be brought under control by the 1603 Union of the Crowns. It has a long and shady history of raids, reprisals, and feuding between the great riding families of the Charltons, the Robsons, the Grahams and the Armstrongs, who ignored political boundaries, forging allegiance instead through time-honoured loyalties such as ancestry. The men of Tynedale and Redesdale were constantly opposed to those of Liddesdale and Teviotdale in border warfare, and indeed they still are rivals, although now, it has to be said, on a friendlier basis. However, it is reported that a great football match took place between them at Kielder Castle in 1790 in which the North Tynedale lads were eventually victorious!

A few miles to the north of the castle sits a huge block of sandstone marking the English-Scottish border. The Kielder Stone, as it is known, was used in medieval times as a neutral 'postbox' where messages and requests could be left in a small hole in the rock. Carved on two of its faces are the initials 'D' for Douglas and 'N' for Northumberland to mark the respective allegiances.

This landmark is also the subject of a grim legend. It is considered unlucky to ride 'widdershins' – against the travel of the sun – three times around the rock. According to folklore, a 14th century border lord named the Cout – or Colt – of Kielder did just this, tempting providence. Bad luck followed when he and his companions were lured into the castle of their deadly enemy, Sir William de Soulis of Hermitage. The young chieftain escaped a horrible death by fighting his way past the guards, leaping onto his horse and fleeing from the forbidding castle, with its occupants in hot pursuit. Then, the Brown Man of the Moors – a malignant fairy – appeared to Sir William and revealed the secret of the Cout's protection: he was wearing charmed mail and a sprig of the mystic holly and rowan leaves in his helmet, and the only thing he had no protection from was running water.

As the Cout tried to cross Liddel Water to escape his pursuers, he stumbled and fell; the unfortunate young lord could do nothing as Sir William and his men held his head under the water until he drowned. The spot where this is reputed to have happened is still known as 'the Cout Of Kielder's Pool' However, retribution did overtake the wicked Lord Soulis in a most terrible form; afraid of his dark deeds and black magic, his enemies captured him and boiled him alive in a lead cauldron on the Nine Stane Rigg.

KIELDER WATER AND FOREST PARK

In the middle to late 20th century Kielder became a landscape of superlatives. The Forestry Commission's largest forest surrounds the largest man-made reservoir in Europe to produce a harmonious, pleasing landscape. It was officially opened by Her Majesty the Queen in 1982.

The planting of Kielder Forest began in 1926 at Smales Farm, Falstone, but for the first few years the work was mainly experimental, because up until then afforestation in peaty areas had not been tried. The forest now covers a total area of more than 250 square miles, with around 150 million standing trees at any one time. Most of the trees planted are conifers – the demand for softwood exceeds that for hardwood – and the main species grown is the Sitka spruce, because it thrives best in this type of wild countryside. This species accounts for around 75% of the forest area; the remaining quarter comprises 12% Norway spruce and 9% lodgepole pine, plus Scots pine, larch and other broadleaf trees. The current trend is to plant more broadleaf trees, which will increase the percentage of hardwoods in the forest from 1% to 8% by 2025.

Half of the wood produced goes to sawmills in the north of England and the south of Scotland, where it is sawn into construction timber, fencing rails and posts, and packaging material. The other half – wood from smaller trees and the tops of bigger trees – goes to the paper mill in Workington, Cumbria, where it is processed into cardboard for cereal packets and boxes; some of this wood is also used in the production of chipboard. When it was opened, the Kielder Water Scheme was one of the largest and most forward-looking projects of its time. Construction of the reservoir took place between 1975 and 1982, at a cost of £167 million. The scheme is a 'regional transfer system' that allows water from Kielder to be released into the Rivers Tyne, Derwent, Wear and Tees, maintaining minimum flow levels at times of low natural rainfall.

Electricity generation is a by-product of the release of water into the river. Two hydroelectric generators installed at Kielder dam convert water energy into electricity for the national grid. A water release of 1,300 million litres a day can produce enough power to illuminate a town about the size of Hexham, which has

Kielder Dam

around 11,000 lively inhabitants. Kielder Water can provide as many as 909 million litres a day, almost the sum total of all the other sources in the region. The water authority, in close consultation with the Environment Agency, sets the release plan for the reservoir; these releases are timed to encourage migratory salmon and sea trout to move up the river to spawn by helping with the shallow flow in the lower stretches of the Tyne.

The dam, designed by Sir Frederick Gibberd and Partners, has its downstream face carefully shaped and planted to merge as far as possible with the surrounding landscape, while the shores of the reservoir are sympathetically planted with deciduous trees.

The need for a major water storage scheme in the North East goes back to the Industrial Revolution of the late 18th and early 19th centuries and the growth in demand from fast-growing businesses on Tyneside, Wearside and Teesside. Expansion continued well into the 20th century, and a group of three reservoirs were built between 1892 and 1915 in the south of the region, in Teesdale. These were further supplemented by three more in 1960, 1965 and 1971 to keep pace with the ever-increasing requirements of the huge industrial complex on Teesside.

The rest of the region needed water, too, and this led to the construction of a further three reservoirs in the north of the region between 1905 and 1966 to supply Tyneside and Wearside.

The industry continued to grow with the consequent increase in demand, but rising prosperity added to this with a surge in new uses, including washing machines, showers, garden sprinklers and carwashes. Because of the pressure of having to supply such an enormous amount of water in the area, the Northumbrian River Authority had to act promptly to ensure efficiency.

Engineering consultants Babtie, Shaw and Morton were employed to find the most suitable locations for new reservoirs. Eventually, it was decided that the North Tyne Valley would offer the biggest potential supply to all the region's rivers, and would also have the flexibility to meet all future demands.

Because of the sheer scale of the Kielder Water Scheme, in 1972 the Department of the Environment commissioned a public inquiry, which was held across six weeks at Newcastle's Civic Centre. Despite around 200 objections, approval was granted, although additional objections and comments led to the inquiry being reopened the following year for the consideration of alternative schemes. The original decision was upheld, however; construction of the Kielder Water Scheme could begin. The site chosen was just upstream of Falstone, with the dam located at one of the narrowest points in the valley. This minimised the amount of material needed for construction, and the gentle gradient of the valley would allow good storage capacity. The reservoir basin was rich in deposits of sand, gravel, rock and boulder clay, all of which were used in construction; a clever bonus was that the quarries from which they were excavated were all submerged when the reservoir was filled.

The lake is capable of holding 200 billion litres of water, has a shoreline of around 27 miles, and is 170ft at its deepest point – for comparison, Nelson's Column is just short of this in height. This outstanding border forest park is considered to be one of the top five tourist and leisure areas in Northumberland. With visitor centres, waterside parks, and activities from boating to birdwatching, cycling to canoeing, and walking and windsurfing to watching wildlife, there is something to interest every visitor.

The graceful Kielder Viaduct, situated at the northern end of the reservoir, was built in 1862 by William Hutchinson for the Border Counties Railway. It is said that the then Duke of Northumberland, who owned the land, insisted that the viaduct should match the Gothic style of Kielder Castle, his nearby hunting lodge. The viaduct, with its skew arches and castellated parapet, was designed by Newcastle architect Peter Nicholson, and is a notable example of Victorian engineering. Unusually, its arches are not square to the trackbed above, meaning that each stone had to be individually shaped to follow a complex mathematical formula devised by Nicholson.

The first train ran on the railway in 1864, and the service linked all the villages of the North Tyne Valley while also providing connections to Carlisle, Allendale Town, Morpeth and Hawick. When the line through Kielder was closed in 1958, the viaduct fell into disuse; however, thanks to the intervention of the Northumberland & Newcastle Society in 1969, it has been preserved for use by ramblers and walkers.

Kielder Viaduct

The Minotaur, Kielder

Nine Stane Rigg

LANGLEY CASTLE

Midway between Hexham and Haltwhistle, just to the south of Haydon Bridge, stands Langley Castle. This magnificent, much-restored, four-square tower house is now a comfortable hotel, but the building has a rich and varied past.

Construction of the castle – built for one of King Edward III's favourite knights, Sir Thomas de Lucy, and his family – began in 1350. Sadly, it was not completed until 1365, a year after the knight's death, so passed into the ownership of his daughter, Maud de Lucy, later the wife of Henry Percy, First Earl of Northumberland. Unfortunately, the castle was destroyed again within 50 years by King Henry IV during his campaign to put down the rebellion of Archbishop Scrope. Throughout its succession of owners – the Umfravilles, the Percys, the Nevilles, and finally the Radcliffes – the history of Langley Castle has been stormy.

Following the execution for treason of James Radcliffe, Third Earl of Derwentwater and Viscount Langley in 1716 the forfeited estates passed to the commissioners of the Royal Naval Hospital at Greenwich, London. Now ruined and neglected, the glory that was Langley Castle had died with the Jacobite uprising.

In 1882, the estate was bought by Cadwallader Bates, the renowned local antiquarian and historian responsible for distinguished works including *Heddon-on-the-Wall: the Church and Parish* and *A History of Northumberland*. When Bates died suddenly in March 1902, at the early age of 49, he was buried in the grounds of his beloved Langley Castle. His wife, Josephine d'Echarvines, dedicated the chapel on the roof to his memory and stayed on at the castle alone, carrying on his restoration work until her own death in 1933.

Langley Castle

Linnel's Bridge, Devil's Water

LINNEL'S BRIDGE

Two miles south east of Hexham, on the B6306, crossing the Devil's Water at severe right angles is Linnel's Bridge.

The present-day bridge was built in 1698, although on its east side there is an inscribed tablet bearing the details of an earlier crossing: "GOD PRESARVE WMFOIRA ERENGTON, BELLDETE THIS BREGE OF LYME AND STONE 1581"

Linnels Mill is just upstream from the bridge, on the west bank of the tumbling river. Although very small, the mill, which dates from the 17th century, was of enormous importance to the surrounding area. It was driven by an early water turbine and worked right up until the end of the 19th century. Unfortunately, examination of any remaining machinery is out of the question, as the mill stands on private land; however, there is a good view of the structure from the centre of the bridge.

It was on the banks of the Devil's Water in 1715, just prior to the Jacobite Rising, that – according to legend – the young James Radcliffe, third Earl of Derwentwater, came face-to-face with a mysterious figure in a grey hooded cloak who presented him with a crucifix that would protect him against sword or bullet. Unfortunately, Radcliffe was made a scapegoat for the whole rebellion and beheaded on Tower Hill the following February.

TYNE VALLEY

LOW CLEUGHS BASTLE

Low Cleughs Bastle, which can be found about a mile west of West Woodburn in the parish of Corsenside, is thought to have been built just before 1600. With walls more than 3ft thick, and small windows, the emphasis is placed firmly on defence. Buildings such as this were constructed by farmers who were slightly better off than most. Bastles usually consisted of a lower basement, for sheltering livestock, which supported an upper floor where the farmer and his family would live.

This bastle is unusual in that the upper doorway is sited directly above the lower one, about a third of the way along the south side. This upper entrance must have been added later, when the need for ease of access was greater than the necessity of defence, because in earlier times the higher level would only have been accessible by ladder, through an aperture that could be easily blocked in times of danger.

Abandoned in the mid-1800s, Low Cleughs Bastle has been a scheduled monument since 1969 and is a fine example of a fortified Northumbrian farmhouse.

West side, Low Cleughs Bastle House

St Mary's Church, Ovingham

OVINGHAM

Ovingham holds an annual Goose Fair on its two village greens, complete with stalls of every kind, Morris men, sword dancers, folk and country music, and, naturally, a gaggle of geese. This tradition dates back to the 13th century. Drovers en route to Newcastle from the great ivestock fairs of Dumfries and Carlisle would break their journey in Ovingham to enjoy a few days' rest and holiday, and naturally this attracted a gathering of peddlers, travellers and wandering performers.

The village church of St Mary the Virgin has a Saxon tower, although the interior dates mainly from the 13th century and was further restored and improved during the 17th and 19th centuries. In the chancel, there is a black n marble slab with a beautifully carved coat of arms, but strangely it carries no inscription; this is supposed to commemorate a member of the Addison family who is reputed to have gone insane and died in 1735.

In the porch, there is a large stone slab dedicated to the engraver Thomas Bewick, who is buried alongside members of his family in the churchyard. Bewick was born at Cherryburn house in the village of Mickley, just over the river. Much of his work is in the Hancock Museum in Newcastle, and his illustrations in *The History of British Birds* are wonderful examples of his art. Born in 1753, the eldest of eight children, Bewick received his early education at Mickley School. His talents as an artist were obvious from a young age: Bewick spent most of his time sketching on his slate, and, when no other materials were available, he drew pictures in chalk on the gravestones in the churchyard of St Mary the Virgin. Birds and animals were his favourite subjects, and the wealth of wildlife knowledge he accumulated in his native Tyne Valley brought him fame and fortune in later life.

Bewick served a short apprenticeship with Ralph Beilby, a copper plate engraver, who paid him a guinea a week for his work. Following a move to London, he eventually returned to the north and set up a workshop close to what became the Cathedral Church of St Nicholas in Newcastle. A small memorial and inscription mark the site of the workshop, which was demolished when Milburn House was built.

The name Thomas Bewick became known throughout the land, and his work was brought to the notice of King George III, who refused to believe the engravings had been transferred from wood – until he was shown the blocks. Although he became famous and prosperous, Bewick never forgot his birthplace in the Tyne Valley, and every weekend he walked the 12 miles from Newcastle to Cherryburn to visit his family. On his retirement, Bewick moved across the river to Gateshead, and his son carried on the business in the workshop his father had founded. Bewick died on 8th November 1828. Cherryburn is now in the care of the National Trust and is open to visitors from 1st April to 31st October.

Mabel Carr, the mother of George Stephenson, was also a native of Ovingham before her marriage to his father, Robert. She was the second daughter of Robert Carr, a dyer in the village. Several generations of her family owned a house adjoining the churchyard, and the family tomb can still be seen.

The beautifully wooded dell of Whittle Dene is reputedly haunted by fairies. The water of Whittle Burn is especially soft and clear, and at one time it was celebrated for its effectiveness in bleaching linen.

The 18th century packhorse bridge that spans the burn beside the modern road to the west of the church is worth seeing and serves as a reminder of a time when there was a gentler form of transport.

Almost opposite the eastern corner of the churchyard, a most unusual and fragile-looking bridge crosses the Tyne. Featuring eight spans with stone abutments and steel tube pylons, built in 1853 and fabricated by Dorman Long of Middlesbrough, the bridge carried horse and cart traffic 490ft across the river. It's only wide enough for one-way traffic, but has a "passing place" halfway across. (There's no room for pedestrians, either – they have their own adjacent bridge, built in 1974.) It was operated as a toll bridge until 1945, when the toll house was demolished. The bridge was closed for four years and underwent a £4 million-pound refurbishment before being reopened in September 2016 – a worthy exercise to preserve this unusual structure.

Thomas Bewick Memorial, St Mary's Church, Ovingham

Prudhoe Castle

Stagshaw Bank, where the famous fair was held

PRUDHOE CASTLE (English Heritage)

Prudhoe Castle is magnificent. Strategically sited on a spur of land between a deep ravine and the river, it affords commanding views of the Tyne Valley.

The barony of Prudhoe was granted to Robert de Umfraville by William the Conqueror in the 11th century. For almost 300 years, Prudhoe was the seat of this powerful family, except for a short period in the early 13th century, during the reign of King John, when Richard de Umfraville was out of favour.

The castle is thought to have been founded by Odinel de Umfraville between 1161-82, probably on the site of a former stronghold – it is said that a wooden structure, surrounded by a wooden palisade, stood on this spot in the 11th century. William the Lion, King of Scotland, attacked the castle in 1174 after raiding Carlisle and then sacking and destroying the massive fortresses of Harbottle and Wark. Three days of siege proved unsuccessful and he was forced to retreat to Alnwick, where he was taken prisoner by Odinel de Umfraville, Bernard de Balliol and other northern lords.

The last feudal baron was Gilbert de Umfraville, who died in 1381. His widow, Countess Maud, became the wife of Henry de Percy, the First Earl of Northumberland, and so Prudhoe Castle came into the hands of the Percys, with only brief interruptions to the family's ownership during the Wars of the Roses and the eventful contests that followed the Reformation. Algernon Percy, the Fourth Duke of Northumberland, was named Baron Prudhoe in 1816.

The castle is an important example of its type, having a free-standing keep in the inner bailey, along with an outer bailey and gatehouse. The curtain wall of the outer bailey is very well preserved, and the gatehouse is thought to be one of the best examples in Northumberland. A barbican was added in the 13th century and lengthened in 1326; this, too, is regarded as one of the finest of its kind in the county. The roadway up through the barbican and gatehouse provides a steep, dramatic entry into the castle.

The medieval bridge over the dene just to the east of the castle has curiously shaped arches, probably from different periods, and is believed by some historians to be one of the earliest in the North.

STAGSHAW BANK

Stagshaw Bank, four miles to the north-east of Hexham, was the site of the famous Stagshaw Bank Fair. Reputed at one time to be the largest in the whole of Britain, the livestock fair was held at Stagshaw Bank from before 1200 until 1926 and attracted visitors from all over the country.

Stagshaw Bank Fair was actually a series of fairs on various dates: 6th May for cattle, pigs and sheep; Whitsun Eve for horses and cattle; 4th July for horses, cattle and sheep; and 26th September for cattle, pigs and sheep. There were also two 'wiste' fairs: one on 5th August for the sale of lambs, and a second on 24th August for ewes. More than 100,000 head of livestock would be traded at the fair, which drew a great assortment of showmen, tinkers, salters, broggers, badgers, piemen, drovers and gypsies. Featuring stalls and sideshows, the fair became a major social attraction as well as a business event.

With the advent of the railways, droving as a means of moving livestock began to die out, but the Stagshaw Bank Fair continued to be held, albeit mainly as a leisure and pleasure event. As the showmen began to abandon any restraint, their activities and sideshows became more dangerous, macabre and horrific. Upper-class Victorians believed such attractions contributed to a serious decline in standards, so in 1871 Parliament passed the Fairs Act to protect the morals of the lower classes by giving the Secretary of State the power to abolish any fair that was "the cause of grievous immorality".

On 5th July 1926, Stagshaw Bank Fair was held for the last time, and exactly eight months later it was abolished under the Fairs Act. An event that had been held for centuries was gone for good. But its name lingers on to this day: when a house, workplace or farmyard is untidy, a true Northumbrian will say it's "like Stagshaw Bank Fair" or "like Stager Bank Fair".

STUBLICK CHIMNEY

Stublick Chimney, a dramatic relic from the days of lead mining in the North Pennines, stands just off the B6305, two miles south of Haydon Bridge. This 100ft chimney stack served as the vent at the end of a long horizontal flue – partly underground – that carried lead fumes from Langley Smelt Mill more than a mile away. Built in 1767 by the Greenwich Hospital for the smelting of lead ore from its mines around Alston, Langley Smelt Mill became one of the biggest smelting mills in the area at a time when the North Pennines were producing more than a tenth of Europe's lead.

The first flue was constructed in 1802, and by 1859 this was extended to the present site where, three years later, the chimney was built to provide a stronger draught to draw up the fumes. The upper part of the flue was lined with stone and high enough for a man to stand in; particles of lead and silver would collect on the walls as the fumes cooled, and the smelting mill would shut down its furnaces to allow the metal-rich deposits to be scraped off and collected for further smelting.

The mill finally closed in 1887, but its reservoirs, flues, chimneys and watercourses can still be seen across the North Pennines. Hollowed packhorse trails still lead to the mill from the south, although most of these old carriers' routes are now utilised as modern roads.

Nearby are the buildings and chimneys of Stublick Colliery, which supplied coal to Langley Smelt Mill. Coal was mined on this site from around 1700 and the remains of hundreds of bell pits pockmark the area. Deeper mining made the driving of a drainage level necessary; this discharged into the smelt mill reservoir. Eventually, in the early to mid-1800s, a beam engine was installed to pump out water and allow even deeper work; the engine house, boiler house and chimney can still be seen from the nearby road. Many of the buildings were converted to agricultural use, including a second engine house which may have housed a winding engine, although the structure was described as a sawmill on the first Ordnance Survey map of the area.

The standing remains of Stublick Colliery serve as a striking reminder of the coal mining industry that supported lead mining into the second half of the 19th century.

Stublick Chimney

Stublick Colliery

TARSET AND DALLY CASTLES

Tarset Castle is a huge green mound above the junction of the Tarset Burn and the North Tyne. This ancient fortification once belonged to Sir John 'the Red' Comyn, Lord of Badenoch, who was assassinated by Robert Bruce in Dumfries in 1306. In 1526 it was occupied by Sir Robert Fenwick and 80 riders who had been sent by the March Warden to apprehend William Ridley, an outlaw who was known to have been involved in the murder of Sir Albany Featherstonehaugh. The locals didn't care much for the presence of Fenwick and his men, because their loyalties lay with the fugitive. A group of them, led by William Charlton of Bellingham, set about Sir Robert and drove he and his men out of Tynedale. Just to emphasise their point, they set fire to the castle; it was never rebuilt.

Legend has it that there is an underground tunnel linking Tarset with Dally Castle, just over a mile to the south. It is said that carriages have been heard rumbling along this dank, dark passage and then seen to emerge from the other end, drawn by headless horses. There is another story that links these two grim old fortresses: it tells of a dangerous romance between Gilbert of Tarset, an extremely powerful border warlord during the dark days of the border reivers, and the sister of his sworn enemy, Lord of Dally. Meetings between the lovers had to be arranged in secret, but ultimately the couple were caught out, resulting in hand-to-hand combat between the two lords. Gilbert was defeated and fled for his life, hotly pursued across the Tyne by his adversary to the highest point of the moors of Hareshaw; there, another fight broke out and, sadly, Gilbert was killed. A memorial known as Gibb's Cross once stood at the spot where the Lord of Tarset died for his forbidden love.

Dally Castle

Site of Tarset Castle

The remains of Thirlwall Castle

THIRLWALL CASTLE

Thirlwall Castle stands half a mile to the north of the village of Greenhead and guards the northern entrance to the 'Busy Gap' – a through route much favoured by the Border Reivers on their nightly forays. The nearby Roman fort of Carvoran provided the ready-made materials for the castle's construction, although the exact date is uncertain; some historians believe it was built in the first half of the 14th century. Close by is a group of crags known as the 'Nine Nicks of Thirlwall', which have been partly destroyed by quarrying. The *'thirl'* part of the name is an archaic word for a hole or entrance, which suggests a gap in Hadrian's Wall; it is thought that this may have been the location where the Caledonians broke through the fortification.

The castle is a wonderful example of a border stronghold. It was here, in 1306, that the Thirlwall family entertained Edward I en route to his aborted invasion of Scotland. A local story tells of a Baron of Thirwall bringing great riches – including a table made of solid gold – back from the wars, the news of which soon spread far and wide. The Scots attacked and took the castle, killing the baron and his followers, and immediately the search for the treasure began. The gold table was known to be watched over day and night by a hideous dwarf, but it, along with the baron's money and its diminutive guardian, was nowhere to be found. Legend has it that during the heat of the battle the dwarf threw the hoard into a well, then jumped in himself and closed the cover. He is said to be there to this day, guarded by a spell that can only be lifted by the son of a widow. So far, however, the well remains undiscovered…

WARDEN

About two miles to the west of Hexham lies Warden, a picturesque village with a church that is of special interest. St Michael and All Angels is in the Early English style, with some traces of Saxon construction visible in the tower, but the main fabric of the church was built from ready-cut stones plundered from the nearby Roman Wall. However, it is the three graves just inside and to the right of the church gate that attract particular attention, for they are fitted with wrought-iron covers to deter grave robbers.

Great advances were made in the field of surgery in the 18th and early 19th centuries, and 1834 saw the foundation of the School of Medicine and Surgery in Newcastle. By this time, surgeons had established that an understanding of human anatomy was key to safe and effective operations, so, to assist in gaining this knowledge, bodies were required for dissection during lectures. Cadavers were provided for demonstrations at the medical schools, but their numbers were insufficient, since supply was limited to the bodies of hanged criminals.

It was this unsatisfactory situation that forced surgeons, students and lecturers to make use of whatever 'subjects' they could lay their hands on. Some teachers of medicine purchased bodies from London where gangs of 'resurrectionists', as these men were known, made a strange living by robbing graves. The corpses were transported in sacks or barrels disguised as perishable goods for tradesmen, but there was trouble when some of these containers were opened by mistake! Other teachers managed to obtain cadavers locally – and, in some cases, students were even expected to provide specimens themselves. This led to an increase in body-snatching from graves in Northumberland and beyond, inciting outrage among the population.

Some of these 'resurrectionists' were rough types for whom grave-robbing was only one of many dishonest activities, while others were men who no doubt felt justified in sourcing essential scientific material for the medical profession. Their method of working was an acquired skill. To avoid detection, they left little or no evidence of disturbance to the grave – items such as flower vases were carefully replaced. The whole grave was not opened; instead, a small hole was dug at one end, through which the body was hauled by a rope – no part of the coffin or shroud would be taken, since that would be stealing!

In the eyes of the law at the time, a corpse had no legal rights or value, and magistrates were often reluctant to convict these men for merely opening graves.

Eventually, however, by-laws were introduced, watchtowers constructed in graveyards and watch committees formed to combat the ever-increasing problem of this stealthy, ghoulish nocturnal activity.

Grave covers, St Michael's, Warden

St Michael's Church, Warden

Stephenson's Cottage and the old Wylam Waggonway

GEORGE STEPHENSON'S BIRTHPLACE, WYLAM (National Trust)

In the 18th century, Wylam was a thriving centre for coal mining and ironworking, associated with the Blacketts, the wealthy family of colliery owners and shipping magnates who built Wallington Hall, near Morpeth. It was also here in this village that some of the most inventive minds of the time began their work.

The track known as the Wylam Waggonway was the first in the north of England on which a steam locomotive engine was tested. It was in the early 1800's that the Blacketts commissioned their first locomotive, built to the plans of inventor Richard Trevithick, but the wooden wagonway was too weak to carry it, and the engine was sold. Two more engines were equally unsuccessful – the track bed by now was in such a bad state that they often ran off the rails. This was best summed up by a workman who, when asked how they had got on, replied, *"We don't get on – we only gets off!"*

The first successful engine was the Puffing Billy, designed by industrial engineer William Hedley and brought into use in 1813, which operated between Wylam Colliery and the staithes at Lemington, five miles to the east. A story is told at Wylam of a stranger arriving late one night and being almost frightened out of his mind by the unexpected approach of the engine – it must have been a terrifying sight as it emerged from the dark, its piston loudly pounding, snorting out huge blasts of steam from either side and belching fire and smoke as it thundered along. No wonder the stranger fled through the hedge and across the fields, crying out to the first person he saw that he had just been chased by "a terrible devil on the High Street Road!".

About a mile from the village, on the north bank of the river, is the cottage where legendary engineer George Stephenson was born on 9th June 1781. It is a typical Northumbrian cottage of two storeys, and has been in the care of the National Trust since 1949, when it was donated by the North East Coast Institution of Engineers and Shipbuilders. Originally, the cottage would have directly faced the Wylam Waggonway, which was re-laid in 1876 as the Scotswood, Newburn and Wylam Railway.

The brilliant Stephenson – inventor of the most advanced locomotive of its day, the Rocket, and regarded to be the 'Father of the Railways' – was a completely self-educated man; indeed, he was illiterate until the age of 18. At the time of his birth, George's father – a colliery fireman – was earning just nine shillings a week to support his wife and family. The young Stephenson's first job was herding cows on Throckley Fell, for which he was paid tuppence per day.

Aged 23, he became an engine man at Killingworth Colliery and was already working on plans for future machines, including the Rocket; his first engine was the Blucher, which was built in 1814 and used at Killingworth. The colliery inspired Stephenson's next invention, too: in 1815, he came up with the design of the first miners' safety lamp, known as the Geordie Lamp, months before the eminent scientist Sir Humphrey Davy presented his own version. In the meantime, Hedley had developed his latest engine, the Wylam Dilly, which replaced the Puffing Billy and was in use at Wylam Colliery right up until 1862.

Commemorative plaque, Stephenson's Cottage

The fast pace of development in steam locomotion led to the formation in 1823 of Robert Stephenson and Company, a railway-engine manufacturing firm set up by George Stephenson, his civil engineer son Robert, and businessmen Edward Pease and Thomas Richardson. The engines would carry people and coal on the world's first public steam locomotive railway, which initially ran from colleries in County Durham to Stockton-on Tees and Darlington. On 27th September 1825, the company's latest creation, Locomotion No 1, carried the first passengers on the new Stockton and Darlington Railway.

The railway station at Wylam is worthy of investigation – opened in 1835, it remains one of the earliest stations in the world still in use by passengers. The nearby road bridge has a fascinating history, too, having started out as a combined road and railway bridge to connect the newly opened Newcastle to Carlisle Railway with local colleries.

The bridge originally had timber decking supported on stone piers, with a toll collector's hut on its south-east corner. It would appear that coal wagons did not use the bridge after the late 1800s and by the end of the century the wooden superstructure was replaced with steel by the Wylam Toll Bridge Company, which also built the tollhouse that can still be seen at the northern end.

West Wylam Railway Bridge from the east

WEST WYLAM BRIDGE (Hagg Bank Bridge)

West Wylam Bridge – also known as Hagg Bank Bridge, Points Bridge or Half-Moon Bridge – stands about half a mile outside the village of Wylam. Now a footbridge and cycle path, the structure was originally built to carry the Scotswood, Newburn and Wylam Railway across the River Tyne at Hagg Bank, to connect with the Newcastle & Carlisle Railway.

Located in an attractive position on a bend in the river, this graceful single-span arch was built at a cost of £16,000 and opened to traffic on 6th October 1876. Several north-east companies were involved in the construction: WG Laws carried out the design engineering; WE Jackson and Co of Newcastle built the foundations and masonry; and Hawks, Crawshay and Sons of Gateshead manufactured the ironwork. Work began in 1874, and the bridge was in use for almost a hundred years before its closure, prompted by the Beeching cuts, on 11th March 1968. The tracks were taken up in 1972, and the bridge was converted to a footbridge and cycle path three years later. In 1997, at a cost of £224,000 – which included £157,000 of support from the Heritage Lottery Fund – the original paintwork was removed, and the bridge was restored to its former glory with a lead-free alternative.

The single-arch design was prompted by the necessity to avoid building piers in the river, the foundations of which would have disturbed shallow mine workings below. The single span of 240ft consists of three ribs connected with diagonal braces to prevent cross strain and distortion. The track bed is suspended from these ribs by 19 girders, at a height of 28ft above the river.

Some historians believe that West Wylam Bridge may have provided the inspiration for the Tyne Bridge in Newcastle and the Sydney Harbour Bridge in Australia, though there are major differences in their load-bearing designs. West Wylam can also lay claim to being one of the world's earliest rib-arched bridges, and it is thought to have been the first to carry a railway, hence its Grade II listing.

During World War II the bridge was subject to mistaken identity by the crew of a Luftwaffe Heinkel 111K who thought it was the Tyne Bridge and released their bombs; fortunately, they missed the bridge and their load allegedly dropped between West Wylam and Crawcrook.

Cycling over West Wylam Railway Bridge

Sycamore Gap

EXPLORING NORTHUMBERLAND HISTORY:
HADRIAN'S WALL

Hadrian's Wall is one of the best-known visitor attractions in Northumberland. It has, of course, been designated a UNESCO World Heritage Site – a fitting tribute to the superb skills of the Roman engineers and masons who worked on it.

The building of the Wall, commissioned by the Emperor Hadrian for the purposes of defence and communications, began in AD 122; however, a substantial amount of the Roman remains in Northumberland date from the arrival of Gnaeus Julius Agricola, the newly appointed governor of Britain, in AD 78. The Romans had been in Britain since AD 43 and spent the first 35 years of their occupation securing their frontier, which stretched from Exeter to York, along the line of the road known as the Fosse Way, before making their advance into Wales.

However, the Romans' policy of 'divide and conquer', along with the heavy-handed way in which they collected taxes, provoked serious revolts. In AD 71, the Brigantes – a confederation of Celtic tribes who controlled Yorkshire and Northumberland – fought a major battle with the occupying forces at Scotch Corner, close to the Yorkshire village in Middleton Tyas, but were driven back to North Northumberland and over the Scottish border.

The Romans were now ready to march north into Scotland. The first frontline they established was between Corbridge and Carlisle, along the Stanegate, much of which can still be seen. This was followed by a series of forts along the line, at Corbridge, Newbrough, Chesterholm, Haltwhistle Burn, Carvoran and – as far as Northumberland is concerned – Throp, near Gilsland. Around AD 81, Agricola and his army marched into Scotland, following the line of Dere Street from Corbridge to Chew Green, then crossing the border and continuing on to Newstead, near Melrose. A secondary force followed the Devil's Causeway, which branched off Dere Street at the Portgate and led directly to Berwick-upon-Tweed, at which point they were supported by their fleet. These two routes were linked by a road from Rochester that joined with the Devil's Causeway at Whittingham, a major crossing point on the River Aln.

By AD 84, Agricola had reached the Moray Firth and forced the Caledonians into a declaration of peace. The governor built a new series of forts to secure his Highland line, and a new legionary headquarters was established overlooking the River Tay. Unfortunately, most of this effort was for nothing; following Agricola's recall to Rome in AD 85, it was decided that the army was too extended, and, as a consequence, there was a withdrawal to the River Tweed.

Just as Emperor Hadrian came to power in AD 117, there was another uprising in northern Britain, a bloody conflict that resulted in the Ninth Legion being wiped out. As a consequence, Hadrian himself paid a visit in AD 122 and, after appraising the situation, ordered the immediate building of the Wall. He entrusted the management of its construction to Aulius Platorius Nepos, Britain's new governor.

The original plan was to build a wall from Newcastle to Carlisle that spanned almost 80 miles in length and was punctuated by milecastles, with two turrets or signal stations evenly sited between them. It was to be 20ft high and 10ft thick, with a rampart 15ft above the ground. Legionary soldiers and locals formed the workforce, and, as various inscriptions confirm, each 'century' was allocated a stretch of about 45 yards to construct. However, just after work commenced, there was a change of plan that reduced the Wall's width to 8ft. This modification, known as the 'Narrow Wall', can be first seen just after Turret 26b at Low Brunton, leading up to Chollerford Bridge, although perhaps it is better observed as the Wall leaves the western edge of the fort at Chesters. Thus, the Wall continued from Chollerford Bridge right across to Gilsland on the western border of Northumberland as a narrow wall on a broad foundation. It was also thought at this time that it would be a good idea to extend the Wall eastwards from Newcastle to Wallsend, to guard against any outflanking movements.

Much of the construction work was done in four years, from AD 122 to AD 126, but during the first 10 years there were many alterations and additions; in fact, some of the early building work was destroyed to make way for later ideas. Also included in Hadrian's original plan were a number of forts projecting beyond the line of the Wall so that troops could be quickly deployed to the north if needed. About 20ft north of the Wall lay a V-shaped ditch measuring 10ft deep and 27ft wide; on its north side was a 60ft bank formed from excavated earth, which sloped away so that it would throw any approaching intruders into stark silhouette, day or night.

The Romans also built another ditch – the Vallum – to the south of the Wall. Flat-bottomed and around 20ft wide, the Vallum marked off the southern aspect of the Wall as a military zone, a forbidden part of the frontier; and, of course, it provided further defence in case of attack from the rear. The need to service the Wall with a good road saw the construction of the 20ft-wide Military Way, which linked

Segedunum – Sentius Tectonicus

the whole defensive line post by post, with a branch to each turret. Although it was a service road, there were places where the Wall followed difficult terrain – such as between Sewingshields and Thirlwall – so this was circumnavigated where possible. The Military Way was linked to Stanegate and Dere Street, and this system could have been used to quickly bring reinforcements from as far away as York – through the forts of Binchester, Ebchester and Corbridge – and also from Chester, through Lancashire and Penrith, to Carvoran.

In spite of spasmodic trouble, Hadrian's Wall was in use until AD 383, when the Roman general Magnus Maximus revolted against the Emperor Gratian, set himself up as Emperor of Britain, then left with a large number of his troops to seize control of Gaul; as a result, the Wall was overrun and never repaired. The last of the Roman soldiers left Britain in AD 407 to defend Rome against the threat of the Vandals and the Goths. Almost at once, the Saxons invaded. The Romano-British civilians were left to fend for themselves, their appeal for help from the Roman commander in Gaul went unheeded.

The Wall is probably best explored from east to west. The most spectacular parts are in Northumberland, and there is now a Hadrian's Wall Trail for those who wish to walk its length. The Military Road (now the B6318) is a good way to follow the line of the Wall – in some places the road runs directly on top, the Romans having provided a good base on which to build. Its construction was proposed in 1745 by General George Wade, the British Army officer who had been charged with suppressing the Jacobite uprising. Wade had positioned the Hanoverian troops at Newcastle, waiting to intercept Bonnie Prince Charlie and his army, but the Jacobites invaded England via an alternative route: southwards through Liddesdale, behind the Cheviot Hills, then onwards to Carlisle. The Jacobites' rapid movement through the Highlands was, ironically, thanks to good roads that had been constructed by Wade! Unfortunately for General Wade and his troops, the route cross-country from Newcastle to Carlisle had proved much more difficult and frustrating. Sadly, Wade didn't live to see the Military Road completed: he died on 14th March 1748.

SEGEDUNUM ROMAN FORT
(Tyne & Wear Museums)

Segedunum, the Roman Fort at Wallsend that marks the eastern end of Hadrian's Wall, was garrisoned for just over 300 years. The site, on the north bank of the River Tyne, was carefully chosen for its commanding views of the east (towards South Shields) and the west (towards Newcastle). It is thought that the original plan was to finish the Wall at Newcastle because this was the lowest bridging point of the river, but after a few years this was reconsidered and the construction was extended to Wallsend; at the same time, a new fort was built. The Wall joined the fort at the west gate and extended beyond the south-east corner to finish a short distance below the river's low watermark. From this point to the coast, the river itself forms a natural barrier to prevent any incursions.

Segedunum follows the traditional design of Roman forts with its playing-card shape and central buildings including a headquarters, commandant's house, granary and hospital. The infantry barracks were sited to the north of these, with the cavalry barracks to the south.

The buildings were enclosed within a defensive wall with four main gates – one on each elevation – although at Wallsend there are also traces of a smaller additional west gate. Originally, these buildings were constructed from timber, but within about 50 years they were rebuilt in stone. An excellent reconstruction of the bathhouse – part of the adjoining civilian settlement – can be seen to the south of the fort.

It was usual for single units to garrison the forts on Hadrian's Wall, although sometimes smaller divisions were drafted in to increase manpower. In the third century, Segedunum was garrisoned by the Fourth Cohort of Lingones, which comprised more than a hundred cavalry troops and around 500 infantry soldiers and is thought to have originated from the Roman frontier of Germania Superior (now eastern France). Further evidence suggests that the fort was occupied in the second century by the Second Cohort of Nervians, a unit from Belgium.

Segedunum is said to be one of the most fully excavated forts anywhere in the Roman Empire. This engrossing site with its excellent museum offers highly interesting displays and reconstructions, with ample opportunity for a hands-on experience. Crowning it all is a magnificent viewing tower that provides impressive views of the entire fort and its surrounding area.

In 2017 – the 30th anniversary of the Wall being listed as a UNESCO World Heritage Site, and 1,900 years since Hadrian became Emperor – a sculpture of a Roman centurion was installed at Segedunum. Created by local artist John O'Rourke, the figure is named Sentius Tectonicus: Sentius was the name of a centurion who supervised the building of a section of the wall near Segedunum, and Tectonicus refers to the sculpture's design as an architectural man. The statue was commissioned by North Tyneside Council, constructed from weathering steel by a local engineering firm, WD Close with trainees from AIS Connect and Installed by Capita. It was unveiled on 24th March 2017 by Norma Redfearn, Mayor of North Tyneside.

An interesting inscription was carved in 1895 and placed at the eastern corner of the fort by Frank Buddle Atkinson, he noted the presence of a "Roman Camp", believed to be Segedunum, it concludes, "The inhabitants of Wallsend are requested to co-operate for the protection of this interesting memorial of antiquity from which the town derives its name"

Wall reconstruction, Segedunum

Cavalry barracks, Segedunum

Heddon-on-the-Wall – later built in oven

HEDDON-ON-THE-WALL

The village of Heddon-on-the-Wall is about nine miles west of Newcastle, overlooking the Tyne Valley. As its name suggests, Heddon was part of the Roman military endeavour, and about 100ft of broad Wall – together with its defensive vallum, cut into solid rock – can be seen on its outskirts. At the western end of this stretch of Hadrian's Wall is a small circular chamber that has been cut into its thickness – all that remains of a medieval lime kiln. Also, the village church of St Andrew's, which dates from around AD 630, was constructed mostly using stone from the Wall.

Heddon marks the start of the Military Road, where, in 1752, during its construction, a valuable hoard of Roman gold and silver coins in mint condition was discovered hidden within the fabric of the Wall; another collection, including an excellent example of a coin showing the emperor Arcadius, was found in 1820.

BRUNTON TURRET (English Heritage)

Brunton Turret is thought to be one of the best-preserved turrets on Hadrian's Wall. Also known as Turret 26b, it is reached via a signposted path leading from a lay-by on the A6079, just south of the crossroads with the B6318 (Brunton Bank). The turret, which was first excavated in 1873, stands more than 9ft tall and is recessed about four feet into the Wall. To the western side is a good example of the broad wall- nearly 10ft wide - whilst on the eastern side is a fine stretch of the narrow wall- around 7ft wide. This was obviously the spot where the engineers decided to alter their building plans.

At first, it was thought that this change was implemented in the interests of economy, although the theory put forward a number of years ago by Sir Ian Richmond, the archaeologist and academic, seems more likely. He thought the modification was brought about by the need for greater strength of construction which, of course, would be necessary to build a wall over the narrow and steep crags that were to come, coupled with the fact that it would be easier to dig narrower foundations over this difficult terrain.

Brunton Turret

HADRIAN'S WALL

CHOLLERFORD BRIDGE ABUTMENT
(English Heritage)

Chesters Bridge Abutment at Chollerford is possibly one of Britain's most interesting sites of Roman bridge remains. It is reached by following the riverside footpath leading from the eastern end of the present-day Chollerford Bridge.

These striking remains were first excavated in 1860 by John Clayton, the town clerk of Newcastle upon Tyne; a keen archaeologist, Clayton also did much of the work at his residence, the Chesters estate, on the opposite bank. It was discovered that there had once been two bridges at this point: one was in use while the Wall was being constructed, and this was replaced by a larger road bridge in AD 192. Beneath the remains of a turret was found the hub of a waterwheel – a large circular stone of the undershot variety, with slots for eight spokes. Water mills were one of the many inventions brought to Britain by the Romans and provided further proof, along with baths and aqueducts, of their skill in water engineering. Roman water mills are known only in military areas, especially along the Wall – all part of the policy of making forts self-sufficient.

The abutment itself is constructed of well-dressed stones in alternating courses of headers (laid lengthwise) and stretchers (widthwise) for strength and stability. The upper surfaces of the stones show lewis holes, by which they were lifted into position, and the masons carved a large phallus low down on the north side of the abutment as typically defiant Roman insurance against bad luck. The second bridge probably had a platform built from timber and would have been supported by three piers, two of which can still be seen mid river when the water level is low.

Chollerford Bridge abutment

Phallic relief carving, Chollerford Bridge

Chollerford Bridge abutment and Chesters Bath House

CHESTERS FORT (English Heritage)

The fort at Chesters – or Cilurnum, as it was known to the Romans – is the second largest on Hadrian's Wall, and also its most accessible and important. The former headquarters of the Ala II Asturum (Second Asturians), a unit that originated in Spain, it is regarded as the finest example of a Roman cavalry fort in all of Europe.

Cilurnum was mostly excavated in the mid-1800s by the enthusiastic amateur archaeologist John Clayton who owned and lived in the mansion at Chesters and, moreover, devoted most of his life to extensive research and work on the Wall.

The fort covers an area of just over five acres and has the traditional playing-card shape with rounded corners to its 5ft-thick walls. The museum is an important and interesting part of the site. It is from the inscriptions on the excellent collection of altar stones, glass, metalwork, sculpture and pottery housed here that much information has been discovered about the soldiers, officers and civilians who inhabited this distant outpost of the Roman Empire.

Cilurnum is entered by the north gate – one of six it originally had. Inside the walls are barracks and stables that housed 500 men and their mounts. In the centre is the headquarters building comprising a colonnaded courtyard, the judgment hall and administration offices. The central room of these offices is the chapel with steps leading down to what was the vaulted strongroom. When Clayton first discovered this, he found an oak door studded with iron, but unfortunately, it fell to pieces when exposed to the air. It was possibly the discovery of this strongroom that gave rise to the local legend telling of an underground stable for 500 horses. Just to the east is the commandant's house, where the hypocaust central heating system is still clearly visible.

The fort was built in the early second century, between AD 122 and AD 146, but was restored after the incursions of AD 197, AD 296 and AD 367, which affected numerous fortifications along the wall.

An abundant water supply was brought to the wall via an aqueduct – not only for drinking purposes but also to fill the remarkable bath house that lies just between the fort and the river. All Romans took a daily bath, and the habit was soon adopted by leading Britons, too. Bathing was a very important social occasion; every Roman town had a public bath house, and every military establishment had its

Chesters Bath House

Chesters Barracks

HADRIAN'S WALL

Chesters Hypocaust

Temple of Mithras

own set located just outside the fort for use by the soldiers and, eventually, by the inhabitants of the vicus. (The commander had his own private bath suite.)

The clever secret of the Roman bath house was the hypocaust heating system. Hot air from a furnace was conducted through underground channels to a pillared vault beneath the room to be warmed. If dry heat was required, the furnace would be stoked with charcoal; for moist heat, wood was used. For greater heat, not only the floors were heated but the walls too, using flues made from tiles. The principle was the same as modern central heating, but it was always hot air that circulated, never hot water.

The idea was to be able to go from hot to cold rooms, via tepid and warm, moist or dry and back again, thus generating a good sweat and opening all the pores. The skin was copiously rubbed with oils, which were then scraped off with a curved metal flesh scraper known as a strigil. The Romans didn't have soap, but they made ample use of sponges, both for washing and as an alternative to toilet paper. In the unctorium, the room where oils were applied, a masseur would be on hand to pound and pummel the flesh. Baths were commonplace for the 300 years or so that the Romans were in Britain, but when they left, the practice of daily bathing was abandoned. In medieval England, and indeed as late as the Victorian era, Britons must have had an unpleasant aroma: it's only fairly recently that the regular bath has again become habit.

TEMPLE OF MITHRAS (English Heritage)

About three-and-a-half miles west of Chesters is Carrawburgh – pronounced Carrawbruff – the site of the Roman fort of Brocolitia. The fort covers quite a large area, approximately three-and-a-half acres, although it has not been excavated and therefore the site has the appearance of a bumpy grass-covered field. One of the last forts to be added to Hadrian's Wall, Brocolitia was garrisoned in the third and fourth centuries by the First Cohort of Batavians from the low countries.

A path leads across the field to a small marshy valley where the best-preserved Temple of Mithras on Hadrian's Wall can be seen. The Mithraic cult was based on the struggle between light and darkness, and men would be initiated into the secret society in this small, dark temple. The inner sanctum has three replica altars depicting gods with torches raised and lowered; the originals of these were removed to the Museum of Antiquities in Newcastle and are now on display in the city's Great North Museum. The god Mithras – believed by the Romans to be of Persian origin, although this has since been disputed – was portrayed killing the bull at the dawn of time, thus releasing the forces of creation for the benefit of mankind; light radiating from behind pierced relief carvings would illuminate the murky interior of the temple, heightening the tension and mystery for the nervous initiate.

Nearby, just to the north-east of the temple, is the site of Coventina's Well, excavated by John Clayton in 1876. It was here that a small shrine built around a powerful spring and dedicated to the Celtic water goddess Coventina was discovered. The altar stones and other sculptures are now in the Clayton Museum at Chesters. Many votive offerings of jewellery were also recovered, along with a hoard of 16,000 Roman coins.

There is evidence to suggest that both the well-shrine and the Mithraic temple were violently destroyed, possibly by a later Christian commander of the fort.

Housesteads Fort

Housesteads latrine plumbing

HOUSESTEADS (English Heritage)

Of all the Wall forts, Housesteads has the most impressive position, being spectacularly perched on the 900 feet contour of the Great Whin Sill, overlooking Broomlee and Greenlee Loughs, and surveying a large tract of wild country to the north. It is, perhaps, the best-preserved fort on the Wall, giving good access to its line in each direction along the crags. On the approach slopes from the south are the remains of early cultivation terraces associated with the vicus, or civilian settlement; the ruins of houses and shops can also be seen. This is the area that would have served the needs of the soldiers at the fort. It has been estimated that as many as 2,000 civilians resided here, living on the upper level of their two-storey houses and using the ground floor to trade and display their goods.

The main purpose of Housesteads was to guard the way through the Knag Burn valley, which lies to beyond its south and east walls. Known to the Romans as Borovicium, the fort covered more than five acres and was garrisoned by around 1,000 men of the First Cohort of the Tungri, a tribe from Tongres in Belgium. Excavations have shown that Housesteads was built after the foundations for the Broad Wall were laid, but before the Narrow Wall reached this point. Discoveries have revealed the foundations of Turret 36b, which was almost certainly demolished to make way for the fort. Here, the terrain dictates that the fort be set lengthwise to the wall, without the usual projection forward.

Perhaps one of the most interesting aspects of Housesteads' history is its development as a Roman customs and frontier post after civilians were permitted to pass through the Wall in the late third century. The Knag Burn Gateway was let into the wall to allow the passage of traffic using an established drovers' road. One of the very few gateways in Hadrian's Wall for civilians, it was flanked by two guard chambers and had a second door at the rear through which all travellers were filtered, a few at a time, for interrogation and search. The necessary toll was levied by a Roman officer known as a beneficiarius, who would have been stationed at Housesteads.

With its plans and models of Housesteads and displays of pottery and sculpted stones, the museum, along with the well-marked-out remains of the fort, helps build a picture of the Roman settlements on this site – and their inhabitants – almost 2,000 years ago.

The walk from Housesteads to Steel Rigg is perhaps one of the most spectacular along the line of the Wall. The line runs along Cuddy's Crags and Hotbank Crags to Peel Crags and thus to Steel Rigg – a distance of two-and-a-half miles. The route passes the sites of Milecastles 37, 38, and 39, the first and last of which are well-preserved and certainly worthy of close inspection. The space between Cuddy's Crags and Hotbank Crags is known as the Rapishaw Gap; this was one of many '*busy gaps or theeves roads*' used in the days of raiding and reiving, and nowadays is the northern exit from the line of the Wall for the Pennine Way.

By Crag Lough, the Wall descends to Milking Gap near the Bradley Burn, passing the site of Milecastle 38. Beyond the Lough, the Wall climbs to Peel Crags, passing Milecastle 39. Because of the change of tactics by Severus, who became Emperor in AD 193, many of the

HADRIAN'S WALL

Housesteads Granaries

Housesteads Bastle House

turrets on this section of the Wall were demolished by the Romans themselves.

As an alternative to walking the Wall in this sector, it is possible to follow the Military Way – the Roman road that runs along its southern side – which is less strenuous and eventually reaches the same point. Or, for the real enthusiast, the Military Way and the Wall form an excellent circular route from either Steel Rigg or Housesteads fort.

The tiny hamlet of Once Brewed is the centre for much activity along the Wall; there is an excellent visitor centre here, plus a youth hostel. The origins of Once Brewed and Twice Brewed – the name of the local inn – intrigue many visitors to the area. The names originate, it is thought, from the fact that there were two pubs here. There are a number of stories said to explain these unusual names. The most popular tale tells of how the crew working on a section of the Military Road (part of the B6318) were disappointed with the quality of the ale served at the inn and told the landlord to brew it again, hence 'Twice Brewed'; The other pub, to distinguish it from the former, was thence forth known as "Once Brewed".

Milecastle 37 north gate, near Housesteads

HOUSESTEADS BASTLE HOUSE

Being possibly the best-preserved fort on Hadrian's Wall, Housesteads is of great interest to Roman historians, but the Border Reivers also left their mark on this site.

In the 17th century, a bastle house – a small, fortified two-storey farmhouse – was built against the eastern guard tower of the fort's south gateway, and this became the home of one Hugh Nixon, cattle thief, a reputed receiver of stolen goods, and a close associate of the infamous Armstrong family.

The house's 4ft-thick walls were constructed using a readily available supply of dressed Roman stone. As well as accommodation, a small corn-drying kiln was added, and the remains of an external staircase – a feature typical of bastle houses in the 17th century – can still be seen.

In 1599, the noted historian and cartographer William Camden visited the area, but he observed that he could not safely undertake a full survey of Housesteads because of the dangerous robbers in those parts. Although they presented a danger to travellers, the Reivers inadvertently helped to preserve Housesteads by also keeping away those who might plunder the site for building materials.

The view from Steel Rigg towards Crag Lough and Hotbank Farm

STEEL RIGG

Steel Rigg affords one of the finest viewpoints of the high central section of Hadrian's Wall, making it very popular with visitors. The location presents a view of the Wall perched atop the mighty, north-facing crags of the Whin Sill – the geological feature that inspired Hadrian to position the Roman Empire's most northerly border here in AD 122.

With wheelchair access and a dry footpath from the car park, this site offers less-agile visitors an opportunity to see the Wall's dramatic Roman engineering at close quarters. It is also an excellent starting point for a walk eastwards along the National Trail to Housesteads Roman Fort, or west to the Wall's highest point at Winshields. Both routes have breathtaking views over the high, wild landscape.

There are less strenuous perambulations too: head eastwards past Milecastle 39 – or Castle Nick, as it is known locally – to Sycamore Gap and you'll find Britain's most photographed tree, as featured in various productions including the 1991 Kevin Costner movie *Robin Hood, Prince of Thieves*.

The walk to the milecastle and sycamore tree is even less taxing if you take the Military Road, but following the line of the wall adds a little frisson to the journey…

THE SILL (Northumberland National Park)

Just to the south of Steel Rigg is The Sill. This is the National Landscape Discovery Centre and is one of Northumberland's newest visitor attractions. It opened at the end of July 2017 at a cost of £14.8 million and serves to welcome, inform and inspire people of all ages and abilities to explore the landscape, history, culture and heritage of Northumberland.

It blends cleverly into the surrounding countryside and features a marvellous landscape exhibition, along with various seasonal exhibitions throughout the year. It is a hub of modern learning and event spaces, a local food café, a world-class modern Youth Hostel, a rural business hub, and a shop specialising in local crafts and produce. The Sill is a showcase of local pride and passion and an exciting gateway into the beautiful countryside of Northumberland.

It takes its name from the Great Whin Sill, a layer of the igneous rock dolerite in County Durham, Northumberland and Cumbria in the northeast of England. It lies partly in the North Pennines Area of Outstanding Natural Beauty and partly in Northumberland National Park and stretches from Teesdale northwards towards Berwick. It is one of the key natural features of the North Pennines. A major outcrop is at the High Force waterfall in Teesdale. Distinctive outcrops occur on The Farne Islands, and at Bamburgh Castle, Dunstanburgh Castle, Lindisfarne Castle and stretches of Hadrian's Wall all these take advantage of the high, rocky cliff lines formed by the sill.

VINDOLANDA (Vindolanda Trust)

Vindolanda is situated about a mile north of Bardon Mill, about a mile to the south of Hadrian's Wall and was an important fort and civilian settlement on the *Stanegate* – the Roman road from Corbridge to Carlisle. It was one of the original forts established on this ancient road. Archaeologists have detected at least nine forts on the site; the first was built in wood around AD 85 but was replaced by more significant constructions until the first stone fort was built c. AD165, then almost entirely rebuilt c. AD213.

The most striking remains visible date from the 3rd and 4th century and include the headquarters, or principia, as they called it. This building was at the centre of the fort where the commanding officer would reside, and the clerks would have offices. There was a strongroom for soldiers pay and valuables. The Sacellum chapel, the most sacred place in a Roman fort, housed the legion's standard, the Aquila: the sculpture of an eagle with outstretched wings perched on top of a metal or wooden pole.

The commanding officer's residence, or praetorium, was a huge house where he lived with his wife, family and slaves. Its style was based on the spacious residences of Rome and designed around a sheltered courtyard. There were also the granaries or horrea. Every Roman fort was supposed to have enough grain to feed its soldiers bread for six months. Vindolanda would have housed about 500 men.

There were several barracks where usually eight soldiers lived per room, including their armour and weapons. Excavation evidence shows that women and children were also living here and revealed much of the civilian settlement or vicus. This fascinating area outside the fort walls had shops, houses, workshops, butchers, temples and even a tavern.

Sited on the northern edge of the settlement, probably due to the high risk of fire, is the well-preserved bathhouse, which, as well as its latrine, features the usual arrangement of hot and cold plunge baths hypocaust-heated rooms favoured by the Romans. It is underneath these remains that the organic layers survive, preserved due to anaerobic or oxygen-free conditions. The wooden buildings have revealed the most extensive single-site collection of Roman organic objects in Britain, including thousands of leather and wood objects. Many wooden writing tablets have yielded important information about the lives of the soldiers and civilians who lived at Vindolanda. The on-site museum displays these objects, including shoes, jewellery and even a Roman toilet seat.

Among the finds were two sparring or practice *caestus* – ancient boxing "gloves" depicted on Roman sculptures and mosaics. The gloves are cut from a single piece of leather and folded into a pouch shape with straps. The pouch of one of the gloves is stuffed with grasses and bracken to absorb any shock; the other has an insert of stiff, coiled leather designed to inflict damage on an opponent.

Perhaps one of the most impressive artefacts is an almost complete chamfron or horse's ceremonial face mask found in the remains of the residence of Flavius Cerialis, prefect of the Ninth Cohort of Batavians.

The full-height replicas on the south-west side of the site show reconstructions of the stone wall and milecastle built using, as far as possible, Roman methods, together with educated guesses to present a good impression of what the Wall was like for the Roman soldiers and civilians on duty on this lonely outpost of the Roman Empire.

Roman "Boxing Gloves", Vindolanda

Chamfron, horse face armour, Vindolanda

Butchers shop, Vindolanda

THE ROMAN ARMY MUSEUM
MAGNA ROMAN FORT
(Vindolanda Trust)

This fort is also situated on the Stanegate where it joins with the Maiden Way from the south. During Hadrian's time, the fort was garrisoned by the First Cohort of Hamian Archers who came from Syria. The fort stands to the south of both the Wall and the Vallum - it was probably established here to command the valley of the Tipalt Burn, and of course, to guard the road junction.

The fort has not been excavated, but the remains of a tower can be seen to the southwest of the Roman Army Museum. The museum is well worth a visit; it provides an insight into the daily lives of the Roman soldiers through the imaginative use of reconstructions, audio commentary and films, which support and complement the comprehensive display of Roman artefacts.

Exhibits in the museum have been specially chosen to help tell the story of life on the frontier. They include some unique and amazing artefacts which help us to understand aspects of Roman life. Highlights include the only surviving helmet crest made of delicate hair moss and an archer's thumb guard. Lifesize replicas are used throughout the museum to add to the experience. These help to graphically illustrate the scale of some aspects of Roman life. There is replica armour and weapons in the training room and a *scorpio minor* and a *manuballista*, both exciting examples of devastating Roman artillery.

Roman armour, Carvoran

MILECASTLE 42
(English Heritage)

Milecastle 42, near Cawfields, is thought to have been built by the Second Legion – Legio II Augusta. Milecastles were sited at a distance of a Roman mile (around 1,617 yards) along Hadrian's Wall; they have also been found on several Roman frontiers. With a few exceptions, the milecastles on Hadrian's Wall guarded a gateway with a corresponding causeway across the wall ditch to the north and had a garrison of perhaps 20-30 auxiliary soldiers housed in two barrack blocks. On either side of the milecastle was a stone tower (turret) located about one-third of a Roman mile away. It is assumed that the garrison also supplied soldiers to man the turrets. The milecastle's garrison controlled the passage of people, goods and livestock across the frontier, and the fortification likely acted as a customs post to levy taxation on that traffic.

Milecastle 42, Cawfields

Poltross Burn

POLTROSS BURN
(English Heritage)

The Poltross Burn marks the border between Northumberland and Cumbria, and it is here that a remarkable section of Vallum can be seen – the deep cuttings on either side of the burn have been faced with stone to strengthen them.

Milecastle 48 (Poltross Burn) is one of the most well-preserved milecastles on Hadrian's Wall. It is approached by a steep climb from the Burn, which was most likely crossed by a wooden bridge. It has been calculated that the walls originally stood at a height of 15ft, and they were entered via a 9ft-wide gate (later reduced to 4ft). The two barrack buildings were divided into four crowded rooms housing a total of 64 men – the maximum number permitted in a milecastle.

Its most important feature is, perhaps, the flight of three stone steps in the north-east corner. These are thought to be the remains of a wide stone staircase leading up to a walkway, calculated to be about 12ft high, which, in turn, would mean that the outside wall would possibly have been about 15ft in height.

EXPLORING NORTHUMBERLAND HISTORY:
MID NORTHUMBERLAND

St Michael's and All Angel's Church, Alwinton

ALWINTON
St Michael and All Angel's Church

In the 13th and 14th centuries St Michael's Church at Alwinton served as a sanctuary: When Gilbert de Umfraville was master of Harbottle in 1293, "Thomas de Holm, being taken within his franchise, escaped out of the prison at Harbottle, and fled to the church at Alwenton, but Simon Smart and Benedict Gley, porter of Harbottle, beheaded him at Simonseth and hung his head on the gallows at Harbottle"

The church dates back to Norman times but was restored first during the 13th and 14th centuries and then again in the 19th century. It is dramatically situated on a steep slope above the river, and unusually, the chancel is higher than the nave, separated by ten steps.

The chancel floor was raised in the early 14th century to make a crypt for the Clennell family, who held the manor from the 13th century.

Close inspection shows that the second step from the top of the chancel has chamfered ends, allowing it to be lifted out. Once this is done the rest easily follow to allow an entrance to the burial chamber. A door in the north wall provided external access until the 1960s when the whole crypt was permanently sealed.

By the mid 1800s the crypt had been allocated to the Selby family. They were lay-rectors and exercised their right to the privilege of a resting place in the chancel. They lived in the nearby Biddlestone Hall which claims to be the Obaldiston hall in Sir Walter Scott's novel, Rob Roy.

St Michael and All Angels is certainly a most interesting and unusual church – churches on hills were often dedicated to the Archangel, because being closer to Heaven, St Michael could more easily be called upon to ward off the devil.

And, just to add to the enigma there is a local story that says no-one has actually been in the crypt for more than a hundred years.

ASHINGTON

Mining was first established in Ashington in the 1840s, but it was only in 1867, with the sinking of the Bothal pit, that coal production in this area 15 miles north of Newcastle saw a considerable upturn. Under the direction of Jonathan Priestman, formerly managing director of the Consett Iron Company, in association with members of the Lee and Milburn families – the latter prominent North-East shipowners – the Ashington Coal Company went on to experience a period of rapid growth and profitability in the late 19th century.

The company operated what were, effectively, three main collieries around Ashington, earning it the name of "the world's biggest pit village". The first of these, Ashington Colliery, rapidly became one of the world's biggest collieries, and by 1897 it had reached a production figure of a million tonnes of coal. In 1924, a drift mine was added to the workings, and the high-volume production continued; by 1930, a peak of one-and-a-half million tonnes had been reached, with a workforce of almost 5,000. By 1947, when the mines were nationalised, new machinery had been introduced and electric locomotives were being used underground, allowing up to 90 per cent of coal production to be done mechanically. Streamlining introduced in the 1960s saw a reduction in manpower and production, which continued throughout the 70s and 80s until 25th March 1988, when the colliery was finally closed after more than 120 years of coal production.

Following the success of their first venture, the company had opened a second, Linton Colliery, in 1894, and by the 1900s there were more than 1,000 men in its workforce. Further expansion was carried out, and by 1945 a huge investment programme was in place. Nationalisation in 1947 halted this, but after consideration, the NCB came up with an even more ambitious plan, and in 1950 Linton produced almost 400,000 tonnes of coal and employed close to 1,400 men. A glut of coal and cheap oil, combined with the fact that the coal could be more easily worked from the surface, led to the NCB closing Linton on 28th September 1968; fortunately, many of the men were able to transfer to other collieries in the Ashington area.

Woodhorn Colliery was the third colliery developed by the

Ashington Coal Company, also in 1894, two miles to the east of Ashington. The mine was soon achieving good production, but this was marred when two men were killed in a gas explosion. Tragedy struck again with another explosion in 1916; this time, 13 lives were lost.

After nationalisation, production was still excellent, and at its peak, Woodhorn employed nearly 2,000 men, who produced well over half a million tonnes of coal. But eventually, production became uneconomical, and on 28th February 1981 the pit closed, and the few hundred remaining workers were moved to nearby collieries. The world's biggest pit village was left with no deep mining.

The end of deep mining in Northumberland as a whole came on 12th January 2005 with the closure of Ellington Colliery. More than a thousand gallons of water a minute were flooding the only working face, located beneath the North Sea, six miles off the coast. It was after two weeks of unsuccessful endeavour to pump out the mine that the owners, UK Coal, decided to close the colliery once and for all, resulting in the bitter loss of 340 mining jobs. The proud era of what had once been the world's mightiest coalfield had drawn to a close, ending a remarkable way of life for many generations of local families.

Northumberland's proud history of mining is remembered at the Woodhorn Museum and Northumberland Archives (formerly the Woodhorn Colliery Museum), which houses displays of the lives of the coal workers, along with original buildings and equipment from the former colliery, including two headframes, a steam winding engine and stables. The buildings are protected by listed status, and the location is recognised by Historic England as a Scheduled Monument, being the most well-preserved example of a late 19th and 20th century colliery in the north-east of England.

The Woodhorn Museum has a unique collection of more than 80 excellent paintings by the 'Pitmen Painters', officially known as the Ashington Group. The group was largely made up of pitmen, who first came together in 1934 through the Workers' Educational Association to study 'something different' – art appreciation. To help the men foster an understanding of art, their tutor Robert Lyon encouraged them to pick up a paintbrush themselves. What they produced was a fascinating and eloquent illustration of all aspects of everyday life in their mining community, above and below ground – from meals around the kitchen table to working at the allotment to the dangerous and dirty world of the coal face. Back in the '30s, none of the members of the Ashington Group would have dreamt that a few evening classes would bring them fame and attention, but today they are acclaimed worldwide; their work provides a poignant glimpse into the everyday life of pitmen and their families in the Northumberland town of Ashington.

In addition to its mining heritage, Ashington has provided English football with some of its greatest players. Jackie Milburn – one of Newcastle United's greatest-ever centre forwards, and the scorer of more than 200 league and cup goals – is commemorated with a statue in Ashington's main shopping street, as well as another outside St James' Park. And his nephews, the Charlton Brothers; Sir Bobby, one of England's 1966 World Cup winning team and winner of the prestigious Ballon d'Or; Jack, the eldest of the two brothers, was also a member of the famous '66 team and after an illustrious playing career with Leeds United he went on to guide Northern Ireland to the European Championship Finals in 1988 and the World Cup Finals in 1990.

Sadly, he died in July 2020 but will always be remembered as one of the North-East's greatest footballers.

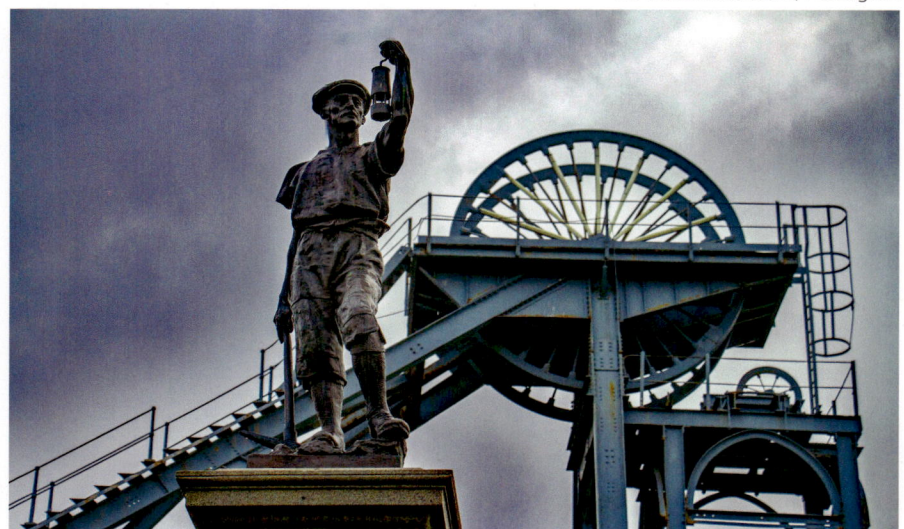

Woodhorn Museum, Ashington

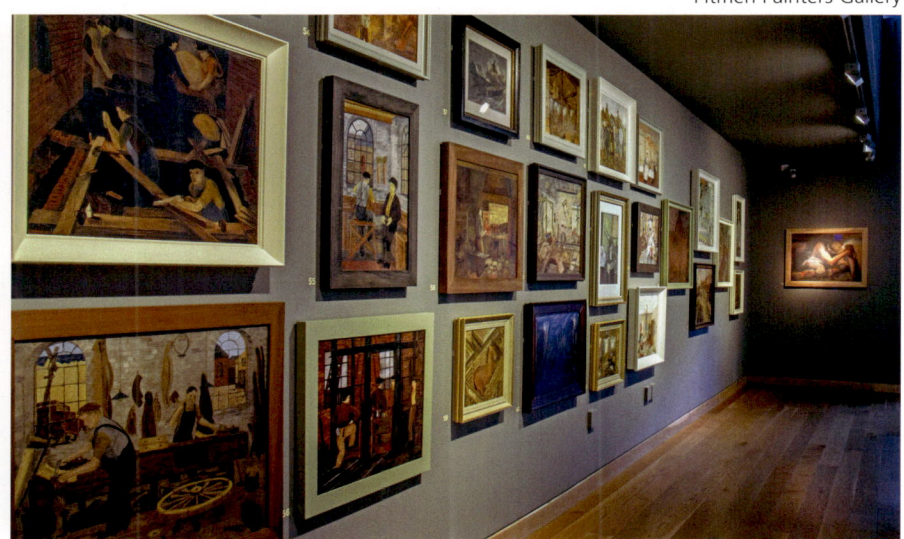

Pitmen Painters Gallery

BATTLE OF OTTERBURN

Battle of Otterburn Monument

The battle that made the village of Otterburn famous was fought on 19th August 1388 and is memorable for having been fought by moonlight. There is some dispute as to whether the site of the battlefield was on the east or west side of the Otter Burn, although it is popularly believed to have taken place between Fawdon Hill and the small valley to the north that runs down to the route of the present A68.

The conflict came about when James, Second Earl of Douglas, seized the opportunity to attack the weakened government of Richard II, gathering an army of about 6,000 hand-picked men and mounting a stealthy lightning strike on Northumberland. His troops penetrated as far south as Brancepeth in County Durham, pillaging, plundering and leaving a wake of devastation. On their return, they camped for three days outside the walls of Newcastle, which was defended by an army under the command of Sir Henry and Sir Ralph Percy, sons of the First Earl of Northumberland. There were several skirmishes, and it was after one of these that Sir Henry (the celebrated 'Harry Hotspur') challenged Douglas to engage in single combat in front of the wooden barriers constructed to defend the New Gate.

Hotspur was unhorsed and lost his spear with its silken pennant to the victorious Douglas, who held it aloft and exclaimed that he would take it back to Scotland and display it as a trophy. Hotspur countered with the threat that the Scot would never get it out of Northumberland. The challenge was laid down. Early the next morning, Douglas' army marched to Ponteland, where they took and burned the town and its castle, before advancing to Otterburn to attack its tower, this time without success. The Scots then camped in the nearby valley with the intention of returning home the next day.

Meanwhile, Sir Henry Percy, eager to make good his threat, had left Newcastle with about 8,000 men and arrived at Otterburn beneath the light of the full moon. Displaying the impulsiveness that had earned him the name "Hotspur", he launched an attack on the enemy, even though his men were weary after the long march. Percy's army broke into the Scots' camp, but mistakenly directed their attack on servants and camp followers, allowing the enemy troops valuable time to manoeuvre around the hillside and attack the English flanks. It seemed at first the superior numbers of the English would be victorious, but soon the tide was turned, and, although the Earl of Douglas was killed, the Scots pressed home their advantage and a complete rout ensued. Sir Henry and Sir Ralph Percy were both taken prisoner, and the fugitives were chased five miles from the scene of the battle.

Meanwhile, the Bishop of Durham had raised an army with the intention of helping the Northumbrians, but not far from Newcastle they met some of the fugitives, who carried word of the disastrous battle. His men were panic-stricken by the news, and the bishop, unable to control their fear, was forced to return to Newcastle. After an indignant and patriotic appeal to the knights and squires of the town, the bishop set out for Otterburn at sunrise the next morning with 10,000 men under his command. His army stopped short of the enemy, who were aware of their arrival. The Scots then blew their hunting horns and made such a noise that, a contemporary account reports, *"It seemed as if all the devils in hell had come thither to join in the noise, so that those of the English who had never before heard such were much frightened."* In spite of this, the bishop did advance further, but seeing how well the Scots had chosen and fortified their camp, he decided not to risk an attack and led his hastily gathered and ill-disciplined army back to Newcastle. Another tactical mistake on the English side.

The Scots then returned across the border, where the body of the Earl of Douglas was buried in Melrose Abbey, and the ransom paid by the English to release the imprisoned Hotspur funded the building of Polnoon Castle for his captor, Sir John Montgomery. Sir Ralph Percy and several other knights were allowed to remain in Northumberland until their wounds healed; they were then required to either give themselves up to the Scots or to pay ransoms.

The spot where the Earl of Douglas fell is marked by a pillar no more than 5ft high, mounted on a circular pedestal of rough stone. Percy's Cross – named after the impetuous loser rather than the pyrrhic victor – stands in a small plantation of fir trees less than a mile north-west of the village. The battle is further remembered in two ballads, one English and one Scottish, each with a different narrative according to its patriotic perspective!

BELSAY HALL AND CASTLE (English Heritage)

The estate at Belsay, considered to be one of the most remarkable in Northumberland, consists of a 14th century tower house (the castle) and an excellent example of a neoclassical house (the hall), built in the 19th century. These two buildings are surrounded by more than 30 acres of landscaped parkland and linked by a wonderful sunken garden.

Belsay was owned by the Middleton family from the 13th century, although by the time the estate was inherited by Sir Charles, Sixth Baronet of Belsay Castle, in 1799, his surname had been changed to Monck to satisfy the conditions of his maternal grandfather's will. The baronet was married in 1804, and, for their honeymoon, he and his wife took a continental tour that included a period of time in Greece. Sir Charles was greatly impressed by Greek architecture, and on his return, he began to build a magnificent Greek-influenced mansion in the grounds of his estate. Some historians believe that he was helped in the design by the young John Dobson, although this has never been conclusively proved.

The exterior of the hall has an air of pure symmetrical simplicity with its square shape and magnificent columns, beautifully constructed from attractive honey-coloured sandstone flecked with small pieces of iron ore. The stone was dressed with a precision that was hitherto unknown; Monck had introduced a new style of masonry that would massively increase the reputation of Northumbrian stone workers countrywide.

Sir Charles made good use of the area of the estate that sourced the sandstone by creating the unusual Quarry Garden. Winding paths lead through the rich planting in this man-made ravine to connect the hall and castle. The ha-ha wall with its arched deer shelters beneath presents an open view across to the lake beside Crag Wood to the south. At the north-west tip of the lake sits the Rhododendron Garden, where many mid-19th/early 20th century specimens still survive, and the Crag Plantation has a wonderful circular walk amid a natural woodland of outstanding mature trees, just waiting to be explored. A magnolia terrace and winter garden with heathers further enhance the aspect of this unusual estate.

The castle, as it is known, is an extended 14th century tower house. A building of this power and strength was essential for safety at that time to protect from the frequent raids mounted by the Scots. After James I came to the throne, his 'Pacification of the Borders' led to more settled times, and the Middleton family added the hall and another wing to the building in the early 1600s, but the castle still serves as a stark reminder of those violent, turbulent days.

After World War II, Belsay was abandoned by the Middleton family, but its future remains assured in the care of English Heritage.

Belsay Hall in Spring

Belsay Castle

Biddlestone Chapel

BIDDLESTONE

North-west of Rothbury and a couple of miles to the west of Netherton is the tiny village of Biddlestone. At the west end of the village, a track leads to Biddlestone Chapel. About 250 yards along this trail are the Biddle Stones from which the place takes its name. There are two of these ancient route markers: one is an uncut block; the other has a socket cut into its upper surface and was once the base of a medieval cross.

Further up the track, in a forest clearing, stands the isolated chapel, formerly the private place of worship of the Selby family, owners of the now-demolished Biddlestone Hall for more than 600 years. The first recorded member of the clan is Sir Walter de Selby of Seghill, who was granted the land by Edward I when it was forfeited by one William Vissard. The Selbys firmly established themselves at Biddlestone, where they built the hall in around 1796 and maintained a Catholic chaplaincy at their own expense. The chapel was built in 1820 on the remains of a medieval pele tower constructed in the 14th century as a solitary defensive building. Its interior, which underwent extensive alterations towards the end of the 19th century, is furnished in the Gothic Revival style with an east-facing stained-glass window that dates from 1862; the glass in the gallery depicts the heraldry of the Selby family.

Biddlestone Chapel is an absolute delight, set in a quiet clearing in a dense pine wood on the slopes of the rolling Cheviot Hills. No wonder, then, that Sir Walter Scott is believed to have used Biddlestone Hall and its setting as inspiration for Osbaldistone Hall in his novel *Rob Roy*; the hero of the title, the outlawed chief of the McGregor clan, is even said to have taken refuge in a cave near Biddlestone Burn.

The Biddlestones

BOTHAL

Bothal is situated on a spur of land with the River Wansbeck on one side and the steep-sided Bothal Burn on the other. Originally an Anglo-Saxon settlement, in 1095 it was given by the king to Guy de Balliol; the local baron then passed on to his daughter's husband, William Bertram, who is believed to have built a hall house on the site.

The castle that can be seen today, standing in a commanding position on private land, dates back to 1343 when Sir Robert Bertram obtained a licence from Edward III to "kernellate" (sic) his manse at Bothal. Sir Robert was one of the 12 knights honoured by the king for their part in the victory at the Battle of Neville's Cross, near Durham, in 1346. His castle must have been an imposing sight with its high walls and towers, supported by huge buttresses, circling the whole of the hilltop and covering almost half an acre. Extra security was provided by the proximity of the river and a moat on the east and west sides.

In 1410, the castle was held by Sir John Bartram while under siege for four days by the army of Sir Robert Ogle; it had been bequeathed to Sir Robert by his father and he sought to take it for himself. He finally succeeded in his quest by mounting a heavy assault on the defences. The castle was later badly damaged during the Civil War in the mid 17th century, and no restoration was carried out for almost two centuries.

In the 1830s, the impressive gatehouse was restored for use as a private home, with further extensions added towards the turn of the century. Three murder holes can be seen in the roof vault of the gatehouse passage; these would have allowed the pouring of molten lead, boiling oil or hot sand onto any attacker who gained control of the archway. On the merlons of the battlements, there were two worn stone statues, undoubtedly placed there to confuse or frighten the enemy, just like the ones at Alnwick Castle. And to the sides of the merlons, there are round holes in which would have been secured the supports for the swing shutters to cover the embrasures: *"Archers could throw up one of these shutters and take a shot at the enemy, and before fire could be returned, the shutter fell again."* It has been discovered that some of the mason's marks at Bothal are the same as those engraved on the barbican at Prudhoe Castle.

Not far from the castle is the attractive little St Andrew's Church, the main fabric of which dates from the 13th and 14th centuries, although major restoration was carried out in the late 1800s – *"In harmony with its ancient character,"* as we are told by Northumbrian historian William Weaver Tomlinson.

Reputedly hidden in the riverside woods are the ruins of the small Lady Chapel. Built by the first Lord Ogle in the middle of the 15th century, it had a stone roof supported by huge wooden roof trusses. On the western side of the ruin is the Jubilee Well, which dates from 1887 and was built to commemorate the first 50 years of Queen Victoria's reign. On the eastern side is the Lady's Well, close to which there was once a board relating the activities of Bertram of Bothal, who is reputed to have seduced one of the daughters of the Umfraville family, powerful landowners in North Tynedale and Redesdale. The Umfravilles are said to have taken a dim view of Bertram's dalliance, and he was shot dead by one of the girl's nine brothers. His dying wish was to be buried at the spot where they usually met, on the bank of the sparkling burn.

Bothal Castle

Brinkburn Priory and Hall

BRINKBURN PRIORY (English Heritage)

The graceful, romantic ruins of Brinkburn Priory are set deep in a wooded dene, on a site almost encircled by the River Coquet. It was founded by William Bartram, the First Baron of Mitford, for the Augustinian canons between 1130 and 1135, during the final years of the reign of Henry I. Tradition has it that the priory was destroyed by Scottish raiders, who, unable to find it in the thick woods, were guided to the very spot by the sounds of the monastery bells ringing, somewhat prematurely, in thanks for supposedly being saved. Consequently, the bells were thrown into a deep part of the river that has become known as the 'Bell Pool'. A local legend says that if the bells are discovered, great treasures will follow, and in 1834 a bell was found buried in the hill opposite the pool, but unfortunately, it was broken while being removed from the ground. Strangely, a little later, an Edwardian copper jug was dug up near the church – it contained almost 300 gold coins dating from the reigns of Edward III, Richard II and Henry IV.

However, there seems to be no doubt that the monks of Brinkburn lived in poverty, and although the priory acquired lands in Northumberland and Durham over the years, it was never considered particularly wealthy. Interestingly, the six small columns supporting the pulpit are fashioned from Frosterley marble, only found in County Durham. Other than this, little of the priory's early history is recorded, although it is known to have survived some difficult times; as late as 1419, it was raided and robbed. It's possible that the priory's poverty was not only due to Scottish raiders: in the mid-1500s, the prior was dismissed with a pension of £11 for some shady misdeed or other, and some of the monks were found guilty of "venerating a girdle of St Peter".

On its dissolution in 1536, the estates were valued at £68 19s 1d, and possession was granted to John Dudley, who later became Duke of Northumberland. Soon after, it passed into the hands of that well-known border family the Fenwicks, who, in the late 16th century, built a manor house on the ruins of the priory buildings and adjacent to the church.

Brinkburn Priory, however, did not fall into disuse, and religious services continued to be held, but there was little income to carry out repairs, and in the 17th century the roof collapsed. It remained in this condition until 1858 when extensive sympathetic restoration was carried out by Thomas Austin at the expense of the Cadogan family. Services continued to be held at Brinkburn, and the church was retained in a fair state of repair till the end of the 16th century. By 1602, it was reported to be in a poor condition of decay, and by 1700 the roof had fallen in and regular services were abandoned. In the 1750s, Thomas Sharp, Archdeacon of Northumberland, initiated repairs to the ruin, but, despite much support for the project, work was called off following a dispute between owner William Fenwick and the Vicar of Felton.

Around a century later, the Cadogan family, then owners of Brinkburn, revived plans for the restoration of the church, and work began in 1858. The roof was completed in the space of a year, and the stained-glass windows had been inserted by 1864; the church, however, was not furnished for another four years. Brinkburn Priory today is a sympathetic 19th century restoration of the medieval original.

Nearby on the estate is Gawen's Field, named after Gawen Redhead, a notorious Reiver outlawed at the time of Elizabeth I. He avoided capture by living here in the hollow of a massive oak tree in which, it is said, half a dozen young cattle could easily take shelter!

Brinkburn Priory, Altar

Cambo model village

Carter Bar, English – Scottish Border

CAMBO

The village of Cambo was built in the 1740s by Sir Walter Blackett, the prosperous owner of Wallington Hall. The existing buildings were demolished and rebuilt in the symmetrical Georgian style, large expanses of woodland were planted, and attractive terraced gardens were carefully incorporated to create a model village for the estate. With a name that means 'camp, or fort, on the hill', Cambo commands excellent views along the vale of the Wansbeck and over the wilder, more remote country towards Rothbury and Elsdon. The centre of the village has a striking granite drinking fountain in the form of a fierce-looking dolphin, which bears a Latin inscription that translates as "Not unmindful of future generations". At one time, Sir Walter had a group of Italian plasterers staying in the village while they worked on the interior of Wallington Hall, transforming its plain and austere interior, it was said, into an aspect of "almost Roman elegance".

The village's post office is a 16th century bastle house, which, unusually, appears to have been built to three storeys; traces of the first-floor entrance can still be seen, despite the staircase having been removed. Former coaching inn The Two Queens – which retains its two-sided sign depicting Elizabeth I looking towards England, and Mary, Queen of Scots, facing Scotland – was closed in the mid-1800s when Sir Walter Trevelyan, first president of the temperance movement United Kingdom Alliance for the Suppression of the Traffic in all Intoxicating Liquors, inherited the estate. The Church of the Holy Trinity, built in 1842, stands on a high ridge to the north of the village. Several interesting old English grave covers, removed from the site of the former chapel, are preserved in its tower and vestry. The interior also contains monuments to the Trevelyan family.

Among those who received their early schooling in Cambo was celebrated landscape architect Lancelot 'Capability' Brown. Headmaster William Robson nicknamed the 'Rhyming School Master', compiled a register that contained the names of all 776 pupils from his 24 years at the school and was written in verse!

CARTER BAR

Carter Bar, where the A68 crosses the Cheviot Hills into Scotland, has always been one of the main routes between the two countries. Packhorses were the main mode of transport for goods well into the late 1700s, and it was here that a stone placed between two high posts marked the route of the old Carriers' Way over the hilltop.

It was graphically described by writer John Murray in his 1863 guide *Murray's Handbook for Travellers in Durham and Northumberland*:

"This lofty ridge is crossed at all times of the year by Carriers from Scotland, who supply the country with groceries and other luxuries. In winter, the cold is frightful. An old carrier, being asked whether he did not find it very cold on the top, replied, "Hoot, man, Hoot; the very Deil himsel' wadne bide there half an hour unless he was tethered."

Ruins of Cartington Castle

CARTINGTON CASTLE

The picturesque ruins of Cartington Castle can be found on the Thropton to Callaly road, just to the north-west of Rothbury. The castle was mentioned in a list of border forts drawn up in 1416, although permission to crenellate the structure was not granted until 1441. A contemporary account in the mid-16th century described it as a *"fortress of two strong towers and other strong houses in good repair"*. It is said that Margaret Tudor, Queen of Scots and widow of James IV, and her baby daughter rested here on the night of 16th November 1515, during her journey from Harbottle.

The first recorded owner of the castle was Ralph Fitz Main, the king's forester in Northumberland; it then passed into the ownership of the Cartingtons, then the Radcliffes and finally the Widdringtons. It was Sir Edward Widdrington who raised a cavalry to support Charles I at the battle of Marston Moor in 1644, and whose daughter, Lady Charlton of Hesleyside, founded an almshouse here for four poor Roman Catholic widows.

Cartington Castle suffered siege by parliamentary forces during the English Civil War and, in spite of stern resistance, was overrun. Over the next few years, it was plundered for building materials. The castle was partly restored in the late 16th and early 17th centuries, but it had fallen into ruin by the early 19th century. Additional repairs and restoration were undertaken in 1887, but, according to some architectural historians, these only served to further obscure the origin of the early fabric of the building.

ELSDON

The village of Elsdon is in a strategic position to guard the two main routes that crossed the border from Scotland and descended into Redesdale. One of these followed the line of what is now the A68 from Carter Bar, the other followed the old Roman road of Dere Street from High Rochester to the camp at Chew Green.

Redesdale had been sparsely populated right from the earliest times, so it's perhaps no surprise that it was considered a lawlessness area where justice and administration were left to those who did live there. As far back as Norman times, the two main areas of the region were declared the 'Liberties' of Redesdale and Tynedale, meaning they were so remote from the centre of power that they were allowed a degree of independence; however, there seemed to be confusion as to the actual ownership of these border provinces.

Towards the end of the 12th century, Tynedale belonged to Scotland and Redesdale to England, and it was not until 1296, when Edward I declared war on Scotland, that both provinces came under the English crown. This, however, proved not to be a permanent arrangement, and when Robert the Bruce crossed the border in 1314, Tynedale immediately acknowledged allegiance to him. Much of the lawlessness in the area was a direct result of the continuous border warfare between the 14th and 16th centuries. This resulted in a large increase in the number of fortifications on both sides of the border – many pele towers and bastle houses sprung up close to farms and churches to offer some form of protection.

At the northern end of Elsdon, there are two strange Mote Hills, said to have been used by both the Romans and the Saxons as a place for dispensing justice. The name could possibly have come from the Saxon 'moot', or meeting place, but is more likely to be derived from the 'motte' of the Normans; there is evidence to suggest there was a Norman castle here in 1080. The Umfraville family were the lords of Redesdale from the early 12th century, although they

The Pinfold with St Cuthbert's Church across village the green, Elsdon

The Mote Hill, Elsdon

moved their main seat of defence at some time between 1160 and 1174 when Harbottle Castle was built. In 1287, Edward I granted a charter for a weekly market to be held in Elsdon, and by 1297 Gilbert de Umfraville was charging market tolls in both Elsdon and Harbottle, as well as extracting a 'crossing tax' from Scots who ventured over the border.

Elsdon's most prominent feature is its large village green. This was used as a meeting place for the Redesdale clans, and as a cattle-holding area – a circular pinfold, or cattle pound, for stray animals can still be seen in the southern corner. The cattle drovers' route from Scotland passed through Elsdon, and the village would have made a convenient stopping point en route where taxes and various dues could be collected. Elsdon's status as the 'capital' of Redesdale remained long after the main defence was transferred to Harbottle, but since the end of the 18th century, this distinction has belonged to Otterburn.

Standing on the village green is St Cuthbert's Church, so named because the site is reputed to have been a resting place for the saint's body during its epic journey from Lindisfarne to Durham. The current St Cuthbert's appears to have been extensively rebuilt in the 14th century on the site of an 11th century church that would have served the whole of Redesdale. It has an excellent rustic bellcote that is characteristic of the 1700s, and the aisles of the nave and transept are remarkably narrow, with half barrel-vaulted ceilings extending directly from the outside walls above the arcades. Preserved in the north aisle of the church is a Roman tombstone that was found near the remains of the fort at High Rochester.

In 1810, a mass grave was uncovered against the north wall of the church, containing around 1,200 closely packed skeletons of young and middle-aged men – it is believed that this was the last resting place of the English soldiers who died at the Battle of Otterburn in 1388. It is interesting to note that similar discoveries were made at Southdean, the closest Scottish church to Otterburn, suggesting that the Scots carried their dead across the border for burial.

To the north of the church is a fine example of a fortified tower house, once used as a vicarage, which dates from around the 14th century, although there is evidence to suggest it was extensively rebuilt two centuries later in the Scottish style. On its outer walls are the crests and shields of the families associated with the house: the Umfravilles, the Percys and the Howards. This handsome building, which is in private ownership, is said to have a wonderful spiral staircase leading up to the battlements on the roof.

St Cuthbert's Church with Bastle House in the background, Elsdon

HARBOTTLE CASTLE

The Castle overlooking Harbottle Village

One of the most famous of all the border fortresses, Harbottle Castle stands on a steep hill overlooking the River Coquet on one side and the village of Harbottle on the other. The mound on which the keep stands is thought to be a mote hill used by the ancient Britons. Its name derives from two Anglo-Saxon words – 'here', meaning 'army', and 'botl', meaning 'dwelling' – and indeed the Saxons had a stronghold here, under the control of Myldred, son of Ackman.

In 1076, the site came into the hands of Robert de Umfraville, who took on the defence of Redesdale on behalf of William the Conqueror. It was for one of Robert's descendants, Odinel de Umfraville, that Henry II had the present castle built to protect this wild area, over which the lords of Harbottle held power. In 1174, not long after the castle was constructed, it was overrun by William the Lion, King of Scots, during his destructive but reckless raid into Northumbria, which ended in disaster when he was captured at Alnwick.

After this, the castle was so strongly fortified that in 1296 the Scots, under William Wallace, had to give up their siege after two days; it eventually fell to Robert the Bruce in 1318. The castle was so badly damaged by the Scottish wars that, in 1336, Gilbert de Umfraville had to seek permission to transfer its many prisoners to his castle at Prudhoe. The Umfraville family died out in the 15th century, and in about 1436 the castle passed into the hands of the Talbot (from the French Taillebois) family; for a long period, it became the residence of the Warden of the Middle Marches.

Perhaps Harbottle's greatest historical connection was a domestic affair: in 1515, Henry VIII arranged for his sister, Margaret Tudor, to use it as a temporary residence. Previously married to James IV, young Margaret had become a widow when the Scottish king was killed at the Battle of Flodden in 1513. Now a Dowager Queen, she had remarried – to Archibald Douglas, Sixth Earl of Angus – and, with a baby due, she was granted use of the castle by Henry.

Just two years after the Battle of Flodden, patriotic feelings were still running high, however, and so Sir Thomas Dacre, Lord Warden of the Marches, forbade all persons of Scottish descent from entering the Queen's chamber unless they were under close guard and, allegedly, wearing clean underpants. Forty-eight hours after she entered the castle, Margaret gave birth to a daughter, Margaret, Lady Douglas, who became Countess of Lennox, mother of Lord Darnley and grandmother of James I of England. When the baby was only two days old, Margaret left for Carrington, near Rothbury. Her presence at Harbottle was declared, *"Uneaseful and costly, by the occasion of the far carriage of everything"*.

After the Union of the Crowns, it was no longer necessary to defend the area and it quickly fell into disrepair. It was the Widdringtons who finally removed most of the stone for the construction of their manor house.

A strange incident that occurred in the 16th century is related by John Murray in his *Handbook for Travellers in Durham and Northumberland:* A vindictive and violent young Scotsman, George Meldrum, in Edinburgh was in disagreement with a judge, Lord Durie. He ambushed him, stole his money, dressed him in old women's clothes, tied him over a horse and took him to Harbottle castle where he was thrown into the dungeon under the watchful eye of the warden, George Ratcliffe. The unfortunate judge was at his wits end, certain that he had become a prisoner of witchcraft and sorcery. After eight days Meldrum returned and Lord Durie was released, no doubt much affected by his dreadful ordeal.

High above the castle on the hillside stands the *Drake Stone,* a huge block of fell sandstone that is traditionally associated with the Druids. This was their Draag Stone and sick children would be passed over this block to speed their recovery.

KIRKHARLE

The tiny village of Kirkharle is pleasantly situated about two miles from Cambo, not far from Wallington. It is, perhaps, best known as the birthplace of the celebrated landscape gardener and architect, Lancelot "Capability" Brown. He earned his nickname through always telling his prospective clients that their country estate had great "capability" for improvement. He was born in 1716, the son of William Brown, a farm labourer, and his wife, Ursula, who was a maid in nearby Kirkharle Hall. He was baptised in the village church where his grandparents, Dorothy and Lancelot, were buried. He had two older sisters and two older brothers: and another sister, three years his junior. Sadly, his father passed away in 1720 while the children were still young.

Capability Brown attended the village school in nearby Cambo until he was sixteen years old. He left school in 1732 and went into an apprenticeship at Kirkharle Hall, the home of Sir William and Lady Anne Lorraine, where he demonstrated his early talent by playing a part in laying out Kirkharle Park. He went on to work for a Mr Robert Shafto who lived in Benwell Tower, in Newcastle.

In 1739 he left his native Northumberland to work for Sir Richard Grenville at Wooten and from there for Sir Richard's son-in-law, Lord Cobham, and his vast estate at Stowe.

It was while he was working there, he met and married a local girl, Bridget Wayet an apothecary's daughter from Lincolnshire. Happily married, and, indeed, quite well off, they had seven children, sadly three of these did not live past infancy, and poor William died when only a few months old. However, Bridget, Lancelot jnr, William, and John all grew to adulthood

His gardening talents were becoming more recognised and more in demand; he was taking bigger and more challenging commissions. He worked on Blenheim Palace and in 1764 was appointed Head Gardener at Hampton Court. As he acquired more and more experience his practice expanded rapidly, and he was even more in demand. In 1767 he bought the manor of Fenstanton, in Huntingdonshire and eventually by 1770 he was appointed High Sheriff of Huntingdon and Cambridgeshire.

Capability Brown died in 1783 after a lifetime of dedication to, as he called it, "being a place maker" - it was not until the 19th century that the term "landscape gardener" was used.

St Wilfrid's Church, Kirkharle

The Lorraine Monument

His vast knowledge and undeniable talent have rightfully earned him recognition as a particular genius of English Garden design.

Between the church and the remains of Kirkharle Hall is the enigmatic Loraine Monument. The present stone was erected in 1728 by Sir William Loraine, 2nd Baronet (the first employer of 'Capability' Brown), replacing an earlier monument to 'This Unfortunate Gentleman' which had fallen into disrepair." The monument, marks the place where Robert Loraine was "barbarously murdered" by a band of Scottish raiders in 1483. Loraine was a Border Officer responsible for prosecuting Scottish Reivers in northern England. But, in common with most shady characters in those days, he was also a Reiver. He kept horses, weapons and men ready to pursue Scottish raiders by the Hot Trod. This was a time of bitter feud, and Loraine must have really upset some of his adversaries; he was killed by 'a party of men' who 'lay in ambush' between his home and St Wilfrid's Church. The circumstances of his death were particularly bloodthirsty. Robert's descendant, Sir Lambton Loraine, 11th Baronet, told the gory details to a journalist from the New York Times in 1874. The latter wrote that the killers *'were determined to strike terror into the hearts of his associates by the brutality of the murder. Robert's body was cut up 'into collops' (Slices - the usual gruesome punishment metered in those days) and placed in the saddlebags of his horse, which was then set loose to wander home'.*

Kirkley Hall

Cup and Ring markings - Lordenshaws

KIRKLEY HALL

Kirkley Hall is set in over 190 acres of garden and parkland and has a beautiful Victorian walled garden with a colourful abundance of plants and shrubs to interest the visitor. It dates from the 17th century and is a Grade II listed building. The estate is sited on the banks of the River Blyth about three miles north of Ponteland.

The Ogles originally had a house on this site – their history dates back to before the Norman Conquest. It was here that John Copeland brought his captive, King David of Scotland, after the battle of Neville's Cross on 17th October 1346.

The Ogles were proud of their Northumbrian heritage as one of the great "Riding Families" and a story relates of how, in 1538, a Milburn protested that the Dacres were as of as good blood as the Ogles, upon which four of the Ogles viciously attacked and killed him.

In 1832 the Reverend John Saville Ogle engaged the well-known architect, Ignatius Bonomi to carry out extensive reconstruction. In 1922 the estate was sold to a wealthy local ship-owner, Sir William Noble. Unfortunately, the house was almost destroyed by a fire in 1928 and again was largely rebuilt, although, this time on reduced scale to a design by Newcastle Architects by Cackett, Burns Dick and MacKellar.

The county council took ownership of the estate in 1948, which led to the opening of the Kirkley Hall Farm Institute – which would become the Northumberland College of Agriculture – three years later; the site currently serves as a land studies campus for Northumberland College.

The Hall is also now a popular and elegant venue for weddings and conferences and many other events. There is also a popular and excellent zoological garden on the estate which has over a 100 species of animals and a vast range of birds where visitors can meet the keepers and learn about the animals; and enjoy other activities, play areas, forest trails and a tea room.

LORDENSHAWS

Lordenshaws Hillfort and rock carvings are easily accessible from the Simonside car park to the west of Rothbury, along the B6342. A short walk along the marked footpath leads to the crest of the hill and the main rocky outcrops with carvings. Most of the markings in Northumberland are found on outcrops and may have been carved to indicate routeways, territory boundaries, or even 'significant' places for its ancient, nomadic people. This site affords excellent views in every direction, and there are many items of great interest in close proximity to each other. A little exploration reveals several Bronze Age cairns, an enclosure around the top of the hill that is believed to date from the Iron Age, and many excellent examples of cup and ring markings, along with several deeply fluted stones.

According to the historian William Weaver Tomlinson, Lordenshaw Farm was a popular place for beekeepers to leave their hives during July and August so that the bees could extract particularly delicious honey from the local heather blossom. This was such a popular spot among apiarists, he reported, that there could be as many as a thousand hives in the area at any one time.

Mitford Castle

MITFORD CASTLE

Although Mitford Castle is believed to have been built as an earth-and-timber motte and bailey by Sir John de Mitford in the late 11th century, the earliest surviving record of its existence dates from 1138. In this record, the owner is named as William Bertram, the son of the Norman knight Sir Richard Bertram and Sybilla de Mitford, Sir John's sole daughter and heiress. Sybilla is said to have been bequeathed to Sir Richard by none other than William the Conqueror himself.

Now little more than a romantic ruin on its high knoll above the River Wansbeck, Mitford Castle suffered greatly from the ravages of hostile armies in the three centuries following its construction. In 1215, it was overrun by the Flemish troops of King John, and a year later it was put under siege by Alexander II of Scotland. From 1316 to 1317, it was occupied by the rebellious Sir Gilbert de Middleton and his army of bandits, from whom it was forcibly seized by Ralph FitzRobert, First Baron Greystoke. Then, in 1318, the castle was captured and badly damaged by the forces of Alexander III of Scotland, and over the course of the next five years, it was totally destroyed.

The estate was owned by the Bartram family until 1264 when it was forfeited to the crown by Roger Bartram, who had taken arms against Henry III at Northampton. During the reign of Edward II, the barony of Mitford was granted to Aymer de Valence, Second Earl of Pembroke, who was involved in the capture of the Scottish patriot William Wallace in 1305. In 1324, the earl held a tournament to mark his third marriage, but he was killed just three days into the celebrations, leaving his wife a maiden, a bride and a widow all at once. It is said that for several generations afterwards a father never saw his son, "He was always snatched by the hand of death before the birth of his issue".

Three centuries later, during the reign of Charles II, the castle and manor became the property of the Mitford family once more, by way of a royal grant.

Several members of the Mitford family have distinguished themselves in literature, among them the author and dramatist Mary Russell Mitford, who, in her 1852 book Recollections of a Literary Life, described the River Wansbeck as *"a wild, daring stream, now almost girdling, as a moat, the massive ruins of Mitford Castle"*.

Arguably the most eccentric of this literary clan was the notorious 'Drunken Jack Mitford', who was born at the castle and served with distinction in the Navy under Admirals Samuel Hood and Horatio Nelson until drink-fuelled bad behaviour led to him being cashiered. Thanks to his abilities as a writer, however, Drunken Jack landed a commission to create a semi-auto-biographical novel titled *Johnny Newcome in the Navy*, for which his publisher paid him a shilling a day until it was completed. He spent 43 days writing the book, during which he resided in a nearby field, washing his clothes in a pond and living on a daily ration of tuppence-worth of bread and cheese; he spent the rest of his income on gin. Mitford finished the book, but he died a miserable and drunken wreck of a man in St Giles' workhouse in London.

MORPETH

Morpeth Chantry and Bagpipe Museum

The bustling market town of Morpeth grew up beside a crossing point of the River Wansbeck. The major buildings such as the castle and the parish church are on the southern bank, while the town itself is situated on the north side of the river. The three main streets leading from the Market Place – Bridge Street, Newgate Street and Oldgate – still form the centre, although the town has grown considerably over the centuries.

The name Morpeth is generally believed to be derived from the words 'moor path', although some have suggested the alternative 'murder path' (from 'mord', the Anglo-Saxon word for murder), recalling the numerous raids by the warring Scots.

There is evidence of two castles at Morpeth. The remains of one can be seen at Haw (or Ha') Hill in Carlisle Park, immediately to the south of the river; this flat-topped mound or 'motte' was the site of a motte-and-bailey castle, believed to have been constructed in the late 11th century by William de Merlay, the First Baron of Morpeth. The earliest documented reference to the castle tells of its capture in 1095 by William Rufus, William the Conqueror's third son and his successor as King of England. In 1216, it was burned and destroyed by King John in his quest to break the power of the Northern Barons, although a local story claims the people of Morpeth set fire to the castle themselves to stop it falling into his hands. This would seem to be quite likely as the king was bitterly hated by the Northumbrians for the vicious attacks he ordered upon their county.

The existing castle, situated on the southern side of the Postern Burn, is thought to have been built between the late-13th and early-14th century by the de Merlays. When the last of the family's male heirs died, the castle passed into the possession of Lord Greystoke, then of the Dacres, and then of the Howards, one of whom was made the First Earl of Carlisle, which also carries the courtesy title of Lord Morpeth.

After the Battle of Flodden, Margaret Tudor, the widowed queen of James IV married the Earl of Angus. She gave birth to a daughter at Harbottle castle in Coquetdale, but found it too primitive and remote and so made the journey to Morpeth where she stayed for some time with the baby. This little girl, Margaret Douglas, grew up to become the mother of Henry Stuart, Lord Darnley, who married Mary, Queen of Scots in July 1565.

In 1644, Morpeth Castle itself was described as "a ruinous hole, not tenable by nature far less by art", most likely the result of attacks by the Marquess of Montrose and his army during the Civil War.

Standing on a small mound known as the Kirkhill, not far away from the castle, is the Parish Church of St Mary the Virgin. There is evidence of a building here prior to the construction of the present church, which dates from the 14th century. The current structure remains largely original, although it is thought that the south porch was added in the 1500s. An interesting building in the churchyard serves as a reminder of Morpeth's more macabre history: almost two centuries ago, notorious body-snatchers eagerly carried out their gory business in the area, so a watch-house was built to allow members of the 'watch committee' to guard the graves.

MID NORTHUMBERLAND

Telford Bridge over the Wansbeck and St George's Church

Morpeth Courthouse

At the bottom of the hill stands the imposing Court House, which effectively acted as an awesome gateway to the prison. Dating from the 1820s, it was designed by John Dobson and is said to have been inspired by the Gothic architecture of Conwy and Beaumaris Castles in north Wales. It was convenient to have the courthouse and jail linked so that, following their trial, the guilty could be moved in to start their sentence with speed and efficiency; the vaulted passageway originally led into the prison courtyard. The prison – built to an octagonal design for ease of operation – was eventually demolished in 1891, following the removal of its inmates to another prison in Newcastle.

Completed in 1831, the Telford Bridge – or New Bridge – across the River Wansbeck bears an inscription that credits the Scottish civil engineer Thomas Telford, although some historians believe he was working to the designs of Northumberland architect John Dobson. Among its interesting features are the original cast-iron lamps with their beautiful scrolled ironwork.

Morpeth Old Bridge was originally built in the 13th century, but so steep and narrow was the structure that it was found to be extremely dangerous for loaded wagons; in the early 1800s, there was a dreadful accident here when two mail coaches crashed through the stone balustrades of the bridge and plunged into the river with their horses and passengers. As a result of this, the present iron footbridge was built in 1869, with the remains of the fabric of the former bridge incorporated into its construction.

Standing at the end of the old bridge is Morpeth Chantry, formerly All Saints Chantry, founded by Richard of Morpeth in the late 1200s. The Grade I listed building has undergone much reconstruction and alteration over the years that wasn't always in keeping with its history, but extensive work carried out in the 1980s restored it to a more sympathetic aspect.

One of Morpeth's most striking and unusual buildings is the Clock Tower that stands in the Market Place. The tower dates back from the early 17th century when it was used as the jail for the town and surrounding areas, and there are many gruesome stories of the unsavoury characters imprisoned there; murderers, robbers and violent thieves were among the inmates. It would appear that the building had no great strength: it was not unusual for an angry mob to break down the walls to get at the prisoners. Morpeth is steeped in history. It is the only market town in the county that has a mayor and one of only two towns in the county where the Boundaries of the Borough are traditionally ridden by a group of horsemen led by the mayor – the only other being Berwick-upon-Tweed.

In September 2018, a statue of Emily Wilding Davison – sculpted by well-known Durham artist Ray Lonsdale – was unveiled in Carlisle Park to commemorate a hundred years since the vote was granted to women over the age of 30. The suffragette died after running out in front of the king's horse during the Epsom Derby on 4th June 1913; her purpose was unclear, but she was trampled and died from her injuries four days later. The incident was captured on three different newsreel cameras, and recent studies of the images have suggested that the 40-year-old campaigner was not, as was assumed, attempting to pull down Anmer, the royal racehorse, but in fact reaching up to attach a banner to its bridle.

Emily Davison by Ray Lonsdale, Carlisle Park

Davison was born in London in 1872, but moved back to the family home in Longhorsley, near Morpeth, after the death of her father in 1893. She later joined the women's suffrage movement, signing up for Emmeline Pankhurst's Women's Social and Political Union in 1906. Three years later, she gave up her job as a teacher and went to work full-time for the suffragette movement. Davison was a tenacious campaigner who resorted to radical methods to drive her message home: she was arrested several times for offences ranging from causing a public disturbance to burning post boxes, and she spent quite a number of short periods in jail. In 1909, she was sentenced to a month's hard labour in Manchester's Strangeways prison after throwing rocks at the carriage of the chancellor of the exchequer, David Lloyd George. In aid of her cause, Davison was arrested on 10 occasions, went on seven hunger strikes, and was force-fed 49 times.

The verdict of the inquest into her death was that *"Miss Emily Wilding Davison died of fracture of the base of the skull, caused by being accidentally knocked down by a horse through wilfully rushing on to the racecourse on Epsom Downs during the progress of the race for the Derby; death was due to misadventure"*. Her funeral on 14th June 1913 was organised by the WSPU. A total of 5,000 suffragettes and their supporters joined the procession, and an estimated 50,000 people lined the route through London; her coffin was then brought by train to the family plot in Morpeth.

Morpeth Castle

Northumberlandia

NORTHUMBERLANDIA

Northumberlandia is an impressive land sculpture in the form of a reclining female, located near Cramlington, Northumberland. More than 100ft high and over a quarter of a mile long, the huge figure was constructed from 1.5 million tonnes of earth from the neighbouring Shotton surface mine and is beautifully set in a public park almost 50 acres in area.

The idea for 'the Lady of the North' originated in 2004 when the Blagdon Estate and the Banks Group applied for permission to develop an opencast site for the extraction of coal and fire clay (for bricks) on farmland near the new town of Cramlington.

The consortium recognised that in addition to its primary purpose – recovering huge amounts of coal for UK energy generation and providing local employment – the operation provided an excellent opportunity to create a spectacular work of art that would provide a legacy for future generations. After consulting Charles Jencks, the architectural historian and 'godfather of postmodernism' whose unequalled skill as a landform and earthworks architect was world-renowned, Northumberlandia was born.

Northumberlandia is a 'restoration first' project, meaning that the local community benefits immediately from the mining operations. In this instance, the Blagdon Estate donated a piece of adjacent land to provide a new landscape for the community to enjoy while the mine is still operational. The cost of the project – £3 million – has been privately funded by the Banks Group and the Blagdon Estate.

Work commenced in 2010, starting with the transportation of carefully selected rock, clay and soil from Shotton to the neighbouring part of the estate that would become Northumberlandia's home. Here, the major landscaping was done, followed by 'hydroseeding' – a quick and effective method of planting seed by spraying – which began to transform the sculpture into a living landscape. To this, Northumberlandia's face, paths and viewing platforms – all in hard stone – were added. The project was completed in 2012.

The concept behind the Lady of the North is that rather than become a formal landscape garden, the landform will be allowed to develop naturally with minimal interference; consequently, it will change with the seasons and continue to mature over many generations to come. Northumberlandia is owned by the Land Trust and managed in partnership with the Northumberland Wildlife Trust.

OTTERBURN TOWER

Otterburn Tower is now a comfortable country-house hotel, but it stands on the site of an old pele tower that played a part in the Battle of Otterburn in 1388. On their way back from Newcastle to the border, the Scottish forces attempted to take the tower at dawn, but the pele was so strong and well-defended – in what was at the time difficult, marshy terrain – that their enthusiasm and stamina was soon exhausted, and they retreated to their nearby overnight camp. Many of the Scottish leaders were in favour of continuing their journey home over the border, but they were overruled by the Earl of Douglas, who insisted the tower must be taken. However, before the next morning, Harry Hotspur and his men arrived at Otterburn and the importance of taking the tower was forgotten.

At the beginning of the 1400s, the tower passed into the possession of Sir Robert de Umfraville and thereafter into the ownership of the Halls, a large and powerful Redesdale clan who were feared and hated on both sides of the border. The family became infamous after an act of betrayal and treachery against Percival (aka Parcy) Reed, the Keeper of Redesdale. Reed's appointment as Keeper had upset the Halls, who felt that they were the more important clan and therefore one of their own should have held the position; his enthusiasm for the post had also earned him the hatred of the Croser family in Liddesdale. The Halls had the motive to rid themselves of Reed, and the Crosers certainly had the means, so soon a plan began to unfold.

The opportunity presented itself when Reed invited the Halls to go hunting with him. They eagerly accepted and invited him to their home to discuss the next day's sport over a meal. Reed failed to notice that the bread on the supper table was upside down – a traditional sign of impending doom. While he was enjoying their hospitality, the Halls sabotaged Reed's weapons, dampening the powder in his gun and ensuring his sword would be jammed in its scabbard – an old ploy was to pour in raw egg, which would dry and make it impossible to draw the blade.

The next day, when the hunting party stopped to feed and water their horses on the lonely fells, the Halls pointed out a group of approaching Crosers. Parcy Reed felt it was his duty to tackle them, but he was unable to draw his sword, and his gun blew up when he fired it – he stood no chance. According to the traditional Border ballad The Death of Parcy Reed, *"They fell upon him all at once, and mangled him most cruellie…"* In fact, he was so badly mangled that his remains were taken home wrapped in a sheet.

For many years after the incident, the Halls were viewed with doubt and suspicion. If they asked for hospitality and were lucky enough to receive it, they would find the cheese placed upside down on the table – a sign of disrespect. Such was the Borderers' fear and horror of betrayal.

Otterburn Tower

MID NORTHUMBERLAND

Robin of Pegswood Sculpture

Ponteland Pele Tower

ROBIN OF PEGSWOOD

Affectionally known as "Robin of Pegswood", but officially entitled "Fire", this 39ft high bronze and steel statue by local sculptor Tom Maley graces the roundabout on the A197 near Bothal. His design has a bronze figure standing near the top of a stainless-steel girder. The girder rises from the ground at an angle and its tip is curved into the shape of a bow with the bronze figure firing a symbolic "arrow-shovel". The miner is depicted symbolically firing his shovel against an imaginary coalface, to be interpreted as a permanent reminder of the strength and determination of the miners who worked in some of the most challenging conditions, sometimes in coal seams as narrow as 18 inches.

Commissioned by landowner Bothal Estates – a subsidiary of Welbeck Estates – at a cost of between £60,000 and £70,000, the work is a permanent tribute to local miners who braved arduous conditions, sometimes in seams as narrow as 18in, to provide fuel for the nation. Welbeck Estates also owns part of Sherwood Forest, home of the legendary Robin Hood, hence the nickname for the sculpture.

PONTELAND TOWER

Ponteland is a pleasant historic village that marks a crossing point on the River Pont. It was here, in 1244, that a truce was called between the English and the Scots, and an agreement – the Treaty of Newcastle – was signed by King Henry III of England and King Alexander II of Scotland to determine a definitive border between the two countries. This did not, however, prevent the Scots from burning the castle and the town in 1388 on their way back from Newcastle to the Battle of Otterburn, or Sir Haymon de Alphel, the Lord of the Manor and valiant defender of the castle, being taken prisoner.

The position of Ponteland on the well-trampled path taken by warring Scottish and English armies dictated that the local vicar would be safer with a pele tower, such as the one at Corbridge. The tower here was attached to the vicarage, making for easy access in times of danger. The earliest documented evidence of its existence dates back to 1415, though it is said that its construction involved the conversion of a 13th century building. In 1555 and 1584, Acts of Parliament were passed that stated all fortresses, castles and towers within 20 miles of the border should be put into good order. All surrounding ground was to be enclosed by a perimeter of wooden palisades or pales; eventually, these defences were replaced by oak trees bound together and covered with earth – this made them difficult, if not impossible, to burn.

The border tower house was built of stone and mortar, with massive walls up to 10ft thick. The only entrance was by a special double door at ground level; the inner door would possibly be made of iron grating, while the outer door would be of thick oak, reinforced with iron. The bottom floor was used for storage, and the two top floors would be living accommodation, reached by a narrow and easily defendable stone staircase. At the very top of the building, there would be a beacon to summon help in the event of an attack.

The pele tower was simple and strong: it was impervious to fire and, in fact, anything short of artillery bombardment. Once the defenders were locked safely inside with the doors firmly closed, they could easily hold out against forces with superior numbers. A determined force could, of course, eventually overcome this defence, either by breaking in through the roof or by 'scumfishing' – the practice of breaking down the door and then filling the bottom floor with material that could be easily burnt to smoke out the defenders.

Armstrong Cross, Rothbury

All Saints Church, Rothbury

ROTHBURY

The attractive market town of Rothbury is regarded as the 'capital' of Coquetdale. It feels like an ancient town and indeed it dates from Celtic times – the name is said to be derived from the Celtic, *Rhath*, 'a cleared spot' - in those days a dense and almost impenetrable forest covered the area. A large camp, known as *Old Rothbury*, is complete with defensive ramparts and occupies a hillside to the north of the town.

The Saxons had a settlement here called *Rodeberia* – the richly carved shaft of a Saxon cross has been used as the pedestal for the font in All Saints Church. The fragment of cross dates from 800Ad but the bowl is marked with the date 1604.

The movement by the Normans into the area seems to have been very gradual, and its history remains strangely quiet until the time of King John when the manor was granted to Robert Fitzroger of Warkworth. With this position came an exceptionally wide range of powers frequently misused by Fitzroger – he put on trial and punished anyone he took a dislike to, wrongdoer or otherwise. He also deprived the townsfolk of their free grazing rights by incorporating the land into his own estates. The town's market charter was granted by King John himself in 1201 when he visited.

It is said that Fitzroger built Rothbury Castle, although not one stone remains in its original position which was on the site of what is now the town's cemetery. Although the castle does not seem to have played an important part in the defence of the town, its stones found their way into many of its buildings, providing a vital link in its social development.

The position of Rothbury meant that its tough inhabitants were often subject to Scottish raids and in between these the smouldering rivalries of the local border families would ensure that peace was not maintained. When all else failed the Forest Laws were there to be broken. Even the men of the church seem to have shared this general spirit of unruly behaviour and at least one rector was heavily fined for breaking Forest Laws.

In the 16th century Rothbury Church was one of the fourteen visited by Bernard Gilpin, *The Apostle of the North*, during his incumbency at Houghton-le-Spring, near Durham City.

It was at a time when ill-feeling between the rival Coquetdale families ran high and even the sanctity of the church counted for nothing when rival kinsmen met within its walls.

On one occasion when Gilpin was in the pulpit there was a clash of swords and a heated exchange of words - two men quickly advanced towards each other, but Gilpin quickly came between them and restored the peace. He then returned to the pulpit and preached a special sermon condemning the use of violence in church, and he secured a promise from the protagonists that there would be no further scenes of disorder while he was in Rothbury. Although he could not end the old deadly feuds, he was held in high enough regard for there to be no further violent breach of the peace while he was in the vicinity. Gilpin was greatly respected and had great influence over the unruly people of the area. On another occasion a glove was left pinned up in the church as a challenge to anyone who would take it – Gilpin took the glove and put it inside his gown – no challenge was accepted. As an example of another incident, a thief is said to have stolen some of his horses but when he found out who they belonged to instantly returned them, saying that he was frightened that "the Devil would have seized him directly knowing them to be Mr. Gilpin's horses!" The 22ft high Armstrong Cross, in the centre of the town, was worked from sandstone from Cragend Quarry on the Cragside Estate. The south side is decorated with an endless Celtic knotwork pattern, similar to that on the original Rothbury Cross which now forms the base of the font in the parish church. The inscription reads, *"This monument was erected in the year 1902, on the site of the ancient market cross, by the inhabitants of Rothbury and other friends, in admiration and grateful remembrance of the long and useful lives of William George Baron Armstrong of Cragside, 1810-1900, and of Margaret his wife 1807 – 1893"*.

Gilpin 500 Anniversary Plaque, Rothbury Church

The skyline ruin of Rothley Castle

ROTHLEY CASTLE (National Trust)

Rothley Castle was built as a romantic ruin in the mid-18th century by Sir Walter Calverley Blackett, owner of the Wallington Estate. This eye-catching, Grade-II listed folly stands dramatically against the skyline at Rothley Crags, which was once the site of a vast deer park. Designed by the architect Daniel Garrett in the Gothic style, Rothley Castle has a two-storey central tower with two lower towers linked by screen walls with cruciform arrow slits spaced at regular intervals. The end towers are thought to have housed large statues, and there is evidence to suggest that the crenellated walls were once decorated with the griffins' heads that now stand on the east lawn of Wallington Hall.

This "castle" must be the only one in the country that was purpose-built as a ruin for the visual pleasure of a wealthy country estate owner.

The folly is now in the care of the National Trust.

Shittleheugh Bastle House

SHITTLEHEUGH BASTLE

The ruins of Shittleheugh Bastle can be found two miles to the north of Otterburn in Redesdale. It stands almost at the crossroads of two ancient routeways – one led through Hopehead and on to Holystone, the other followed the Durtrees Burn – and no doubt these tracks would have been well used when the building was constructed, possibly between the mid-16th and the mid-17th centuries.

From the remains, it is obvious that Shittleheugh was a substantial building: the walls, built from huge blocks of stone, are more than 4ft thick and remain as high as 6ft tall; presumably the gable ends are still at full height. The bastle would have been built to two storeys and measured 30 to 40ft long and more than 20ft wide. As was usual with a building of this type, the emphasis was very much on defence. The door frame is formed from seven massive stones, and the windows are, in effect, loopholes with their jambs angled at about 45 degrees, which would have given a wider line of fire when under attack. Unusually, access to the upper floor appears to have been by a small staircase in a porch, rather than by the traditional wooden ladder; also, the door to the ground floor is situated in one of the long sides – a feature only used on the 'more elaborate' bastles.

Shittleheugh is an inspiring place with mesmerising panoramic views – especially towards those enigmatic Scottish hills. Standing on the fellside, it is easy to imagine the stealthy approach of a band of reivers, the sound of their advance barely discernible when mingled with the wind whispering through the ancient remains of this atmospheric building.

WALLINGTON ESTATE
(National Trust)

The Wallington estate is recorded as having been first owned by the Strother family during the reign of Henry IV, before being inherited by the notorious Fenwick clan in the late 15th century. A well-known family of Border Reivers, the Fenwicks were Jacobites during the 1600s; one of their number, Sir John Fenwick, was beheaded in London in 1697 for his part in the plot to assassinate William III.

In 1688, faced by financial difficulties, the Fenwicks were forced to sell Wallington to Sir William Blackett, the son of a wealthy businessman and politician from Newcastle. Sir William largely demolished the Fenwicks' Tudor house and castle, incorporating the cellars and foundations into a new, larger house of a simple square design around an open courtyard. The Blacketts always regarded offering great hospitality as

Great Spotted Woodpecker

highly important, and his son – also Sir William – carried on the rowdy tradition; it is said that he kept half a dozen strong lads in employment for the express purpose of carrying drunken guests up to bed.

This Sir William died in 1728, leaving no direct heir, but he bequeathed Wallington to his nephew Walter Calverley on the condition he married William's illegitimate daughter, Elizabeth Ord, and changed his name to Blackett. Walter Calverley Blackett, as he was now known, became the new owner. He was a most remarkable man; popular and respected, he showed great aptitude for business and demonstrated excellent taste. Walter inherited a baronetcy from his father and sat in seven Parliaments; he was also Mayor of Newcastle five times.

Under Walter's ownership, the Wallington Estate was completely transformed: roads and bridges were constructed; a clock tower and courtyard were added; woods were planted; and the park and gardens were laid out. His estate workers were also well looked after – he built them modern stone cottages and rebuilt nearby Cambo, a model village, for their comfort. The infant River Wansbeck was dammed to widen it, and a graceful bridge, designed by James Paine at a cost of £300, was built over the river to provide a more memorable approach to the house.

Sir Walter loved follies, and there are several on the estate: the Arches, seen from the East Wood, were placed there because, as one of the main entrances, they were too narrow for a coach and horses to be driven through; Codger Fort, above Rothley Lakes, housed cannon that *Sir Walter* would fire to summon friends to hunting or fishing; and Rothley Castle was built as a ruin to enhance the skyline.

The formal East Wood, with its beautiful ponds and buildings, was laid out by Sir Walter in the

East Side of Wallington with Griffins heads

Wallington Gardens, Spring

1730s. The Walled Garden is perhaps one of the most charming aspects of Wallington. It is about half a mile from the house, a pleasant walk along the formal paths, passing rhododendrons, the Portico House and the Garden Pond leads to the Neptune Gate and into the garden, a relaxing, fragrant corner with quiet paths and sheltered seating where the shrubs and flowers can be enjoyed in tranquillity. The conservatory, heavy with the scent of heliotrope and full of fuchsias and exotic climbing plants, was added in 1908 by Sir George Otto Trevelyan, perhaps to revive the 19th century tradition at Wallington of growing rare plants under glass. The collection of lead figures on the wall opposite the conservatory make an unusual and interesting feature.

The West Wood covers roughly the same area as the East Wood, but is less formal, wilder and quieter. It has three ponds, one of which was originally for boating, and the secluded footpaths eventually link with Paine's Bridge over the sparkling Wansbeck.

Sir Walter Blackett also turned the house into a magnificent showpiece that attracted much praise and admiration. Making great improvements to his grandfather's original design, he had the roof heightened, introduced a pediment, enlarged the main rooms, had a wonderful staircase built, and added a fine front entrance. Today, the house is remarkable for its craftsmanship in wood, marble and plaster; it is a treasure store of beautiful period furniture, ceramics, and rococo plasterwork – and, of course, there is the famous Wallington collection of doll's houses.

Sir Walter had no surviving children, and when he died in 1777 he left Wallington to his sister Julia's son, Sir John Trevelyan of Nettlecombe in Somerset. Among Sir John's friends were the eminent potter Josiah Wedgwood and Thomas Bewick, the talented wood engraver.

In addition to Wallington, Sir John owned a large estate of some 20,000 acres in Somerset, but eventually, he found owning two such large estates a burden, so he passed the Northumbrian estate to his eldest son, also John, when he married in 1791.

It was in 1853 that the last major development took place at Wallington when Sir Walter Calverley Trevelyan and his wife Lady Pauline employed John Dobson of Newcastle to install a roof over the hitherto open courtyard of the house to create a central hall. They commissioned William Bell Scott to decorate it with eight murals depicting finely detailed scenes from Northumbrian history, and the Scottish artist demonstrated great care with the work: all the portraits were based on real people, and he borrowed a chasuble for the St Cuthbert scene and an authentic piece of wall for the Hadrian's Wall picture. Some of the plants on the pillars were painted by Lady Trevelyan, while others are by John Ruskin – the balustrade is copied from an illustration in his treatise on Venetian art and architecture, *The Stones of Venice*.

On the lawn guarding the east side of the house are four stone griffins' heads that once supported the coat of arms of the City of London above Bishopsgate and were brought north by Sir Walter Blackett in one of his ships.

There is an interesting entry about Wallington in *Murray's Handbook for Travellers in Durham and Northumberland* that reads: *"Tickets admitting five persons may be obtained at Mr Handyside's shop at Cambo. The pictures are only shown on Saturdays from 12 to 4. No gratuities are permitted to be given to the servants – Sir Walter Calverley Trevelyan, Bart."*

In 1942, the Wallington estate was handed into the care of the National Trust by then-owner Sir Charles Trevelyan.

Winter's Gibbet and the base of Steng Cross

WINTER'S GIBBET

Winter's Gibbet stands beside the lonely moorland road just under three miles to the south-east of Elsdon. It is said to be the last gibbet used in England and serves as a grim reminder of a gruesome murder. Near to this remote spot, known as the Raw, are the remains of Haws Pele, the home of an old woman called Margaret Crozier, who ran a small shop here selling drapery and other goods. William Winter, a dangerous and unsavoury travelling man, together with two female tinker accomplices, Jane and Eleanor Clark, broke into old Mrs. Crozier's house on 29th August 1791, brutally murdered her and stole her goods. They mistakenly believed her to be wealthy because she had shown great kindness to the travellers earlier in the week.

The day before the murder the three ruffians had rested and dined in a sheepfold overlooking Haws Pele. They had been seen by a young shepherd boy who had taken particular notice of the unusual pattern and number of nails in Winter's boots; and he had noticed the large gulley, or butcher's knife, that Winter had used to divide the food. On his evidence, they were arrested and brought to justice.

The three of them were condemned to death and hanged at the West Gate in Newcastle. Afterwards, Winter's body was brought to Steng Cross by wagon and hung in chains in sight of the spot where the murder took place.

Long after the dreadful object had rotted away, one piece at a time, on the Gibbet the place was still regarded with awe and superstition. Local superstition says that toothache can be cured by rubbing the affected tooth with a splinter from the gibbet.

But much more chilling is the belief that anyone passing the gibbet at night may still hear the eerie sound of chains……rattling in the wind……………

The large block of stone at the foot of the Gibbet is the base of the Saxon Steng Cross which marked the highest point on this ancient drove road down which Scottish cattle were driven to the English markets; near to this point was a smithy where the cattle were shod before reaching the metalled English roads; interestingly several cattle shoes have been found near this spot.

EXPLORING NORTHUMBERLAND HISTORY:
NORTH NORTHUMBERLAND

Iron Age hill fort remains, Alnham

St Michael's and All Angels Church, Alnham

Saxon cross socket, Alnham

ALNHAM

The tiny village of Alnham – or Yalham as the locals call it – stands just about at the confluence of the two streams that form the source of the River Aln.

The Church of St Michael and All Angels was built on the site of a small Roman camp and is said to date from around 1200, although some architectural historians believe it may be much older. Close to the entrance to the beautiful walled churchyard are three stones carved with 'socket' holes for use as bases for crosses. These are thought to originate from Saxon times, meaning they would pre-date the present church.

When St Michael's underwent extensive restoration in 1870, it had been in ruinous condition for a great many years. More recently, in 2018, another major restoration project was completed; as a result, facilities were upgraded, and the church – now a Grade I-listed building – was removed from Historic England's Heritage at Risk register.

Inside the church is a font bearing the date 1664 and carved with heraldic symbols that appear to refer to the house of Percy. Nearby, carved into one of the tomb slabs set into the floor of the nave, is the curious epitaph to a farmer who was drowned while crossing the ford at Kelso. Another unusual feature is a fireplace in the north wall of the nave – probably there to provide physical warmth while the congregation sought comfort of the spiritual kind!

The building to the west of the church is now a private home but was once the vicarage, strongly fortified in the style of those at Corbridge and Etal. Just across the road, a few hundred yards to the south-east of St Michael's, are the turf-covered ruins of Alnham Castle, which suffered greatly at the time of the Border raids. It was mentioned in a Border warden's report in 1405, but in 1532 the Earl of Northumberland reported to Henry VIII that *"the Scots had burned the place with all the corn, hay, and household stuff in the said building, and a woman"*.

On nearby Castle Hill are the remains of an Iron Age hillfort. It is quite small, only about a hundred yards in diameter, and of a typical oval shape with triple banks and ditches. The old smugglers' route, The Salters' Road, passes close by the site.

NORTH NORTHUMBERLAND

ALNWICK

Alnwick, the ducal town of Northumberland is a busy, bustling place – it was once a major halt for coaches on the Great North Road – and has succeeded in retaining its old-world charm and atmosphere. It is a place that has borne the full brunt of Border turbulence: the remnants of its mighty city walls and the magnificent castle bear testimony to its important position during these troubled times. In days gone by Alnwick learnt from bitter experience that London was a long way away and the Northumberland town would have to defend itself. Throughout history, its loyalty has been mainly to the Percies – the Earls and Dukes of Northumberland who have made the castle their home – but there have been times when the policies of these traditional leaders have not always agreed with those of the Crown.

From the time that the first market was held, in 1291, Alnwick has been a great commercial centre for its surrounding villages and farms. The traditional fair has been revived and is held for a week at the end of June when everyone in the town seems to take part in this colourful and entertaining event. There were several small but important industries established in Alnwick during the 16th century. Leather was an important by-product of livestock farming, and there were several small tanneries in the town. Textiles were also important; near Walkergate, there was a fulling mill and a dye house. Ropemaking was a development of the textile trade, and a small business that manufactured fishing tackle was established – this is still in the town today.

The town is dominated by the castle, although there are many interesting buildings scattered throughout.

The Hotspur Gate, Alnwick

Hotspur Tower

The narrow medieval archway of Hotspur Tower divides the main street of Bondgate into Bondgate Without and Bondgate Within (though the latter is now simply known as Bondgate) and was built by the Second Earl of Northumberland in the 1430s as part of the town's fortifications. It is the only one of Alnwick's four original gates to have survived: although they can no longer be seen, the other three – Clayport, Pottergate and Bailiffgate – still have streets named after them. Hotspur Tower was once the county jail, but in more recent times it has served a variety of purposes, including its use as a practice space for the town band. Its name commemorates one of the heroes of the county, the charismatic 'Harry Hotspur' – Sir Henry Percy, father of the Second Earl – whose great deeds in battle have been immortalised over the years, not least in the imagination of William Shakespeare.

Percy Tenantry Column

This monument – a fluted Doric column standing 83ft high and topped by the Percy lion with its tail extended stiffly, with four lions *couchant* at its base – stands just opposite the old railway station. It was erected in 1816 by grateful tenants, it is said, as a mark of respect after Sir Hugh Percy, the Second Duke of Northumberland, had reduced their rents. There are several unkind stories about what happened, including the suggestion that before the reduction, the duke had doubled and quadrupled rents Another relates that Percy subsequently increased the rents again, suggesting that if the tenants could afford to waste their money on a monument, they could easily afford to pay him more. For this reason, the column has earned the nickname 'The Farmers' Folly'.

The truth is that it was erected by a group of men who were known as the Percy Tenantry Volunteers, founded by the Duke during the Napoleonic Wars to deal with any invasion attempt by the French on the Northumberland Coast. The inscription on the monument reads:

"To Hugh, Duke of Northumberland KG. This column is erected, dedicated, and inscribed by a grateful and united tenantry. Anno Domini MDCCCXVI."

The column is also inscribed on each side with the Percy family motto: *"Esperance en Dieu"*.

Ye Old Cross Inn

In Narrowgate is an 18th century coaching inn that would have served travellers on the Great North Road. Ye Old Cross Inn – or The Dirty Bottles as it is now named – comes with a popular local legend attached: it is said that almost 200 years ago the innkeeper suffered a massive heart attack and died after touching a collection of dirty bottles sitting in its small bow window. The story goes that a friend then tried to help by completing the task of dressing the window, but he too died. As a result, the innkeeper's widow became convinced that anyone who touched the bottles would be struck dead. Superstition has it that this dreadful curse is still at work and no one has tried to clean the window or attempted to move these eerie cobweb-covered objects ever since.

St Michael's Church

The parish church of St Michael, which stands on the junction of Bailiffgate and Canongate, was mentioned as early as 1147, although the present building, perpendicular in style, dates mainly from the 14th and 15th centuries. Parts of the nave may be of Norman origin, and there is some typical zig-zag carving in the chancel porch. The chancel and aisles were rebuilt in the 15th century at the time of the Fifth Earl of Northumberland; the capitals display some unusual carvings, and the floor is paved with old gravestones. At the south-east corner of the aisle is a strange stair-turret leading to a priest's chamber. It is quite possible this turret was also used as a lookout post – it faces towards Heiferlaw pele tower, around two miles to the north of the town, where a beacon would have been lit to warn of any raids by the Scots.

Inside St Michael's is an early 14th century Flemish chest,

Percy Tenantry Monument

The Dirty Bottles Curse, Alnwick

thought to be one of the finest examples of its kind in an English church; it is carved with a hunting scene and patterns depicting foliage and dragons. Outside the porch are a series of gravestone slabs with unusual emblems including a hammer and anvil, bows, a hunting horn and a mason's square.

The Lion Bridge

Designed by John Adam in the Gothic Revival style and built in 1773, the Lion Bridge carries the old Great North Road out of the town over the River Aln. A striking construction, it has battlemented parapets with a cast-lead Percy lion proudly displayed on its eastern side. An old local tale tells of a young boy who, not long after the bridge had opened, was swinging on the outstretched tail of the lion when it broke, and he fell into the river. The mischievous lad was pulled out of the water, but sadly he had sustained a serious head injury. Unfortunately, he never recovered and, sadly, became known as the town idiot, for the rest of his life.

The Lion Bridge features prominently in JMW Turner's wonderful painting of "Alnwick Castle" in moonlight, attributed to him around 1829.

Alnwick Castle

Alnwick Castle has been the home of the Percy family since the early 14th century *and the time of Edward II.*

It is widely believed that there has been a fortification on this site since the 11th century when Gilbert de Tesson (also recorded as Tyson) – standard-bearer to William the Conqueror – was granted the lands for his loyal service. His 'castle' was probably a simple construction of earthen ramparts and wooden palisades, although there are no remains to prove this.

Shortly after de Tesson took possession of his lands, several events took place that would lead to his downfall. In 1093, Scottish king Malcolm III was killed just outside of Alnwick by an army of knights led by Robert de Mowbray, Earl of Northumbria, and the Scots were forced back northwards. Within two years, de Mowbray's influence was

NORTH NORTHUMBERLAND

St Michael's Church, Nave & Altar, Alnwick

Lion Bridge and Alnwick Castle

so great that de Tesson joined his rebellion against William Rufus; this was defeated, however, and a now grossly out-of-favour de Tesson was forced to give up his possessions at Alnwick. Ownership was awarded to Ivo de Vesci, a Norman knight, and it was he who laid the foundations for a motte-and-bailey castle.

Following de Vesci's death around 1133, the castle passed into the hands of Eustace FitzJohn, the husband of de Vesci's daughter Beatrix. In his role as Baron of Alnwick, FitzJohn played an enthusiastic part in the political disagreements of the day, taking sides with the Scots' King David I against England's King Stephen. David took possession of the castle at Alnwick in 1136, but, following the Scot's defeat two years later, FitzJohn gained Stephen's favour once more and ownership was returned to him. He settled down and completed the construction of the castle, much as it is today, by the time he died in 1157.

FitzJohn's descendants, however, did not enjoy a time of peace; the castle was attacked twice in the late 12th century by William the Lion, King of the Scots. Both raids were repelled by FitzJohn's son, William de Vesci, who even managed to capture the Scottish monarch in a clever ambush and held him to ransom. When de Vesci died in 1184, the estate went to his son Eustace.

In 1199, King John ascended to the English throne, and over the next few years fighting and feuding again dominated the North. Eustace de Vesci fought against the king in an unsuccessful rebellion by the Northern barons and ended up losing Alnwick. He made peace with the monarch and regained his estate, only to lose it once more in another revolt, and this time the castle was burnt in revenge. De Vesci continued his part in the rebellion against King John and was eventually killed in 1216 during the siege of Barnard Castle on the southern boundary of County Durham.

Peace reigned for a while, but in the 1260s Eustace's grandson, John de Vesci rebelled – in the family tradition – against the English ruler, this time Henry III. He was defeated and yet again the castle was lost. But after being heavily fined, de Vesci was pardoned by the king and regained his estate.

Following the death of John de Vesci in 1288, Alnwick became the property of his brother William. The castle was still at the centre of the continuing conflict between England and Scotland, successfully holding out against a savage attack by William Wallace and his army during their rampage into England in 1297.

Shortly after this, William de Vesci died, leaving no legitimate heir; he did, however, have an illegitimate son, William de Vesci of Kildare, so Alnwick Castle and its estate were placed into the care of Antony Bek, the Prince Bishop of Durham, to be held in trust for the young man.

It is generally believed that while he should have been looking after the interests of young de Vesci of Kildare, the reputedly shady and unscrupulous Bek sold the estate to Lord Henry Percy in 1309. Although many historians view this sale as grossly dishonest, an equal number firmly believe the bishop did nothing wrong. The truth is shrouded in mystery, and, of course, the lack of documentation prevents a definitive verdict. This is further compounded by the fact that William de Vesci of Kildare was killed at the Battle of Bannockburn. His heirs laid claim to Alnwick, but they were paid a substantial cash settlement instead. Lord Henry Percy paid

Alnwick Castle Gatehouse

Harry Hotspur Statue

just over £4,500 for Alnwick. It was quite a financial risk - his existing annual income was £900 and the Alnwick estate would bring in £475 per year and although this would increase his income by half as much again, he still had to borrow £2,600 to pay Bishop Bek.

Alnwick became the Percy stronghold. Ransom money received for Scottish prisoners captured at the Battle of Neville's Cross, near Durham, in 1346 provided the finances for the building of the two towers to guard the inner bailey. It was after the coronation of Richard II in 1377, when he made Lord Henry the First Earl of Northumberland, that the Percies came to full prominence as prodigious warriors and clever statesmen.

The First Earl and his son – the redoubtable but likeable Harry Hotspur – rebuilt the keep, the postern gate and the Constable's Tower. Their duties included keeping Scottish reivers under control as Wardens of the Eastern Marches, as well as protecting the unstable border area. The Percies' traditional enemies were the Scottish Douglases, and perhaps the most memorable confrontation between the two families came in 1388 with the Battle of Otterburn. Although the Scots claimed victory, it came at a price: James, Second Earl of Douglas, was killed. Harry Hotspur and his brother Ralph were taken prisoner but were subsequently ransomed.

The Percies took their revenge at the Battle of Homildon Hill, near Wooler, in 1402.

It was after this battle that the relationship between the Percies and King Henry IV, who they had helped to gain the throne, became strained when the king upset them by disputing ransom payments and holding back money that was rightfully theirs. The Percies entered into a scheme with English nobleman Sir Edmund Mortimer, backed by Welsh patriot Owain Glyndwr, to remove the king. They even allied with the old enemy, the Scots, and in July 1403 the rebel forces marched on Shrewsbury in Shropshire. However, they were intercepted by the king's army, and in the ensuing battle Harry Hotspur was killed and his uncle Thomas, First Earl of Worcester – along with Archibald, Fourth Earl of Douglas – was captured. It was a dreadful disaster that was to haunt the Percy family for years.

Harry Hotspur's father, the First Earl, was pardoned by the king within six months, but in 1405 he revolted again, this time helped by kinsman Richard Scrope, Archbishop of York. However, their aborted attempt at an uprising on Shipton Moor, just outside York, was unsuccessful and resulted in the arrest and execution of the archbishop. The earl escaped and remained at large until 1408 when he suffered a resounding defeat and was killed at the Battle of Bramham Moor, near Tadcaster. As an example, to all traitors, his severed head was mounted on the middle tower of London Bridge, and his body was quartered, pickled and sent to the 'four corners' of his northern lands.

In 1414, Harry Hotspur's son was restored to his grandfather's estates as the Second Earl of Northumberland by his close friend, Henry V. During the Wars of the Roses, the Percies supported the Lancastrian cause, and two of the earls were killed – the Third Earl was died in 1461 at Towton in what is believed to have been the bloodiest battle on English soil, claiming the lives of more than 28,000 men.

The Fourth Earl took part in the famous Battle of Bosworth Field in 1485 – he started out on the side of Richard III, but when things began to go wrong he changed sides to that of Henry VII, for whom he eventually became a collector of taxes. It was while he was performing this unpopular task near Thirsk in Yorkshire that he was attacked by a mob and killed. Early in the following century, his son – the Fifth Earl – was entrusted with the job of providing a protective escort for Princess Margaret, Henry VII's daughter, on her journey north to marry James IV of Scotland.

Henry Percy, Sixth Earl of Northumberland, was betrothed to Anne Boleyn when Cardinal Wolsey intervened and she was stolen from him to become the second wife of Henry VIII. Percy eventually married Mary Talbot, daughter of the Fourth Earl of Shrewsbury, but died without leaving any direct heir. The estate, therefore, passed to a nephew, and thereafter the family fortunes took an unfortunate downturn.

The Seventh Earl, Thomas Percy, was executed in 1572 for his involvement in the Rising of the North – an unsuccessful attempt by Catholics in northern England to place Mary, Queen of Scots on the throne; his successor, also suspected of being a keen supporter of the Scottish monarch, died in the Tower of London in 1585 under suspicious circumstances.

The Ninth Earl was involved in the ill-fated Gunpowder Plot in 1605 and was fined £20,000 and made to swear that he would not return north again. However, in the first English Civil War of 1642-6, his son Algernon – the 10th Earl – would take the side of the Parliamentarians against King Charles I. In 1670, on the death of the 11th Earl, Joceline Percy, the estate passed to his sole heiress, Lady Elizabeth, who later married the 6th Duke of Somerset.

When, in 1750, the latest heiress – another Lady Elizabeth Percy – married the Yorkshire squire Sir Hugh Smithson, her husband took the family name and became Hugh Percy, First Duke of Northumberland. By the 1760s, the great Percy strongholds of Alnwick and Warkworth were in ruins, so the duke decided to transform the former from a fortress into a residence, securing the services of architects James Paine and Robert Adam to carry out the task.

Many of Adam's Gothic Revival-style additions to Alnwick Castle were replaced less than a century later, however, by Algernon Percy, the Fourth Duke. Much influenced by Italianate styles, in 1854 he commissioned English architect Anthony Salvin to carry out a large-scale restoration at the cost of around a quarter of a million pounds. The duke planned to restore the medieval style of the exterior, while the interior would be made into a comfortable palazzo-style residence. A pleasing balance was achieved, successfully converting the castle into the magnificent and stately mansion it is today.

Alnwick Castle is an absolute treasure house, with paintings by many famous artists including Titian, van Dyck and Canaletto; a collection of beautifully crafted classical furniture; and a superb collection of Meissen china and other historical heirlooms.

The castle, which remains the home of the Duke and Duchess of Northumberland, has undoubtedly earned its affectionate title of the 'Windsor of The North'.

Hulne Park

Hulne Park is, in effect, the castle estate and comprises more than 2,500 acres of landscaped parkland bisected by the River Aln to the north-west of Alnwick. It is surrounded by a wall more than nine miles long and was partly laid out by the famous landscape gardener Lancelot 'Capability' Brown. In and around the park are several sites of great interest:

Malcolm's Cross is said to mark the spot where, in 1093, King Malcolm III of Scotland was killed along with his son during the siege of Alnwick Castle. An older cross stood on this site until 1774 when it was replaced with the existing monument by the then Duchess of Northumberland.

St Leonard's Hospital is now in ruins, but this medieval building was founded sometime between 1193 and 1216 by Eustace de Vesci in memory of the fallen King Malcolm III. The small hospital had fallen into ruin well before the Restoration and was only rediscovered during ploughing in 1845.

Hulne Priory is sited on a spur above the River Aln, about three miles upstream from Alnwick. It was founded around 1240 by William de Vesci for the Order of Carmelites (or White Friars) and is believed to be the best example of its kind in the country. The massive curtain wall that was necessary at that time for any religious settlement in or near the borders is almost complete, only missing its battlements and defensive turrets. The tower was added in 1488 by the Fourth Earl as a refuge for the friars in the event of Scottish raids.

Connected to the tower by a bridge is a summer house built for Hugh Percy, First Duke of Northumberland, in around 1777. The church nearby is almost square in shape and, like others of this order, has no aisles. Interestingly, there is a tau cross – a pre-Christian symbol based on the Greek letter tau – carved onto a gravestone set

Malcolm's Cross

St Leonards Hospital remains

into the floor. The sacristy has a piscine and a recess with a shelf, a flue and a bowl, and is thought to have been used for the preparation of wafers for Holy Communion. The large yew tree growing in the cloister garth is said to have been recorded as far back as the late 1500s.

Brizlee Tower

Standing almost 90ft high, Brizlee Tower is dramatically sited on a hilltop about a mile south of the priory, across an ornamental footbridge. This striking tower – built in the Gothic Revival style by Robert Adam in 1781 and topped with a huge cast-iron fire basket – was part of the First Duke's restorations and would allow him to survey all his estates, from south of Alnwick to almost as far as the Scottish border.

Hulne Priory

Brizlee Tower Hulne Park

Fountains – Alnwick Garden

The Poison Garden, the front gate warning …Alnwick Garden

The Alnwick Garden

The original walled gardens of Alnwick Castle were first laid out in the middle of the 18th century, but in a little more than 100 years they enjoyed the reputation of being some of the finest in Europe. It was, perhaps, the first four Dukes of Northumberland who were mostly responsible for their development – all were well-known as men of science, and it was a love of nature that encouraged them to build an excellent collection of exotic botanical specimens. During Victorian times, walking and relaxing in country house gardens became a popular pastime for the general public. The improved transport system brought about by the introduction of the railways allowed people to travel further afield, and this, coupled with an enthusiasm for the development of better horticultural techniques, led to the gardens at Alnwick being opened for the enjoyment of the public; this continued until well into the 20th century.

World War II saw the gardens put to a different use, again to the benefit of the public: this time, they were part of the 'Dig for Victory' campaign – a successful drive to encourage the British people to grow their own food during such times of hardship.

The difficult economic climate that followed the war saw the gardens fall into disuse, and eventually, they were put to use as a tree nursery. Then, in 1995, the present Duke of Northumberland inherited the estate from his elder brother, and the duchess – a keen gardener for many years – saw potential in the old walled garden.

A combination of great vision, technical innovation and horticultural advances led to the development of a garden that is now seen as a milestone in the history of Alnwick Castle.

Its centrepiece is the Grand Cascade, a magnificent water feature with more than 7,000 gallons a minute tumbling over a series of stepped waterfalls, and, at regular intervals, a spectacular display of jets shooting almost 100 gallons of water 20ft into the air every second; a state-of-the-art computer system synchronises and controls the 120 jets that provide these breathtaking performances.

However, the Alnwick Garden is not only about water: a system of interlinking pathways, open spaces and hidden corners lead the visitor through a range of sensory experiences that make this one of the most imaginative public gardens ever created.

The Alnwick Garden

Flodden Field Monument and Battlefield

BATTLE OF FLODDEN

Flodden was a disastrous and unnecessary confrontation for Scotland. James IV, the Scottish king, was married to the sister of England's King Henry VIII and a treaty of friendship existed between the two countries. However, early in the summer of 1513, James made the fatal decision to invade England. The official reason was to avenge the death of Robert Ker, Warden of the Scottish Middle March, who was killed in a brawl involving one of the Herons of Ford Castle. However, some historians have suggested that it was because the Scottish monarch was unhappy with the dowry he received on his marriage to Margaret Tudor, although another well-known legend tells how the Queen of France sent James her glove and a ring, accompanied by a love letter urging him to attack England under the agreement of the 'Auld Alliance', to ease the military pressure on her own country.

James gathered an army – estimated to have contained between 60,000 and 100,000 men – and marched south, crossing the Tweed at Coldstream and destroying the castles of Wark, Norham and Etal before making Ford Castle his headquarters. The English needed a little time to respond and it was 18 days after James crossing the Border that an army was finally gathered. While James dallied at Ford Castle – occupied, it is said, with the charms of the attractive Lady Heron – some of his army left, reducing his number of men to around 30,000. Meanwhile, Thomas Howard, the Earl of Surrey, commanding on behalf of Henry VIII, had landed archers at Tynemouth and marched them to meet the forces of Northumberland, led by the Percies, and the army of Thomas Ruthall, Bishop of Durham, commanded by Sir William Bulmer.

In all, Surrey assembled an army of some 30,000 men just west of Alnwick before marching to Wooler Haugh, where he made his headquarters. James had taken up a strong position on Flodden Hill. Surrey divided his forces, sending the vanguard and artillery, under the command of his son Edmund Howard, to cross the River Till by Twizel Bridge, circling the Scottish position. Surrey himself took the infantry and cavalry across the fords between Etal and Ford. James remained in position on his hilltop. Only when the English forces were reunited and making their way to the adjacent Branxton Hill did the Scottish king take action.

At 4 pm on 9th September 1513 – a day to be henceforth known as Black Friday – James set his tents ablaze and, under cover of the smoke, charged downhill to engage the English. The king had allowed an almost unassailable position to be outflanked and rendered useless – however, he had the flower of Scottish nobility under his command and a great victory was still a possibility.

Edmund Howard was in command of the English right flank and his men were first to take the powerful Scottish onslaught. His line wavered but did not yield – it was strengthened by a tough contingent of border reivers under the command of Lord Dacre. The Scots regrouped to attack again and might have easily crushed the English flank and turned the field, but then a strange thing happened – they simply disappeared! Tradition has it that they found looting more profitable than fighting, and of course, these men were also reivers, under the command of Lord Home.

Possibly the best and the worst sides of the reivers' character came out at Flodden, and there are many conflicting stories about their part in the battle. Surrey commented that "they were the boldest and the hottest I ever saw of any nation". But Home is reported to have said that the man who did well that day was the man who stood and saved himself. Home and Dacre were heavily criticised after the battle and were accused of collusion to minimise casualties. They denied it, of course, but bearing in mind the borderers' cynical attitude to national allegiance it could possibly have been true, although the real truth will never be known.

The battle ebbed to and fro for hours until Sir Edward Stanley and his men outflanked the Highlanders, wheeled and charged downhill into the back of the Scottish royal division. The end was now in sight; in fact, by nightfall, it was all over. James himself is said to have died bravely, cut off and surrounded by only a handful of his men. The dawn of the next day revealed the truth. Scotland's military might was no more; at least 10,000 men lay dead on the field, although some English eyewitness accounts put the numbers as high as 15,000 or even 17,000.

It is estimated that the English lost about 1,700 men, including five knights and 10 squires. Scotland, however, lost almost its entire nobility, gentry and ruling class – among the dead were an archbishop, a bishop, 10 earls, 19 barons and masters, the Provost of Edinburgh, and more than 300 knights, lords and gentlemen.

As well as a whole generation of nobility, entire companies of shire and burgh levies had been wiped out, such as the men of Selkirk, of whom only one, a pikeman named Fletcher, returned to tell the tale.

During the night after the battle, the Scottish reivers pillaged the bodies of the dead, while "false borderers" from Tynedale also plundered tents and baggage, and removed several horses belonging to the English army. One English officer is quoted as saying that "the borderers did full ill". The Bishop of Durham was particularly aggrieved and complained bitterly that they had removed some of the Scottish prisoners and ransomed them, and that they had done more damage to the English army than the Scots had. He also went on to say the English borderers were "falser" than those north of the border, and that his men were more worried about these reivers than they were about the Scots.

King James' body was identified by Lord Dacre and laid in the 12th century church at Branxton, from whence it was taken to Berwick and from there to London. It remained unburied until the reign of Queen Elizabeth. It is said that at some point the head was hacked off the body by workmen for "sport" but was eventually claimed as a trophy by the royal glazier, who later had it buried in an unmarked grave at the now-long-demolished church of St Michael, Wood Street, in London.

A sombre granite cross marks the spot on the battlefield where King James is traditionally believed to have fallen. However, the centuries-old lament *The Flowers of the Forest* provides perhaps the most emotive reminder of this dreadful Scottish tragedy:

"We'll hear nae mair lilting at our ewe milking,
Women and bairns are heartless and wae,
Sighing and moaning on ilka green loaning,
The flowers of the forest are a' wede away.

England had taken its revenge for Bannockburn, but, once the battle was over, Surrey disbanded his army and left the affairs of the border to be managed in the traditional manner by the enthusiastic Lord Dacre, who ordered huge raids to be mounted in the Scottish West and Middle Marches. There is evidence that in one raid more than 4,000 head of cattle, plus horses, were taken and that the areas were left "burning from daybreak to late afternoon".

There was a certain amount of retaliation by the Scots, but it could not match the English attacks. Liddesdale, Eskdale and Teviotdale were all but devastated, and Dacre boasted that all was quiet from Bowness to the Hanging Stone in the Cheviots. There had never been so much robbery and raiding in Scotland, and the lord added that he hoped it would continue.

St Paul's Church, Branxton

The Monument, Halidon Hill

BATTLE OF HALIDON HILL

The Battle of Halidon Hill was fought on 19th July 1333 – however, there were several events in the preceding years that contributed to the event. In 1318, Robert the Bruce captured Berwick – it was a sentry on the "Kow Gate" who turned traitor and allowed entry to the Scots. In 1328, Edward III renounced any claim to Scotland in return for £20,000 paid by the Scots as compensation for any damage done to England. Later that same year, Joan de Terribus, Edward's sister, married David, son of Robert the Bruce – great hopes for the future depended on this union and earned the princess the name of "Makepeace", but it was not to be. When Robert the Bruce died, Edward III invaded Scotland and laid siege to Berwick on 12th April 1333. However, the town was well prepared. Realising he could be in for a long siege, Edward took a large army of men further into Scotland, laid waste to the Borders and captured Edinburgh Castle. Meanwhile, Lord Archibald Douglas brought his army to relieve Berwick and, in an attempt to lure the English away, laid siege to Bamburgh Castle. The plan did not work: Bamburgh was strong enough to hold off a siege for as long as was necessary.

By 15th July, the town of Berwick had agreed to surrender in five days hence, and Sir Alexander Seton, the deputy governor, consented to his eldest son, Thomas, being held as a hostage. Seton's youngest son was already being detained by the English, and Edward, fearing that the town may be relieved before the five days were up, demanded immediate surrender, threatening to execute Seton's sons if it was not forthcoming.

It is recorded that Sir Alexander would have agreed to the terms but was dissuaded by his mother – and both sons were put to death in view of their parents on a small hill still known as "Hang-a-Dyke-Neuk". There is a record of two skulls, reputed to be those of Seton's sons, being on display in the poorhouse in Tweedmouth in 1873.

Lord Archibald Douglas returned from his unsuccessful siege of Bamburgh and decided to engage the English in battle. His troops crossed the Tweed and found the English army firmly established on Halidon Hill, about two miles to the north of Berwick.

It is said that, prior to the battle, a challenge to single combat was issued by a gigantic Scottish ruffian named Turnbull, who hailed from that notorious family of reivers from West Teviotdale, associates of the Olivers, the Trumbles and the Rutherfords.

Turnbull advanced boldly, accompanied by a huge mastiff war dog. The challenge was taken up by a Norfolk knight named Sir Robert Benhale. The growling mastiff with dripping jaws suddenly launched a ferocious attack on the knight, who deftly sidestepped the dog's attack and, with one mighty blow, cut the enormous beast in half. Turnbull moved quickly forward into the attack, but Benhale cleverly avoided the fierce blows aimed at him with amazing agility and, with great dexterity, turned and lopped off Turnbull's left hand and, before he could react, swiftly cut off his head.

The battle began with the Scottish army advancing up the hill, but it would be the English archers who would once again prove their superiority. They showered the close Scottish ranks with a rain of arrows, followed by a powerful advance by the spearmen and men-at-arms. The Scottish army, unable to stand the tremendous onslaught, fled in disarray and panic. Thousands of Scots, including their illustrious commander, lay dead on the battlefield. Halidon Hill became known as one of the greatest military disasters in Scottish history. Berwick immediately surrendered.

BATTLE OF HUMBLETON HILL

Just a few miles north-west of Wooler stands an ancient monolith known as the Bendor Stone, which is said to mark the spot where the Battle of Humbleton (also known as Homildon) Hill was fought on 14th September 1402. This battle, celebrated in ballad and song as the encounter where the Percies took revenge for their defeat at Otterburn 14 years earlier, also led to the Battle of Shrewsbury.

To understand the importance of the Battle of Humbleton Hill, we first have to consider trouble and unrest on another border – that with Wales. Henry IV sat uneasily on the English throne while a Welsh patriot, Owain Glyndwr, had plans to re-establish independence for his country and to regain the old titles of the native princes for himself. In the Welsh borders, many people still supported the deposed Richard II and believed he was still alive. It was Harry Hotspur who was entrusted with the job of maintaining peace in the area. Naturally, with Hotspur absent from his own lands, this presented a great temptation to the old enemy, the Earl of Douglas. Reports of the Scottish incursions, and the fact that he had established a kind of uneasy peace there, allowed Hotspur to return north and engage the Scots in battle.

Hotspur was a shrewd politician as well as a great soldier – he had as part of his force hundreds of Welsh archers, and to leave them behind on the Welsh border at a time when Glyndwr was gaining support with his patriotic fervour would have been asking for trouble; also, the supporters of Richard II were on the lookout for more followers. Hotspur was too clever and too experienced to risk these highly trained men being recruited by others, so he brought them back with him to Northumberland.

Douglas led around 10,000 men, representing the very best of the Scottish army, on his raid of northern England. It was very successful – they laid waste the lands of Northumberland as far as the gates of Newcastle, before beginning the journey home, laden with spoils. Douglas and his army camped near Wooler but found their retreat cut off by Henry Percy, the Earl of Northumberland, and his son, Harry Hotspur.

The Scots took up position on the lower slopes of Humbleton Hill; however, the English were drawn up on the higher ground. Before the Scots could engage in battle with the English infantry, Hotspur's archers inflicted great losses on them. It is said that the situation was so serious for the Scots that even sworn enemies Sir John Swinton and Adam de Gordon united to try to break through the English line. The charge failed and almost every Scot was killed or captured. The ragged remnants of the routed Scottish army were pursued to the River Tweed where many drowned trying to cross. More than 80 knights and nobles were captured as prisoners, including the Earl of Douglas, who was badly injured and lost an eye in combat. The battle was over, but the repercussions were far-reaching.

Hotspur thought the ransom from the Scottish prisoners would do much to balance the expense he had incurred on behalf of the king on the Welsh border, but Henry demanded that they are handed over. There followed a heated exchange, and Hotspur declared his intention of rising against the king. The Percies made a secret agreement with the Scots to put Sir

Humbleton Hill Battlefield

Remains of a possible bastle near Humbleton

Edmund Mortimer on the throne in place of Henry. The combined armies of Northumberland and Scotland marched south intending to meet up with Owain Glyndwr's men, but the king intercepted them at Shrewsbury and inflicted a massive defeat. Hotspur fell in battle and his body was exhibited in Shrewsbury market place so *"that all the world might know that this dangerous firebrand of the north was, in truth, dead and that even his name could be used to conjure with no more"*.

Chillingham Castle

CHILLINGHAM CASTLE

Chillingham Castle was a Border tower in 1298 when Edward I stayed as a guest, but by 1344 Sir Thomas de Heton had been granted permission by then-king Edward III to crenellate. He upgraded the fortification in the usual 14th century style: four square towers connected by a curtain wall. When the Heton family died out at the end of the same century, Chillingham passed into the ownership of the Greys of Wark. Sir William Grey became Lord Grey of Wark in 1623, and in 1695 his son was made Viscount Glendale and Earl of Tankerville. On his death in 1701, these titles became unused, but they were revived 13 years later when Sir Charles Bennet, Lord Ossulston, married an heiress of the family. By 1933, the castle had sadly fallen into neglect and decay, and it stayed this way until five decades later when Sir Humphry Wakefield and his wife Lady Katharine (née Grey) took over the estate and began the enormous task of restoring it to its former glory.

Over the years, Chillingham has become associated with eerie tales and supernatural events, leading to an unsettling reputation as the most haunted castle in Britain.

Beneath the balcony in the courtyard is the famous 'toad-stone', an oblong slab of fine-grained limestone in which a live toad is said to have been discovered, imprisoned in a small cavity. The slab is about five-and-a-half feet in length and two-and-a-half feet wide and was used as a mantelpiece until it was removed and hidden for many years.

On the north-east side of the castle is the old prison; this dark chamber is only illuminated by the light filtering through a narrow slit in the thick wall. The wretched prisoners have left their mark here with roughly carved letters and rows of long and short lines crudely scored into the walls. An old trapdoor in the floor leads to a dark, dank dungeon.

Chillingham's most famous apparition is perhaps the 'Blue Boy' (or 'Radiant Boy') who would regularly appear to guests in one of the castle's rooms at the stroke of midnight, crying, screaming and moaning as if he was in dreadful pain or great fear. The noises always emanated from the direction of an old passage that led to a tower adjoining the room. As the cries grew weaker, a bright light began to appear beside the bed, and from within it the figure of a young boy dressed in blue 17th century clothing would materialise.

It wasn't until the 1920s that building work in that particular section of the castle revealed the bones of a man and a boy, along with some fragments of blue clothing, within a wall. They were removed and buried in consecrated ground, and the Blue Boy has not appeared since.

The ghost of Lady Mary Berkeley, wife of the aforementioned Viscount Glendale and Earl of Tankerville, is also reputed to haunt Chillingham Castle. It is said that Lady Mary's husband became infatuated with her sister, the attractive Lady Henrietta, and the pair ran away together, causing a great scandal and leading to a lawsuit presided over by the infamous and ruthless Judge Jeffreys. The outcome was that the poor Lady Mary was left in the cold castle with only her fatherless baby girl for company; she never got over this dreadful desertion and eventually died heartbroken and grief-stricken. To this day, it is said, the sound of the rustle of her dress and the sensation of a rush of cold air can be discerned as she wanders the corridors and staircases in search of her heartless husband. There have even been reports that Lady Mary's ghost "escapes from her portrait" to wander the castle; it is claimed that when her picture was hanging in the nursery she would "step out of the painting" and terrify the children and their nurse by following them around.

Butchers' "Cratch" or "Creddle"

Fountain Head

Stocks and Dungeon Entrance, Chillingham

THE WILD WHITE CATTLE OF CHILLINGHAM

Wild white cattle have grazed in Chillingham Park for – it is believed – at least 800 years. A great wall was constructed around it in the early 13th century, possibly it is thought, to contain the herd for food and also to protect them from cross-border raiders – the fact that these cattle are wild and fierce make them impossible to drive like domestic animals!

Opinions differ as to the origin of the herd; Darwin and his contemporaries thought *the beasts were descended from a native white cattle similar* and *to the now-extinct Great White Aurochs* that roamed the ancient forests. Others suggested they were the descendants of cattle brought over by Danish invaders, while yet another theory claims that their direct ancestors were Italian cattle bred by the Romans. In the 19th century, local superstition had it that the herd appeared as if by miracle: at sunset, there was nothing in the park; by sunrise, they were grazing among the trees and on the hills.

A wild, rugged area covering about 1,500 acres, Chillingham Park has fine open green spaces for feeding, and dense thickets and woods for cover, together with extensive bogs profusely fringed with alders – the perfect habitat for these rare, enigmatic creatures.

Ever since first being enclosed in the park – believed to have been some time in the 14th century – the cattle have inbred with the minimum of human contact. Any animal carrying human scent is attacked by the rest of the herd, making it impossible to provide veterinary treatment when needed, and difficult to help cows in trouble when calving.

The strongest, fittest bull becomes leader – or King – of the herd, and he holds this position as long as he can fend off challenges from other bulls. He will sire all the calves born during his 'reign', thus ensuring that only the best bloodline is carried forward.

When another bull offers a challenge, he will move a little way out of the herd start to call and stamp on the ground. If the King Bull accepts the challenge, he too will move away from the herd and, facing his opposing number, will go through the same ritual. Then, suddenly, one of the animals will attack. After a brief skirmish, they will both resume grazing, keeping a careful eye on each other, but if one is caught off-guard there will be another sudden, brief clash; this process will continue until one of the bulls slinks away, admitting defeat.

The loser will live away from, but in sight of, the herd until he cools down. During this time, he'll be very quick to anger and highly dangerous to approach – a bad loser no doubt! It is very rare for the bulls to seriously injure one another during these fights, but, on occasion, animals have been discovered badly hurt or dying – a reminder of the terrific strength of these powerful creatures.

The cows always leave the herd to give birth, and during the first couple of weeks, the calf is well hidden, lying quite still with its chin on the ground, concealed in a dense clump of bracken or grass, rather like a young hare. However, should the mother see anyone near her young, she will attack without hesitation. Eventually, the calf is introduced to the herd. The mother and her offspring will approach, and the King Bull will come out to escort them. Then the rest of the herd will inspect the calf as if to decide whether it is welcome – once this is done, it is an accepted member of the herd.

Wild White Cattle of Chillingham

Thomas Bewick, the Northumbrian naturalist and wood-engraver, made a portrait of the King Bull in 1789. It is, perhaps, one of his best-known engravings; however, it was not achieved without difficulty. It is said that when Bewick was drawing, the bull gave chase and the artist only escaped by climbing a tree. While he was thus trapped by the beast bellowing and stamping just below, Bewick was able to finish the drawing to his satisfaction!

The herd have been in the direct care of the Chillingham Wild Cattle Association (CWCA) since the death of the 8th Earl of Tankerville in 1971. However, they fell under threat nine years later when – following the demise of his son, the 9th Earl – the decision was made to sell Chillingham Park and the surrounding woodlands. A personal intervention by the Duke of Northumberland secured its purchase by the Sir James Knott Charitable Trust, which granted the CWCA grazing rights for 999 years. In 2005, the association took ownership of the park as well as the cattle.

A small breeding group of these unique and attractive beasts has been established at a secret location in Scotland in case of any unexpected and disastrous eventuality. And so, hopefully, the future of Chillingham's wild white cattle is now positively assured.

Cragside House

CRAGSIDE (National Trust)

Perched high on the eastern side of the Debdon Valley, near Rothbury, Cragside is aptly named. This Victorian country house stands at the centre of a 14,000-acre estate, surrounded by varied and extensive woodland – a more romantic situation would be difficult to imagine. It was created as a country retreat by Lord William Armstrong, an inventor, engineer, industrialist and armaments manufacturer and supplier who is regarded to have been one of Britain's greatest scientific geniuses and perhaps the mightiest of the Victorian industrialists. Cragside clearly illustrates his originality, boldness, power, wealth, romance and sentiment.

The house forms a dramatic but picturesque outline against the crags; it has an interior with intriguing rooms ranging from the small and intimate to the large and grand, and all have their original furniture – indeed, some of it was specially designed for Cragside. Lord Armstrong used Cragside not only as a country retreat but also as a comfortable home to which he would invite many of the important clients from all over the world who bought armaments from his Elswick Works on Tyneside.

Lord Armstrong's love for the area began when he was a boy, enjoying country pursuits during annual family visits to Rothbury in the 1820s. In 1863, he made a nostalgic return visit, and it was during this that he decided to buy as much as he could of the beautiful Debdon Valley. By the end of the year, he had purchased a small plot of land, about 20 acres, and started building a small house "to be used for occasional visits in the summertime".

The original Cragside, dating from 1864, was a modest, two-storey lodge built in stone; some historians believe that its design was possibly influenced by John Dobson, who had worked on Lord Armstrong's house in Jesmond Dene, although by then he had retired.

The surrounding hillsides were quite bare, so the next thing that Lord Armstrong and his wife, Lady Margaret, did was to start a scheme of extensive planting and landscaping to improve the aspect of the estate. As well as this, Armstrong introduced the latest hydraulic technology to Cragside. Debdon Burn had dried up in 1865, causing a severe water shortage, so, to avoid this happening again, he dammed the stream to form Tumbleton Lake, and below it he installed a hydraulic ram that pumped water up to the house and gardens. Around this time, Lord Armstrong also purchased much of the land surrounding his original site, and his estate began to grow quite considerably.

It was around 1869, possibly influenced by the proposal to extend the Northumberland Central Railway to Rothbury, that he decided to make Cragside his main house. Architect Richard Norman Shaw was employed to enlarge and improve Cragside in the 'Old English' style, albeit with modifications to blend this with the more rugged and less refined traditions of Northumbrian building. Shaw is said to have sketched out his plans in one day, but the extensions, alterations and improvements took another 15 years.

Cragside was the first house in the world to be lit using hydroelectric power, and by the end of 1878 Lord Armstrong was illuminating his now extensive collection of valuable paintings with an arc lamp – one of the earliest domestic experiments of its kind. The power came from a dynamo run from a small turbine connected to the dam at Debdon Burn. In 1880, the scheme was extended using the newly invented incandescent lamps designed by Joseph Swan of Newcastle, a great friend of his lordship. Forty-five of these lamps were installed; however, they were never all used at once. Lord Armstrong extended and modified the equipment several times over the next few years to improve its efficiency, and by 1887 a permanent hydroelectric powerhouse had been constructed at Burnfoot. This was fed by water from Nelly's Moss Lakes, situated high in the country park above the house, rather than from Debdon Burn.

NORTH NORTHUMBERLAND

Cragside Lower Lake

In the 1880s, extensive alterations and improvements were carried out by Lord Armstrong at Cragside as it began to assume greater importance than his house in Jesmond. It was at this time that the buildings in the inner courtyard were added, and by the early 1890s, the home farm and stables by Tumbleton Lake had been greatly extended.

The First Lord Armstrong of Cragside died in 1900 and very few alterations were carried out after this. His great-nephew, William Watson-Armstrong, inherited his estate and was made "the First Lord Armstrong of the second creation". For a while, the new lord divided his time between Cragside, Bamburgh Castle and the South of France, but by 1908 his unfortunate business involvement with several companies of "a largely speculative character" saw him accrue debts of almost half a million pounds. On the suggestion of the estate's trustees, many of the great treasures of Cragside, including the prize herd of Shorthorn Cattle, were sold to liquefy his assets.

His son, the Second Lord Armstrong, died in 1972, and five years later Cragside and its estate, plus two farms in the Coquet Valley, passed to the Treasury in part settlement of death duties. Cragside was then transferred to the National Trust through the National Land Fund, helped by a generous gift from the Third Lord Armstrong.

Today, Cragside, together with its surrounding country park, is possibly the National Trust's most treasured property in Northumberland, with visitors from all over the world coming to view the house of one of the North's most dynamic industrialists.

Boathouse, Cragside Lower Lake

Water turbine, Cragside

CUDDY'S CAVE

On the southern slope of Dod Law, near Wooler, is Cuddy's Cave, traditionally associated with St Cuthbert who was an itinerant preacher in the early days. However, a large block of stone nearby, heavily scored with Bronze Age grooves, would perhaps suggest that the cave was in use long before it served as a haven for the saint during his travels.

Cuthbert was made prior of Old Melrose Abbey following the death of his successor and great friend Boisil during a plague epidemic. He had great enthusiasm for the position and showed how the rule should be obeyed both by teaching and by example. Following the tradition started by Boisil, he spent a lot of time travelling great distances to spread the gospel. Cuthbert was usually away about a week on these journeys, but occasionally as long as a month because during the plague epidemic there had been a destructive back-sliding into heathenism. The terrified villagers reverted to the worship of the "old gods" and took to the use of incantations, amulets and what Bede described as "other mysteries of devilish art".

It took all the power of Cuthbert's zeal and charisma to persuade them back to the true faith. He particularly sought out villages situated in the high, wild Northumbrian hills that others feared to visit. Poverty and ignorance prevented other teachers from reaching them in these remote and frightening places.

Cuddy's Cave, near Wooler

Duddo Stone Circle

DUDDO STONE CIRCLE

The stone circle known as the Duddo Five Stones is situated on private land – Grindon Rigg – about three-quarters of a mile to the north-west of the village of Duddo, although it is accessible by a permissive footpath. It is a small circle measuring around 35ft in diameter, with five stones ranging from about 5ft in height to just under 8ft. It is also thought that there were a further two stones at the north-west quadrant.

Excavations have revealed that the stones enclosed an Ancient British burial site; several sepulchral urns along with cremated human remains have been discovered in its centre. Radiocarbon dating on charcoal from the site indicates that the stones may have been erected around 2000 BC, and a recovered bone fragment has been dated to between 1740 and 1600 BC, suggesting the circle was used for burial several hundred years after its erection.

A local name for the site is "the Singing Stones" – a reference, perhaps, to the eerie noise made by the wind as it blows through them. Over millennia, the stones have been weathered by wind and rain into unusual shapes, and some of the markings are believed by some historians to be cup markings; the meaning of these enigmatic symbols, dated to the Neolithic and Early Bronze Ages, is regarded to be one of the great prehistoric mysteries.

Stone circles are usually associated with the Bronze Age (around 2000 BC to 700 BC in Britain), but in the early years of Christianity they were regarded with superstitious awe – their impressive appearance, lonely situation and immense antiquity, along with their ancient use as a temple or burial ground, combined to endow them with magical qualities. To those early Christians, the stones were associated with witchcraft, fairies or the Devil and, indeed, old pagan gods; the mere physical difficulty of erecting such things seemed proof enough of diabolical influence! There are many tales of farmers suffering horrific consequences after trying to move such stones – reason enough, perhaps, to leave them exactly where they stand.

The Duddo Five Stones are dramatically sited on a gentle rise at the centre of a landscape of prominent landmarks, surrounded by the distant Cheviot and Lammermuir Hills, only four miles from the Scottish border.

In the village itself, the scant remains of Duddo Tower are sited on a crag overlooking the settlement, serving as a stark reminder of border troubles. This tower was once the stronghold of the Lords of Tillmouth, but was destroyed in 1496 during cross-border raiding; it was rebuilt by the late 16th century but was destroyed again by the Scots on their way to the Battle of Flodden. It was not rebuilt a second time.

EDLINGHAM (English Heritage)

Edlingham is an interesting little village with a long history. Originally named Eadulfingham – "village of Eadwulf" – it was given to the monks of Lindisfarne by King Ceolwulf of Northumbria, who ruled from AD 729 to 737 before abdicating to enter the monastery on Holy Island. The village church, dedicated to St John the Baptist, dates mainly from the 12th century, although it is widely believed that it was constructed on the site of an eighth-century Saxon building. The west wall is 11th century, but the rest of the church – including a Norman nave and chancel – was rebuilt in the 1100s. The ancient tower with its thick walls and narrow slit windows suggests it was built with an emphasis on defence, providing strong protection from border raids. It is thought that the tower may have also been used as a temporary jail for reivers; the door could be fastened from the outside, and the socket for a sturdy bar is still visible.

Edlingham Castle from the Barbican

Not far from the church are the ruins of Edlingham Castle, which was built in around 1300 by Sir William Felton. Originally, it was thought that the castle was merely a typical border tower, but extensive excavations in the late 1970s and early 1980s proved that this was just one aspect of the building. The excavated remains of the walls show that although Edlingham was small, it was a complex and well-fortified castle, covering an area of about 200ft by 150ft and encircled by a moat.

In the late 17th century, the village became well-known as the home of Margaret Stothard, an old woman known locally as "the Witch of Edlingham". At an enquiry in 1683, a whole range of far-fetched evidence was given against Stothard by several villagers, including John Mills of Edlingham Castle, who swore that while lying awake one Sunday night he felt a great icy blast of air rush through the window and something huge land upon his chest, howling like a cat. He looked up to see a bright light appear at the foot of his bed, and from the light, a vision of the old woman appeared. Mills tried to scream, but he could make no sound. Eventually, he was able to cry out in fear, "The witch! The witch!"

His tale and those of the other villagers, all equally fanciful, did not seem to have impressed the officials of the enquiry – Margaret Stothard was set free without having to undergo any of the usual trials and tests inflicted on supposed witches at that time!

St John the Baptist, Edlingham

The Keep, Etal Castle

ETAL CASTLE (English Heritage)

Etal is a very attractive village, its small thatched cottages and traditional inn providing an air of rural tranquillity. The striking ruins of the castle stand at the lower end of the village, overlooking the River Till. The castle started life as a three-storey tower house, but its position so close to the border exposed it to the threat of attack by Scottish raiders. It was Sir Robert Manners, a local administrator and landowner knighted on the battlefield by Edward III, who obtained permission to crenellate the house in 1341.

The improvements and extensions were carried out by the same masons who built the nearby Ford Castle for Sir William Heron. Originally it was necessary to cross a drawbridge, then pass along a narrow passage and through a strong gatehouse to enter the building. The entrance tower is still standing and has an excellent example of a 'murder hole' under one window – this was a hole in the floor of a bay window that allowed missiles, boiling liquids or hot sand to be dropped onto people trying to force entry through a doorway beneath. In front of the castle are two cannons that once belonged to the ill-fated *HMS Royal George*, a Navy warship that sunk in the Solent in 1782.

Not surprisingly, there was a long-term feud between the Manners family of Etal Castle and the Herons of Ford Castle. This reached a peak in 1428 when John Manners – the grandson of Sir Robert – is said to have killed Sir William Heron and one of his servants. Lady Heron complained to the adjudicating warden's commission that her husband had been killed through malice, but Manners claimed self-defence, saying that Heron had attacked his castle with archers and swordsmen. The commission decided in favour of Lady Heron – Manners had to pay 250 marks as compensation to the widow; he also had to meet the expense of 500 masses for the souls of the deceased.

By the beginning of the 16th century, the Manners family had moved from Etal Castle, and it was left in the care of a constable. In 1513, it was one of the castles destroyed by King James IV of Scotland on his way to the Battle of Flodden. By 1547, the fortification was in the possession of the Crown as part of a project to reduce neglect of strategically sited border strongholds – however, it was never restored.

A quarter of a mile along the riverside from Etal Castle are the moss-covered ruins of St Mary's Chantry, founded by Sir Robert Manners in around 1345. It was here that a wren's nest was discovered in an unearthed human skull – a macabre place to bring up a family. Near to the chantry is St Mary's Well, a natural spring of cool, clear water.

Entrance to Ford Castle

FORD CASTLE

Built as a border stronghold in 1287 by Odenel de Forde, Ford Castle lies on the banks of the River Till, about nine miles south from where it joins the River Tweed. The castle was fortified in 1338 by then-owner Sir William Heron, making it one of the earliest examples in Northumberland of a crenellated rectangular building with four massive corner towers – a style later adopted at Chillingham Castle in 1344 and Lumley Castle, near Durham, in 1389.

In 1385, Ford Castle was overrun and destroyed by a marauding army of Scots commanded by the Earls of Fife, March and Douglas; it was, however, rebuilt when it was later recaptured by the English.

At the time of the Battle of Flodden, the castle suddenly came to prominence. The owner, another Sir William Heron, was being held a prisoner in Fast Castle in Scotland, and his young wife, aware that she could not hold out against the massive Scottish army, is said to have approached the Earl of Surrey asking for his assistance in having Ford spared. The Earl wrote to King James IV, offering to release the imprisoned Lord Johnstone and Alexander Home if he would spare the castle; however, the king refused and advanced on Ford, making it his headquarters.

It is said that Lady Heron became the king's mistress, and, while he dallied, his enemies advanced closer and closer; indeed, she has been accused of betraying James to Surrey, commander of the English forces. But it seems that even the king was capable of double-dealing, allowing his men to pillage and plunder the area while he enjoyed the hospitality of Lady Heron. However ardent the passion between the two, it did not prevent James from burning down the castle and its surrounding village when he left to take up his position at Flodden. Sir William was released after the battle, and following his death in 1535 the castle was placed into the care of a trust, before passing into the ownership of Thomas Carr of Etal, husband of Heron's daughter Elizabeth.

Ford subsequently passed into the hands of the Blake and Delaval families; from Sir John Hussey Delaval, it went to his wife Susannah, and then to their granddaughter Lady Susan, the Marchioness of Waterford. A major restoration of the castle took place in the 1790s, followed by further alterations almost a century later, commissioned by a subsequent Lady Waterford, Louisa Beresford. The imposing building we see today incorporates two of the castle's original towers.

Lady Louisa, who took over the estate in 1860, was also behind the redesign of the nearby village of Ford. It consists of one street: at the eastern end is a single-storey smithy with a horseshoe door surround; at the western end, a granite memorial fountain topped by St Michael and erected in memory of Henry, the Marquis of Waterford, who died in 1859. In the middle of the street is Lady Waterford Hall, built originally as a school but now used as a village hall and museum. It was here, between 1861 and 1883, that Lady Waterford painted a series of biblical scenes in watercolour for the children of the school, mostly using people from the village as her models.

Standing in the grounds of the castle is the church of St Michael and All Angels, which dates from the early 13th century. The church was restored sympathetically by noted local architect John Dobson in 1853 – its original and most unusual bellcote can still be seen.

St Michael and All Angels Church, Ford

The Site of Ad Gefrin

THE ANCIENT SITE OF AD GEFRIN

Ida the Flame-bearer took control of northern Northumbria in AD 547 when, with typical violence, the Anglian ruler added Bamburgh to his rapidly expanding kingdom of Bernicia.

Ida, reputed to be a descendant of the Anglo-Saxon god Woden, made Bamburgh his centre of government, although it was custom at the time for the monarchy to travel widely to dispense their rule. Of course, Ida's subjects wanted and expected to see their leader exercise his regal power in important centres around the kingdom; thus, the royal household moved between various residences, ruling on legal disputes, receiving tributes, feasting, and being entertained and adored.

It was around this time that a royal settlement was established on a stretch of land between the foot of Yeavering Bell and the River Glen; the base, which became known as Ad Gefrin, would provide a provincial residence for some of the greatest kings and queens of the day, including Æthelfrith, Edwin, Æthelburga, Oswald (later a saint) and his younger brother, Oswy.

For more than a hundred years, this ordinary, pleasant field was the setting for some of the most momentous events in early Northumbrian history. In his *Ecclesiastical History of the English People*, written at his monastery in Jarrow in AD 731, the Venerable Bede tells of a time when Edwin (AD 617-633) and his queen, Æthelburga, stayed at the settlement he calls 'Ad Gefrin'. He describes how the queen's Italian bishop, Paulinus, spent 36 days:

"Catechising and baptising; during which days, from morning to night, he did nothing else but instruct the crowds who flocked to him from every village and district in the teaching of Christ, and, when instructed, he washed them in the water of absolution in the River Glen nearby."

Looking towards the Cheviot Hills from Ad Gefrin

HEATHERSLAW MILL

Heatherslaw Mill

There has been a mill on the River Till at Heatherslaw for more than 700 years. The only wholly English tributary of the River Tweed, the Till flows down from the Cheviot Hills and meanders northwards past the castles of Etal and Ford; the mill is sited about halfway between the two.

The Agricultural Revolution of the 18th century saw huge improvements both in the breeding of livestock and the growing of crops – yields were increased dramatically, resulting in greater prosperity for the farming community. It was at this time – specifically between 1768 and 1770 – that Sir John Hussey Delaval rebuilt Heatherslaw Mill, essentially converting it into two mills under one roof to cope with the extra workload. He also built a forge mill on the opposite side of the river to manufacture farm tools.

The prosperity of Heatherslaw Mill continued until the 1800s. There were seven waterwheels in use, and a bustling community of millers, blacksmiths and carters were accommodated in about 30 houses along the riverbanks. It is thought that the building took its present form in around 1830 – the millstones are characteristic of this time. Its two mills worked side by side, and each had its own mill race and waterwheel, with three pairs of horizontal grinding stones, plus a vertical stone for pearl-barley polishing. Also, the weir was raised at this time to provide a more substantial head of water for increased power. Heatherslaw Mill continued to be busy for most of the 19th century – this was due, in the main, to the fact that many farm labourers at that time received part (or, in some cases, all) of their wages in the form of corn.

However, at the end of the 1800s, an agricultural depression brought a decline in business, and by the early 20th century there were only three millers working at Heatherslaw, producing pearl barley for human consumption.

By the mid-1900s, milling at Heatherslaw had stopped altogether, and the building was used merely for storing grain; further abandoned and unused, it rapidly became derelict.

But the 1960s saw a great upsurge of interest in industrial heritage, and by 1972 the Heatherslaw Charitable Trust had been formed, to revive the mill as a working museum.

Extensive restoration was carried out, and Heatherslaw Mill was opened to the public in 1975. The upper mill has been fully restored and produces flour that goes into the bread, cakes and biscuits sold in the shop and tea room. The lower mill is not operational, but it is used to demonstrate the normally unseen parts of the milling process.

The most northerly working mill in England, Heatherslaw provides a valuable insight into a process – the production of flour – that has changed little over many hundreds of years.

Machinery, Heatherslaw Mill

Millers tools

St Michael and All Angels Church, Ingram

Altar and chancel window – Church of St Gregory the Great, Kirknewton

INGRAM, St Michael and All Angels Church

Although the church of St Michael and All Angels in Ingram has changed its appearance dramatically over the last 200 years, it has retained the atmosphere of a small rural medieval church. The building was damaged by fire during the border wars, and, as late as 1597, Scottish raiders stole lead from its roof. Three centuries later, the tower was carefully rebuilt with new foundations, in a style as close to the original as possible: the lower sections still appear to be early Norman, and the upper parts have retained their narrow-paired bell openings. These massive, low square towers with narrow window slits afforded safety and protection to the local people in those unsettled years on the border when raiding and robbery was a constant threat. The font in the church bears the date 1662 and is decorated with heraldic carvings identified as those of the Percy family.

In the churchyard is an unusual tombstone for the rector's wife Isabella Allgood and their two sons, who were killed in a railway accident at Abbots Ripton, near Huntingdon, on 21st January 1876. The slab of rough, natural rock that marks their grave is said to be where Mrs Allgood rested during her last-ever walk in the surrounding hills. Perhaps the most famous rector of Ingram was Walter Reginald, who, in the early 13th century, served as chaplain to Edward I and later became Archbishop of Canterbury and Lord Chancellor of England.

One of the most intriguing features of St Michael and All Angels is a mysterious fragment of a medieval carving showing two angels at the foot of a robed cleric. The attractive lychgate was added as a War Memorial with money raised by public subscription in 1928.

KIRKNEWTON

The village of Kirknewton lies at the confluence of the River Glen and the College Burn. In the past, the village's location close to the border made it highly vulnerable to attack, as the thickly built walls of its buildings attest. A passage in Sir Robert Bowes' report on the state of the borders in 1550 tells of how a band of Scottish reivers set fire to a stone tower and a nearby stone house. This was certainly a wild and dangerous time, although it must be noted that the quality of life in Kirknewton had improved greatly by the late 1800s – according to inscriptions on village gravestones, some of the locals were now living to the grand old ages of 97, 102 and 109! Among the graves that can be seen in the grounds of its parish church is that of the Northumbrian social reformer Josephine Butler.

The church of St Gregory the Great dates from Norman times, but was rebuilt in the late 15th century and underwent further extensive restoration by John Dobson in 1860. The chancel is considered to be quite remarkable – it is thought to be the vaulted chamber of a pele tower built on the ruins of the Norman church. The spring of the chancel arch is only 2ft 9in from the floor. At right angles on the south side is another small chamber – supposedly an ancient chantry, but now known as the Burrell vault.

On the wall to the right of the chancel arch is a curious piece of sculpture that some historians believe to be of Saxon origin; known as "the Kilted Magi", it shows the Virgin Mary and Jesus attended by the Three Wise Men, who appear to be wearing kilts.

NORTH NORTHUMBERLAND

The accompanying interpretation board reads: *"The carving is quite amazing as it appears to show the Magi in kilts (but more probably Roman tunics). The ancient stone relief is a great treasure of the church, being at least 12th century and could possibly be earlier. There is some evidence to suggest that the style of the Magi 'caps' is similar to an example in the Roman catacombs, so there could be the influence of St Paulinus, who was a Roman (he is thought to have preached and baptised at Gefrin, near Kirknewton) and would date the carving at several centuries earlier, pre-dating the church; but the mystery deepens – where was it prior to that?"*

Church of St Gregory the Great, Kirknewton

Kilted Magi, Kirknewton Church

Lady's Well, Holystone

LADY'S WELL, HOLYSTONE

Lady's Well – or St Ninian's Well, as it is sometimes known – is just a short walk north from the attractive village of Holystone. The well, which is now in the care of the National Trust, is set in a circular enclosure, surrounded by trees. An atmospheric spot, this cool, shaded pool of pure spring water is reputed to be the place where St Paulinus baptised more than 3,000 Northumbrians during Easter Week in AD 627, although according to some historians he was actually in York at the time. Even if this mass baptism did occur, it would seem it had no lasting effect on the population: they were soon to be overrun by Penda of Mercia, Cadwallon of Gwynedd and their combined pagan armies.

This was once a useful watering place, being located close to the junction of the Roman roads of Dere Street and the Devil's Causeway. St Ninian was a fifth-century apostle of the Border Country and is associated not only with this well but with several others situated beside Roman roads in Northumberland. It is believed that the site was walled around in either Roman or medieval times, but the name Lady's Well is said to have come into use after the first half of the 12th century when Holystone became home to an Augustine priory of canonesses dedicated to St Mary the Virgin. The sisterhood, which numbered between six and eight, became so impoverished by the Border raids of the Scots that they were forced to ask for assistance from Pope Nicholas IV, who helped the group by assigning them the income from the parish of Alwinton. The remains of the nunnery are scant: an arch on the end of the wall of a cow byre is barely visible, but it is thought that the Church of St Mary the Virgin stands on part of the site.

In 1788, the well underwent extensive restoration and was adorned with a religious statue from Alnwick representing Paulinus; in the late 19th century, this was moved to the south-west end of the site and replaced by a simple cross. It is said that the remains of another stone cross can still be seen on the moors between Holystone and Elsdon, marking a point of prayer for pilgrims making their journey to the Holy Well.

NORHAM CASTLE (English Heritage)

Norhamshire was not part of Northumberland but an outpost of the County Palatine of Durham, and the castle was the main northern stronghold of the powerful Prince Bishops. The fortification, which rises majestically above the village, is strategically sited in a commanding position above a ford on the river. The ground drops steeply away both to the north and south of the curtain walls, and, far below, the river tumbles over a succession of shallow rapids. The east and south are protected by a deep ravine and an artificially deepened ditch. The spectacular position of this huge fortress captured the imagination of Sir Walter Scott, who wrote at the start of his epic poem *Marmion*:

Day set on Norham's castled steep,
And Tweed's fair river, broad and deep,
And Cheviot's mountains lone;
The battled towers, the donjon keep,
The loophole grates, where captives weep,
The flanking walls that round it sweep
In luster yellow shone.
The warriors on the turrets high,
Moving athwart the evening sky,
Seemed forms of giant height;
Their armour, as it caught the rays,
Flashed back against the western blaze
In lines of dazzling light.

The first castle on the site is thought to have been built by Bishop Ranulf Flambard in 1121 and was probably a wooden tower built on a large mound surrounded by wooden palisades and a defensive moat. Fifteen years later, it was overrun by the army of King David I of Scotland. In the aftermath of the English victory at the Battle of the Standard two years later, the second Treaty of Durham handed control of Northumberland to the Scots; Norhamshire, as part of Durham, was restored to the bishop.

The Scots didn't occupy Northumberland for long, and it was retaken by Henry II in 1157. He immediately ordered the timber in the more important border castles to be replaced by stone. Hugh de Puiset (or Pudsey) was now Bishop of Durham, and he set about rebuilding the castle on a grand scale, including the addition of the great red sandstone keep that dominates the site.

For more than a century, Norham Castle stood, seemingly impregnable – a challenge to the Scots who, apart from an unsuccessful siege in 1215, seemed content to wait for the right opportunity. That chance arose when, in 1307, Edward I died and left his inept son to lead England. The Scots were under the

Norham Castle entrance gate

leadership of the powerful Robert the Bruce, who was quickly tempted to test Norham, so in 1318 he brought a huge force across the Tweed to rush the fortress. It stood firm. He followed with a second attempt the following year, lasting more than seven months, but still, the garrison held.

Among the English defenders was a knight named Sir William Marmion, who some believe provided the model for the hero of Sir Walter Scott's poem. Scott wrote mainly of the events leading up to the Battle of Flodden – almost 200 years later – but his use of poetic licence shifted Marmion to a more glorious age. The original Marmion's exploits are well documented. In the *Scalacronica*, a chronicle written in the 14th century by Northumbrian knight Sir Thomas Grey, the author reports that at a banquet in Lincolnshire, a pageboy appeared bearing *"a war helmet to William Marmion, a knight, with a letter from his lady commanding him to repair to the most dangerous place in England, and there to make the helmet famous"*.

Norham seemed a likely spot, so Marmion "repaired" there and gained admission. A chance to enhance his reputation arrived when the Scots made a surprise attack, threatening the castle. The English soldiers rushed for their horses and were preparing to ride against the enemy when the constable, Sir Thomas Grey – father of the author – said to Marmion, *"Sir knight, you have come as knight errant to make that helmet famous, and it is more meet that deeds*

Norham Castle Keep

of chivalry be done on horseback than afoot, when that can be managed conveniently. Mount your horse: there are your enemies; set spurs and charge into their midst. May I deny my God if I do not rescue your person, alive or dead, or perish in the attempt!"

The lone knight charged into the middle of the foe who, it is recorded, *"laid some stripes upon him, and pulled him at last out of his saddle to the ground"*. While the Scots were gathered around Marmion, Sir Thomas and his men galloped to his aid. In the confusion, the Scots retreated, and quickly Marmion remounted his horse and joined the rout.

For another 150 years, ownership of Norham Castle was hotly disputed; it fell into Scottish hands in 1327 but was again restored to the Bishop of Durham by the treaty of Edinburgh-Northampton the following year. During the Wars of the Roses, it changed sides twice: first held by the Yorkists, it was then occupied by Lancastrian supporters in 1463, but following the Lancastrian defeats at Hedgeley Moor and Hexham it once again became Yorkist. At the end of the Wars, the Tudors saw the need to further strengthen their border strongholds, which turned out to be a wise decision. In 1497, the castle was put under siege by James IV, but it resisted for 16 days under the watch of Bishop Fox until the Earl of Surrey came to provide relief. On 23rd August 1513, the Scottish king made another attempt to take it – on this occasion, his favourite cannon, Mons Meg, is said to have been used against the massive walls. After two days' bombardment, the barbican was in ruins and the outer ward had been taken by assault. On 29th August, the garrison commander, Sir Richard Cholmondeley, surrendered. King James and his army went on to their massive defeat at Flodden.

After the battle, Bishop Thomas Ruthall repaired the damage done by the Scots and generally strengthened the fortress. In 1530, the Scots attacked Norham again, but the castle was saved by the bravery of Archdeacon Franklin, who, as a reward, was presented with a coat of arms by Henry VIII. There is evidence that Norham Castle was used as a form of defence right up until 1583, but after that, it slowly and sadly sank into ruin.

NORHAM, St Cuthbert's Church

St Cuthbert's Church, Norham

St Cuthbert's Church in Norham was once affectionately described as being "half as old as time". This is not far from the truth, because Norham's links with Christianity reach back beyond the time when the first church was established. In AD 635, when Aidan was called to the great kingdom of Northumbria by King Oswald, he is said to have crossed the River Tweed by the old ford here on his way to Lindisfarne. And it is quite possible he started his work among the people of Ubbanford, as Norham was called in those days.

The first church on the site would have been a simple wooden construction, but in around AD 835 Egfrid, the 14th Bishop of Lindisfarne laid the foundations of a new stone building dedicated to St Peter, St Ceolwulf and St Cuthbert. The dedication to St Cuthbert serves as a reminder of the story of how the monks of Lindisfarne fled the island with the body of saint and its associated treasures in the face of violent, vicious and terrifying raids by the cruel Norsemen. They made for the comparative safety of Norham, although they did not stay long and soon left on their strange succession of wanderings that would eventually take them all over Cumbria, North Yorkshire and Northumberland before finding a resting place for their saint's body in Durham.

For more than 300 years, this little church remained unchanged. Bishop Ranulf Flambard ordered the construction of Norham Castle in 1121, and the rebuilding of the church, credited to Hugh de Puiset, began four decades later in 1165. De Puiset replaced the original chancel, and eventually, a new nave was added – this still forms part of the present fabric. The church had three chantries and was able to grant the privilege of 37 days sanctuary. By that time Norham had been incorporated into the County Palatine of Durham, under the control of the Prince Bishops.

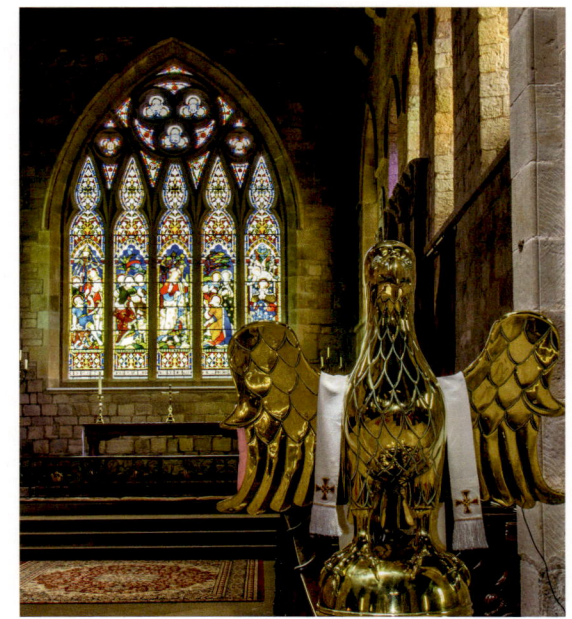

St Cuthbert's Church, Norham, lectern and chancel window

Norham also played a part in the dispute between Bruce and Baliol over the right to the Scottish throne after the death of Alexander III. It was here on 10th May 1290 that King Edward I of England sat on his throne, in the company of Antony Bek, Bishop of Durham to hear the protagonist's claims. The claim was resolved in favour of John Baliol but Any peace was short-lived, however. The king's son and successor, Edward II, was no match for the Scots; in 1318, Berwick fell, and this was followed by a heavily armed attack on Norham Castle, which was under the command of Sir Thomas Grey. The castle withstood the onslaught, but the Scots took refuge in the church, holding it as a fortress for almost a year. It was during this time that the whole of the eastern end – the Norman apse – was destroyed. In 1551, a treaty between England and Scotland was signed within the church.

Much of the church's Norman work was destroyed during the restorations that took place in 1619, 1846 and 1852. In spite of this, there are sufficient remaining features of the fine old 12th century building to show its architectural character. The interior woodwork is of special interest with some outstanding examples of Bishop John Cosin's fine restoration work brought here from Durham Cathedral.

The winding path at the end of the churchyard eventually leads across a stile and the fields to the riverbanks. This is the spot where the 'Blessing of the Nets' is performed at midnight on 14th February each year at the opening of the salmon-netting season.

NORTH NORTHUMBERLAND

Preston Tower

PRESTON TOWER

Preston Tower was originally built in 1392 in a style typical of the 14th century: a tower with four corner turrets, along the same lines as Langley Castle and Tarset Castle. The two south turrets of three storeys and the wall between them still remain, along with parts of the side walls. One of 78 pele towers in existence in Northumberland at the time of the Battle of Agincourt, its owners included Sir Guiscard Harbottle, who was killed at the Battle of Flodden in 1513.

These border tower houses had to be extremely well-built to withstand the constant raiding and reiving that went on in the area from the time of Edward I to the reign of James I. Dwellings were constructed with an emphasis firmly on defence – 7ft-thick walls and tunnel-vaulted rooms provided refuge for people and livestock. Staircases were usually spiral and started on the first floor, which could only be reached by a ladder.

Following the Union of the Crowns in 1603, half of the tower was demolished, and its stone was used in the construction of farm buildings on the estate. The house close by – also called Preston Tower – was built in the early 1800s for Edmund Craster. When the new hall was built, the north wall of the tower was reconstructed and a striking clock installed.

The grim reality of the pele tower's turbulent history is brought to life by informative displays in the building and its grounds, instigated by Major Tom Baker-Cresswell, owner of the estate until his death in 2011.

Ros Castle

ROS CASTLE (National Trust)

Ros Castle once belonged to Sir Edward Grey, Viscount of Falloden, but in 1936 it was gifted to the care of the National Trust. The name is perhaps a bit misleading – while it stands at just over a thousand feet high and dominates the adjacent Chillingham Park, this "castle" is really a large hill crowned with the remains of a double-ramparted Iron Age hill fort.

From the summit, there are splendid views of the Cheviots, the Farne Islands and the coastal castles. A warning beacon was lit here in 1804 to signal a French invasion had begun, but fortunately, it was a false alarm!

ROUGHTING LINN

Roughting Linn can be translated as "Bellowing Pool" – a fair description of this secluded waterfall. The nearby promontory takes its name from the fall, which gushes powerfully over the cliffs on the north-west side. This was the site of an Iron Age fort, with the remains of earth ramparts across the narrowest section and an in-turned gate on the north-east side.

The main attraction at this site, however, is the series of cup-and-ring markings carved into the rocky outcrop that lies among the trees near to the road. These markings are regarded as Northumberland's best examples of this widespread – but still largely unexplained – practice of decorating large stone outcrops. Most of the carvings are deep, hollow cups surrounded mainly by rings and sometimes spirals. This form of decoration is common throughout Northumberland and was perhaps the product of religious inspiration, or – as has been suggested – a small-scale representation of stone circle geometry, carrying astronomical information.

A good description is included by John Murray in his *Handbook for Travellers in Durham and Northumberland*: "The Devil's Rocks, a wild chaos of huge rocks on the edge of the moorland, may be visited on the way to Rowting [sic] Linn. Above the Linn are a number of mounds and dips in the turf, supposed to be traces of a circular British Camp. Here is a rounded Sandstone Rock, 60ft long and 40ft broad on which a few years ago a shepherd discovered a number of hieroglyphical marks consisting of a series of grooved rings, often dotted in the bottom of the grooves. The figures are scattered and vary in size, the largest being little more than a foot in diameter, but they are alike in form and in sculpture. Short parallel leads away, for a few inches, from some of them; but no two circles appear to be connected and would appear to be religious symbols…"

Roughtin' Linn Waterfall

Cup and Ring Marks – Roughtin' Linn

ST CUTHBERT'S CAVE
(National Trust)

To the north-east of Wooler, near Holburn Grange, is a natural stone cave set into the Kyloe Hills. This is St Cuthbert's Cave, one of the places the saint's body is reputed to have rested on its epic journey from Lindisfarne to Durham. The site is on land owned by the National Trust but is open to visitors all year round.

St Cuthbert had warned of heathen raids on Lindisfarne, and in AD 793 the Vikings arrived. Churches were plundered and Holy Island lost most of its treasures. Those brethren who had escaped with their lives fled inland, and the few who later returned were overjoyed to find the shrine of St Cuthbert had not been touched. Monastery life was resumed and continued in peace for 80 years before a second and much more fierce attack was launched. The bishop and the abbot remembered Cuthbert's words and gave instructions for the saint's body to be lifted from its resting place. Other treasures were placed in the coffin, including the head of St Oswald and the bones of Saints Aidan and Eata. The sad procession of monks left their beloved island for the mainland, where they would wander for years on both sides of the border.

Throughout this period of great danger and hardship, the coffin was carefully guarded – only the seven men specially chosen for this sacred task were allowed to touch the bier on which it was carried. They wandered for seven years, only stopping in safe, holy places; locations that have become linked with the name of the saint for over a thousand years.

St Cuthbert's Cave, Belford

The view out of St Cuthbert's Cave

Twizel Bridge

Twizel Castle looming sinisterly over the Twizel Bridge

TWIZEL BRIDGE

Twizel Bridge, which crosses the River Till three miles to the north of Cornhill-on-Tweed dates from 1511.

Said to have been commissioned by one of the female members of the Selby family, this narrow bridge was – at 90ft – the longest single-span stone arch in Britain until Causey Arch in County Durham was built in 1727. The graceful shape of the bridge is further enhanced by its beautiful setting on a bend of the river, with the wooded glen rising steeply to the north-west. On the edge of the ravine are the remains of Twizel Castle – really a mansion house rebuilt in the Gothic Revival style. Landowner Sir Francis Blake began the construction project in 1770, but although the work continued for more than 40 years it was never completely finished.

Twizel Bridge also played an important part in border history. On the morning of 9th September 1513, James IV of Scotland was encamped at Flodden, his position well sited and secure for the forthcoming battle. The Earl of Surrey, however, was intent on out-manoeuvring him, and when the English artillery and heavy baggage crossed the bridge, the Scottish king did not attempt to prevent or intercept them. This action, or lack of it, has been variously described on the one hand as chivalrous and on the other as gross incompetence in the art of warfare. The event was described by Sir Walter Scott in his epic poem Marmion:

"From Flodden ridge
The Scots beheld the English host
Leave Barmore-wood, their evening post,
And heedful watch'd them as they cross'd
The Till by Twizel Bridge."

However, contrary to Sir Walter Scott's version, Twizel Bridge cannot be seen from Flodden. There is no explanation for James' inaction, except perhaps that he was reluctant to leave his well-established position.

NORTH NUMBERLAND

UNION CHAIN BRIDGE, LOAN END

The Union Suspension Bridge from the Scottish approach

Union Suspension Bridge from the English approach

At Loan End, just about a mile to the north-east of the village of Horncliffe, is the Union Suspension Bridge, dramatically linking England with Scotland across the River Tweed. This place also conveniently marks the extent of the tidal river. This bridge is generally accepted to be the first suspension bridge in Great Britain to carry vehicular traffic and was erected in 1820 to a design by Captain Samuel Brown RN who was to eventually gain a knighthood for his further bridge-building efforts.

Large iron suspension bridges were first built in America in the early 1800s but the next developments followed in Britain and France. It was his invention and introduction of the wrought iron chain link that made Captain Brown's contribution to the project so important – some of the link bars in the Loan end bridge are only two inches in diameter.

The Scottish side of the river has a freestanding support tower, but the anchorages on the English side are embedded into the rocky outcrop 40ft above the roadway; this outcrop, however, is faced with stone to match the opposite tower. Originally, there was a small tollbooth on the English side, but this was removed in 1955. The bridge was completed in just 11 months, at a cost of £7,700 – only a third of the outlay for an equivalent stone bridge.

The opening of the bridge attracted great support and excitement; the first person to cross it was Captain Brown in an open-topped carriage, followed by a crowd of spectators, clapping and cheering this new route across the Tweed.

WHITTINGHAM

Whittingham Bridge carries the road across an ancient crossing point on the River Aln

Around eight miles west of Alnwick lies Whittingham, a village that dates from Saxon times. Its name is said to derive from the Anglo-Saxon *Hwita-ing-ham*, which translates as "the home of Hwita's people". Many historians believe Whittingham to be the "Twyford" that is mentioned in the writings of the Venerable Bede – the location by the River Aln where, in AD 684, a synod was assembled in the presence of King Ecgfrith, at which Cuthbert was chosen as Bishop of Lindisfarne. The village was mentioned again in AD 737 when Ceolwulf, King of Northumbria, relinquished the crown to become a monk on Lindisfarne and, as a gesture of devotion, gave Whittingham to the monastery.

Whittingham played a further part in England's history following the death of Halfdan, the first Viking King of Northumbria, in AD 877. It is said that St Cuthbert appeared to Abbot Eadred of Lindisfarne in a vision and advised that the Vikings should give the crown to Guthred – the son of Hardacnut – who had been sold as a slave to a woman at Whittingham. After buying Guthred's freedom, the Vikings installed him as their king; he also gained the acceptance of the Saxons, thus uniting the two opposing groups of warriors, just as Cuthbert had foretold.

The village is divided in two by the infant River Aln. The northern side was once known as the "Church Town" because of the presence of the Church of St Bartholomew, which stands on the site of the original Saxon place of worship. It was the Reverend Robert Goodenough who, in 1840, decided that the existing Anglo-Saxon tower should be pulled down and rebuilt in the Gothic style, but the job was only half-finished, and the bottom part of the tower remains unmistakably Saxon. In this section are the finest examples of Anglo-Saxon long-and-short quoining – long stones set vertically between smaller stones laid horizontally – in all of Northumberland.

The interior of the church contains architectural work dating from the 12th century right through to the early 20th century. Hanging on the walls of the chancel and nave are hatchments – black diamond-shaped heraldic plaques that would have been displayed outside large houses following the death of the head of the family and later moved to the church. The south porch is very old, dating from the 14th century, and has a pointed tunnel-vaulted ceiling strengthened by two transverse ribs. The two entrances to the churchyard from the east and the west are by way of worn stone stiles. An ancient venerable Anglian stone cross, unearthed in 1893, stands on top of the wall near the eastern stile of the churchyard and is thought to predate the church itself. Many of the gravestones are unusual and have been designated as being of Special Historical Interest. Some of those near to the church date from the 18th century and are decorated with a representation of a skull-and-crossbones. Early tombstone carvings were filled with dark images of death and horror; however, by Victorian times funerals had become much more socially important and the enthusiasm for grave markings with gruesome symbols all but vanished.

Across the footbridge below the church and up the wooded lane to the south of the river stands Whittingham Tower. The tower house dates from the late 13th or early 14th century, and in 1416 it belonged to Sir William Heron, a member of the famous reiver family who also owned Chipchase and Ford Castles. As with most of these border defences, Whittingham Tower would have suffered attack, siege and bloodshed; eventually, it fell into ruin. By the mid-1800s, however, it was restored and converted by Maria Susanna, Lady Ravensworth, for use as almshouses. A carved stone tablet above the doorway proclaims that:

St Oswald window detail, Whittingham

By the munificence and piety of
LADY RAVENSWORTH
This ancient Tower which was formerly
Used by the village as a place of refuge
In time of rapine and insecurity
Was repaired and otherwise embellished
For use and benefit of the deserving Poor

The tower house remained in use until the early 1960s when its now-decrepit facilities led to its closure.

Set just below Whittingham's village green, in the middle of the junction to the south of the road bridge, is the Ravensworth Fountain. This unusual and interesting monument, installed in 1905, comprises an octagonal basin with a statue of Athole Liddell, Third Earl of Ravensworth, and his dog on a pillar at its centre.

Once held annually on 29th August, the now sadly defunct Whittingham Fair was a gathering place for the people of the vale. A cavalcade of horses accompanied by fiddlers and pipers opened the event, and there were refreshment tents set up by traders from all parts of Northumberland. Food stalls sold nuts, oranges, apples, homemade toffee, gingerbread, cheese and gooseberries. Tinkers and tailors from Kelso and Rothbury sold their wares alongside shoe and bootmakers from Alnwick.

Statue to Athole – 3rd Earl of Ravensworth

The fair has been immortalised by the ballad that is now a part of traditional Northumberland folklore:

Are you going to Whittingham Fair?
Savoury, sage, rosemary and thyme,
Remember me to one who lives there
She once was a true lover of mine.

The occasion is now remembered by the Whittingham Show, which is held on the third Saturday in August and attracts competitors from across the north of England.

Woodhouses Bastle

WOODHOUSES BASTLE

Woodhouses Bastle is an excellent example of this type of fortified dwelling, and also perhaps one of the most dramatically sited. Standing on a slope in the grounds of Holystone Grange, the bastle house is extremely well-preserved, with the arched vault, the staircase, and the spout over the doorway – for pouring molten tar, boiling water or hot sand over assailants – all clearly visible. The ground-floor doorway arch is inscribed with the date 1602 and the initials WP, BP and TAM; WP and BP are thought to reference William and Bartholomew Potts, former landowners here.

In the 18th century, Woodhouses was the dwelling of William Allan, the father of celebrated Northumbrian piper and sometime criminal Jamie Allan. A thief, bigamist and deserter, Allan's life was one long evasion of the law, although his talent on the small pipes earned him the recognition of the then Duchess of Northumberland. Allan became resident at Alnwick, but, after losing the favour of the duchess, he left to embark upon a remarkable (and irresponsible) itinerant lifestyle throughout Europe, Asia and Africa.

On his return to England in 1803, Allan was convicted at Durham Assizes on a charge of horse stealing and condemned to death. The sentence was later commuted to transportation, but, perhaps because of Allen's advanced age and poor health, this journey was not enforced, and he spent the final years of his life in Durham's House of Correction. Sadly, he died on 13th November 1810, just days before notification arrived that the Prince Regent had granted him a free pardon. Even Allan's request to be buried near his home in Rothbury went unheeded; he was interred in St Nicholas' Churchyard, now part of the city of Durham's busy Market Place.

YEAVERING BELL

Yeavering is a small village on the River Glen, four miles to the west of the market town of Wooler. A roadside monument marks the position of the seventh-century settlement of Ad Gefrin – Old English for "hill of the wild goats" – close to the present-day village. This was the residence of King Edwin and Queen Æthelburga, and, according to the Venerable Bede, it was here that in AD 627 Paulinus worked from dawn till dusk for 36 days, instructing the inhabitants of the surrounding villages in the word of Christianity and baptising them in the River Glen.

Shortly after this, in around AD 632, the site was destroyed during a violent incursion by Penda of Mercia, Cadwallon and their pagan hordes. However, it was soon rebuilt, most probably by Oswald when he took the Northumbrian crown after the Battle of Heavenfield. There are signs that it was burnt down once more in the mid-600s, but by this time Ad Gefrin had been succeeded by a new palace at Maelmin, now known as Milfield.

The site of Ad Gefrin was rediscovered in 1949 and it has been extensively explored by excavation since that time. One very unusual building seems to have been the focal point of life at the settlement: a small type of amphitheatre that would have accommodated about three hundred people - its purpose undoubtedly social and ceremonial.

Paulinus possibly preached here during his evangelising stay in the township. For a long time, local tradition had it that a shepherd's house in the nearby hamlet of Old Yeavering once formed part of Edwin's palace, but although the structure is very old it was more likely part of an old pele tower dating from the times of the border raids.

The conical-shaped hill known as Yeavering Bell rises to a height of 1,182ft above the village. At the base of the hill is a stand of primeval woodland that may well be a part of the ancient Caledonian Forest and is reputed to be haunted by a mysterious apparition known as 'the White Lady'. The panoramic view from the flat summit of Yeavering Bell is regarded to be the finest in the extensive Cheviot range. However, its main point of interest is the remains of a hill fort – believed to date from the Iron Age – covering an area of around 13 acres. Although now reduced to rubble, its massive perimeter wall once stood 7-8ft high and was

Yeavering Bell

more than 10ft thick at its base.

Four gateways would have allowed access to the interior, which was densely crowded with many circular buildings, the remains of which can still be traced. In its day, it must have been a busy but well-defended small town. This ancient enigmatic site is thought to be the finest example of an ancient hill fort in the whole of Northumberland.

Just across a small ford to the north of Yeavering lies the settlement of Coupland. The hamlet takes its name from an ancient family – the first John de Coupland was one of the 12 knights appointed by King Henry III in 1248 to negotiate a settlement with Scottish commissioners over border disputes. It was another Sir John de Coupland who, almost a century later, captured King David II of Scotland after the Battle of Neville's Cross, near Durham. The story has it that, following the conflict on 17th October 1346, the Scottish king took cover beneath a bridge, but his reflection in the water gave away his position. John de Coupland leapt from his horse and went to pull David from his hiding place, at which the Scot, despite being wounded, put up a determined fight, knocking out two of his adversary's front teeth in the struggle. The monarch was eventually ransomed for the sum of 100,000 marks – about £15 million in today's money.

The privately-owned Coupland Castle was built in the late 16th century; scratched into a ground-floor door lintel is the date 1594. The fact that such a stronghold was built after the Union of the Crowns is conclusive proof of the unsettled state of the Borders at that time. Strictly speaking a tower house rather than a castle, the building was constructed (unusually) from volcanic rock and was restored in the 19th century.

Coupland

"the road to Flodden"

Exploration is defined as "to travel through an area in order to learn about it". This has been the pleasure for me – to travel through such a wonderful county with a camera, pencil and notebook; with *Murray's Handbook* and *Tomlinson's Guide to Northumberland* for 'guidance' and reference. These old books are full of character, a mixture of fact and folklore that greatly add to the Exploring Experience.

Of course, you can't cover everything there is to see or learn about on a journey like this. But hopefully, there are things in this book that will help fire the imagination and curiosity, and encourage further exploration of this excellent county, its places, its history and its marvellous people. This is an area you can't get enough of – one story leads to another, all woven into the rich tapestry that is the dynamic essence of Northumberland.

Philip Nixon 2021